WORLDWIDE GROWTH RATE OF CHRISTIANITY

THE BAKER
atlas
of
CHRISTIAN
HISTORY

Copyright © 1997
Tim Dowley & Peter Wyart trading as
Three's Company / Lion Hudson plc

First US edition published in 1997 by
Baker Books
a division of Baker Publishing Group
PO Box 6287, Grand Rapids, MI 48516-6287

Reprinted 2005

Library of Congress Cataloging-in-Publication Data is on file at the
Library of Congress, Washington, DC.

ISBN 0-8012-2248-7

Designed by Peter Wyart,
Three's Company

Co-edition organised and produced by
Worldwide co-edition produced by
Lion Hudson plc,
Mayfield House,
256 Banbury Road, Oxford OX2 7DH,
England.
Telephone: +44 (0) 1865 302750.
Fax: +44 (0) 1865 302757.
Email: coed@lionhudson.com.
www.lionhudson.com

The maps in this atlas have been
computer generated by specialist
cartographers Hardlines for Three's
Company and Angus Hudson Ltd, who
are the copyright owners. The
cartographers and copyright owners
have made every effort to achieve
accuracy, but cannot be held responsible
for any errors or omissions.

All scripture quotations, unless
otherwise indicated, are taken from the
HOLY BIBLE, NEW INTERNATIONAL
VERSION®. NIV®. Copyright © 1973,
1978, 1984 by International Bible
Society. Used by permission of
Zondervan Publishing House. All rights
reserved.

Printed in Singapore

Cartography
by Hardlines, Oxfordshire
Cartographer: Geoff Walker

Photographic Acknowledgments
Tim Dowley: pp. 11, 12, 18, 19, 21, 32, 36,
38, 50, 57, 62, 63, 67, 71, 75, 87, 92, 97, 98,
102, 104, 107, 113, 120
FMB Southern Baptist Convention:
p. 150
Mig Holder: p. 109
Jamie Simson: p. 48
Peter Wyart: pp. 13, 17, 19, 26, 29, 55, 58,
60, 64, 72, 73, 78, 83, 87, 92, 93, 99, 102,
110, 116, 141

Illustrations
James Macdonald: pp. 27, 36, 44, 47, 50,
58, 68
Richard Scott: p. 37
Paul Wyart: p. 96

THE BAKER

atlas

of

CHRISTIAN

HISTORY

EDITOR: TIM DOWLEY

EDITORIAL CONSULTANTS:

Alan Millard
Rankin Professor in Hebrew and Ancient Semitic
Languages, University of Liverpool

David Wright
Senior Lecturer in Ecclesiastical History,
University of Edinburgh

Brian Stanley
Director of the North Atlantic Missiology Project
for the University of Cambridge, and Fellow
of St. Edmund's College

Research: Malcolm Day

INTRODUCTION

We believe that this atlas features several notable innovations. Chief among these is to combine an atlas of the Bible with an atlas of church history and of the development of Christianity in the two millennia since the birth of Christ. Moreover, a number of the maps of recent church history included in this atlas, particularly those covering the twentieth century, present material not previously available in this form. We have aimed to create a book that combines the accuracy and comprehensiveness required by the academic world with a clarity and interest that make it accessible to the general reader.

We believe this atlas breaks new ground too in being almost entirely computer-generated, with the enhanced accuracy and control that state-of-the-art technology affords. We have aided location finding by adding latitudes and longitudes to the maps, and by providing precise reference points in the exhaustive gazetteer at the back of the book.

This atlas, the end product of a number of years' intensive work, is the result of team effort. The original design work was by Tony Cantale of Tony Cantale Graphics, and the huge task of researching every map was completed by Malcolm Day. We are most grateful to the three specialist consultants, Professor Alan Millard, Mr David Wright and Dr Brian Stanley, for their advice and expertise at each stage in the development of the atlas. The page designs were created by Peter Wyart, and the boundary-expanding work of generating the finished maps by Geoff Walker and his team at Hardlines. The index and gazetteer were drawn up by Christopher Pipe. We are most grateful to them all.

Tim Dowley
St Nicholas' Day 1996

CONTENTS

LIST OF MAPS

Old Testament Period

THE PATRIARCHS

ISRAEL IN THE PROMISED LAND

THE UNITED KINGDOM

THE DIVIDED KINGDOM

EXILE AND RETURN

New Testament Period

JESUS OF NAZARETH

The Early Church

The Modern Church

THE GEOGRAPHY OF PALESTINE

When viewing the Holy Land from the air the eyes immediately slide down the long straight corridor that is the Jordan valley. It runs north-south the entire length of Palestine, from Mt Hermon to the Arabah. Although it meanders wildly along its lower course, unlike other rivers the River Jordan is constrained by high-sided valley walls which form part of the Great Rift Valley. This rift is part of a 6,500-kilometre (4,000-mile) geological fault that begins in Syria and ends in Mozambique.

Millions of years ago the subterranean plates, upon which the continents of Africa and Asia rest, shifted towards each other and caused the earth's crust to buckle and fracture. This produced the distinctive features of Palestine. Pressure between the two plates caused the sub-surface sediments to bulge and rise in the west, resulting in the Judean Hills. In Transjordan, the plate tilted upwards to produce the high Eastern Plateau. Between them the sediment dropped, with the result that the surface of the Dead Sea is some 400 metres (1,300 feet) below sea level, the lowest place on earth.

The consequence of this cataclysm for climate and vegetation in the region was huge. Although Palestine is only some 70 kilometres (45 miles) wide, altitudes range from over 1,000 metres (3,300 feet) in the Judean Mountains to minus 400 metres (1,300 feet) at the Dead Sea. Where the land is low lying, away from the coast, temperatures soar and desert conditions prevail. In the mountains temperatures are cooler and relief rainfall can support pastureland or cultivation. Since most of the land north of the Dead Sea is hilly, westerly winds coming off the Mediterranean Sea would bring rain which would support large areas of forest. South of the Dead Sea hot dry winds from Africa and Arabia produced deserts.

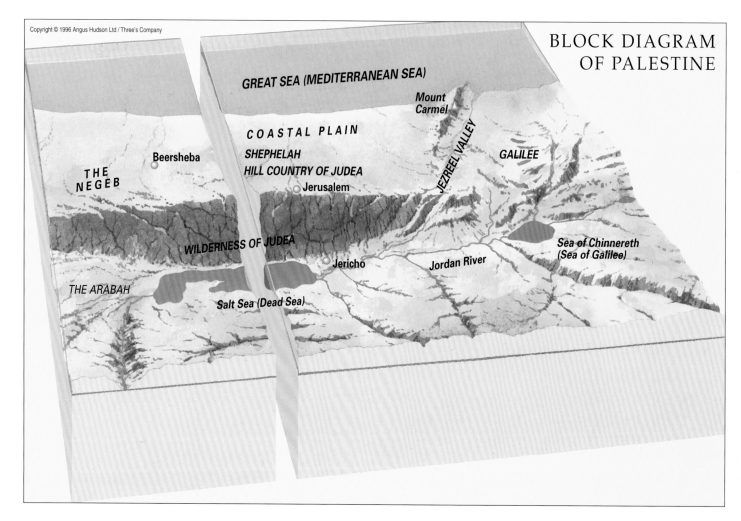

BLOCK DIAGRAM OF PALESTINE

GREAT SEA (MEDITERRANEAN SEA)

Mount Carmel

COASTAL PLAIN

SHEPHELAH

HILL COUNTRY OF JUDEA

Jerusalem

JEZREEL VALLEY

GALILEE

THE NEGEB

Beersheba

WILDERNESS OF JUDEA

Jericho

Jordan River

Sea of Chinnereth (Sea of Galilee)

THE ARABAH

Salt Sea (Dead Sea)

RELIEF MAP OF PALESTINE

Copyright © 1996 Angus Hudson Ltd / Three's Company

Mt. Hermon
(9,232ft / 2,184m)

Tyre

PLAIN OF PHOENICIA

Dan

Lake Huleh

SYRIAN DESERT

ARAM

Hazor

Acco

SEA OF CHINNERETH
(SEA OF GALILEE)

GREAT SEA

(MEDITERRANEAN SEA)

Mt. Carmel
(1,732ft / 528m)

Tiberias

Mt. Tabor
(1,929ft / 588m)

Yarmuk

VALLEY OF JEZREEL

PLAIN OF SHARON

Megiddo

Mt. Gilboa
(1,630ft / 497m)

GILEAD

Pella

Samaria

Mt. Ebal
(3,083ft / 940m)

Jordan

Shechem
Mt. Gerizim
(2,889ft / 881m)

Jabbok

HILLS OF EPHRAIM

ISRAEL

THE ARABAH

AMMON

Joppa

Shiloh

Bethel

Lod

Gibeon

Gezer

Jericho

Heshbon

Mt. of Olives
(2,723ft / 830m)

Jerusalem

Ashkelon

Bethlehem

Mt. Nebo
(2,630ft / 802m)

PLAIN OF PHILISTIA

SHEPHELAH

JUDAH

HILLS OF JUDEA

WILDERNESS OF JUDEA

SALT SEA (DEAD SEA)

Gaza

Lachish

Hebron

Dibon

Arnon

Beersheba

MOAB

THE NEGEB

metres   feet
1,000   3,281
500   1,640
200   656
0   0
below sea   below sea
level   level

THE ARABAH

Zered

0   25   50 km

0   10   20   30 miles

EDOM

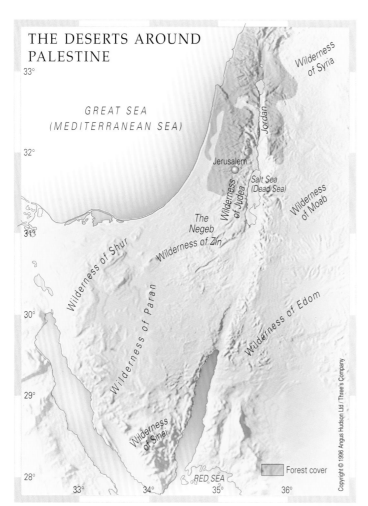

THE DESERTS AROUND PALESTINE

33°

GREAT SEA
(MEDITERRANEAN SEA)

Wilderness
of Syria

Jordan

32°

Jerusalem

Salt Sea
(Dead Sea)

Wilderness
of Judea

31°

The
Negeb

Wilderness of Zin

Wilderness
of Moab

Wilderness of Shur

Wilderness of Paran

30°

Wilderness of Edom

29°

Wilderness
of Sinai

28°

RED SEA

Forest cover

33°   34°   35°   36°

Copyright © 1996 Angus Hudson Ltd / Three's Company

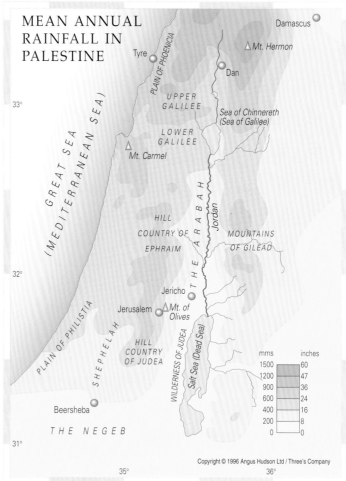

MEAN ANNUAL RAINFALL IN PALESTINE

Damascus

Tyre

PLAIN OF PHOENICIA

△ Mt. Hermon

Dan

33°

UPPER
GALILEE

Sea of Chinnereth
(Sea of Galilee)

LOWER
GALILEE

GREAT SEA
(MEDITERRANEAN SEA)

△
Mt. Carmel

HILL
COUNTRY OF
EPHRAIM

THE ARABAH

MOUNTAINS
OF GILEAD

Jordan

32°

Jericho

Jerusalem

△ Mt. of
Olives

PLAIN OF PHILISTIA

SHEPHELAH

HILL
COUNTRY
OF JUDEA

WILDERNESS OF JUDEA

Salt Sea (Dead Sea)

mms   inches
1500   60
1200   47
900   36
600   24
400   16
200   8
0   0

Beersheba

THE NEGEB

31°

35°   36°

Copyright © 1996 Angus Hudson Ltd / Three's Company

THE CLIMATE, VEGETATION AND ECONOMY OF PALESTINE

Warm air from the Mediterranean brings mild winters to the coastal zone, when over 90 per cent of the rainfall comes, but in the hills and mountains the temperature can drop below freezing and snow may fall in places such as Jerusalem. Summers, from May to September, are hot and dry, soaring to over 100°F/38°C in the Jordan Valley and beside the Dead Sea.

A transitionary steppe climate bridges the area between the mild Mediterranean zone and the harsh, arid conditions of the desert. In this zone, approximately between Hebron and Beersheba and on the western edge of the Transjordanian Plateau, 20-30 cm (8-10 in) of rain will fall in a year, while the desert areas beyond will generally have under 20 cm (8 in) per year.

It is sometimes suggested that the region has undergone a climatic change over time, and that this explains a change in the natural vegetation. However, there is virtually no archaeological evidencè for this. More likely is that successive peoples over-exploited the natural resources, especially timber, causing soil erosion and a slow desertification of the region. The need of timber for building and fuel depleted what was a fairly extensive tree cover of oak, pine and acacia. (Since 1948 the Israeli government has undertaken a huge programme of tree-planting in an attempt to rectify this.) Uncontrolled grazing by sheep and goats also destroyed natural pasture, reducing large tracts of land to scrub. One exception to this deforestation is the centre of the Jordan Valley, which has remained a dense forest of tamarisk and thorn scrub, 'the jungle of the Jordan' (Jeremiah 12:5).

The traditional economy of Palestine was agricultural. Pastoralism predominated on the higher and poorer ground, while arable farming was practised in the valleys where at least 20 cm (8 in) of rain would fall annually. Rivalry for land was frequently a source of conflict in the Old Testament, as portrayed in the stories of Abraham and Lot, and may lie behind the confrontation between Cain and Abel.

MEAN ANNUAL TEMPERATURES

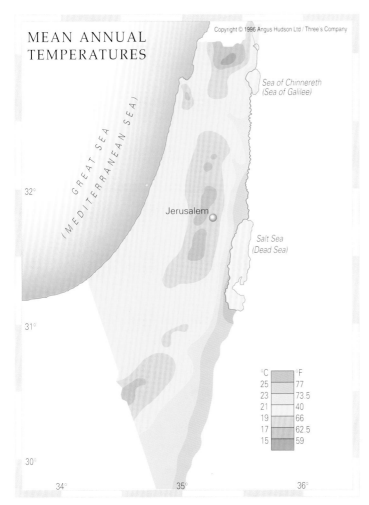

Copyright © 1996 Angus Hudson Ltd / Three's Company

G R E A T   S E A
(M E D I T E R R A N E A N   S E A)

Sea of Chinnereth
(Sea of Galilee)

Jerusalem

Salt Sea
(Dead Sea)

32°

31°

30°

34°   35°   36°

°C	°F
25	77
23	73.5
21	40
19	66
17	62.5
15	59

THE NATURAL VEGETATION OF PALESTINE

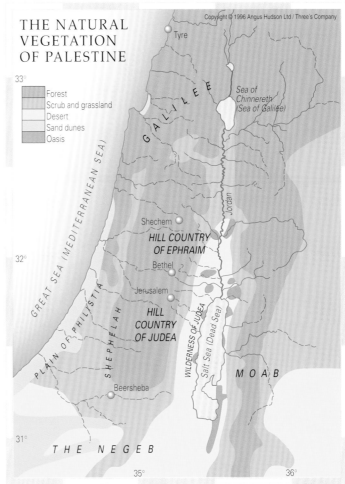

Copyright © 1996 Angus Hudson Ltd / Three's Company

Tyre

33°

Forest
Scrub and grassland
Desert
Sand dunes
Oasis

G A L I L E E

Sea of
Chinnereth
(Sea of Galilee)

Jordan

Shechem

HILL COUNTRY
OF EPHRAIM

32°

Bethel

Jerusalem

HILL
COUNTRY
OF JUDEA

WILDERNESS OF JUDEA

Salt Sea (Dead Sea)

M O A B

Beersheba

31°

T H E   N E G E B

35°   36°

GREAT SEA (MEDITERRANEAN SEA)

PLAIN OF PHILISTIA

SHEPHELAH

Trees and shrubs in the hill country near biblical Shechem.

SOILS OF PALESTINE

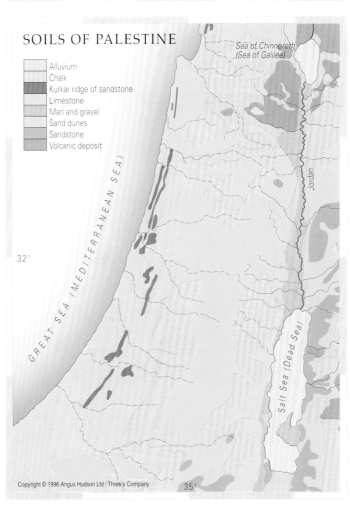

Sea of Chinnereth
(Sea of Galilee)

Alluvium
Chalk
Kurkar ridge of sandstone
Limestone
Marl and gravel
Sand dunes
Sandstone
Volcanic deposit

Jordan

32°

G R E A T   S E A   (M E D I T E R R A N E A N   S E A)

Salt Sea (Dead Sea)

35°

Copyright © 1996 Angus Hudson Ltd / Three's Company

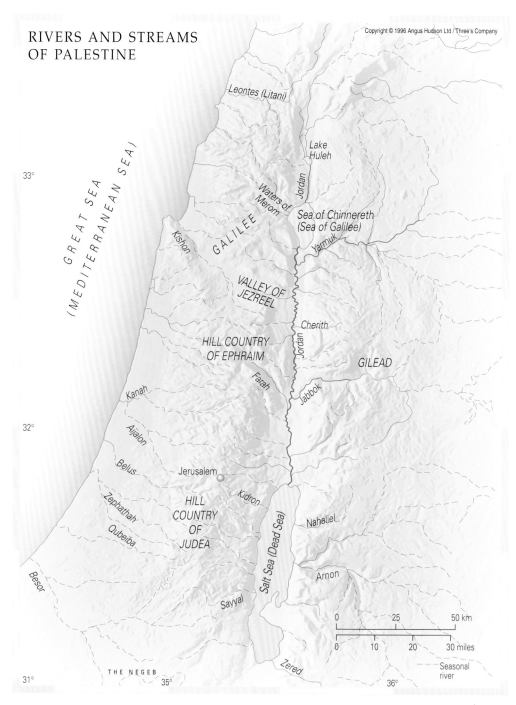

RIVERS AND STREAMS
OF PALESTINE

Leontes (Litani)

Lake
Huleh

33°

Jordan

GREAT SEA
(MEDITERRANEAN SEA)

Waters of
Merom

Sea of Chinnereth
(Sea of Galilee)

GALILEE

Kishon

Yarmuk

VALLEY OF
JEZREEL

Cherith

HILL COUNTRY
OF EPHRAIM

Jordan

GILEAD

Kanah

Farah

Jabbok

32°

Aijalon

Belus

Jerusalem

Zephathah

HILL
COUNTRY
OF
JUDEA

Kidron

Nahaliel

Qubeiba

Besor

Salt Sea (Dead Sea)

Arnon

Sayyal

0   25   50 km

0   10   20   30 miles

THE NEGEB

Zered

Seasonal
river

31°   35°   36°

**The fast-flowing
waters of the upper
reaches of the
River Jordan.**

THE BAKER
atlas
of
CHRISTIAN
HISTORY

OLD TESTAMENT PERIOD

THE FERTILE CRESCENT

The Fertile Crescent is the arc of land running from the Gulf to the Nile Delta, hedged by mountains on the east and north and enclosing the deserts of central Syria and Arabia. Rainfall in those mountains and in the ranges along the Mediterranean coast (the Amanus and the Lebanon) fills the great Tigris and Euphrates rivers and the lesser Orontes and Jordan. The first two make farming possible in Babylonia and so enabled cities to arise there six thousand years ago. Rainfall in Ethiopia fills the Nile, giving life to Egypt.

The earliest farming consisted of grain production in the river countries, while grapes and olives were grown as well in the hilly regions such as Palestine. Animals grazed in the fields and hillsides, sheep being especially important in Babylonia, where their wool supplied a major textile trade (see Joshua 7:21). Horses were raised in the hills of Ararat (Eastern Turkey) and Iran. The usual animal for carrying loads was the donkey. From about 1200 BCE camel breeding began to be important in Arabia.

Copper was the major metal from about 5000 until 1000 BCE. Ores were found in the Arabah and smelted there. Copper was alloyed with tin to make bronze from about 2500 BCE onwards. Iron working developed late in the second millennium and the metal gradually replaced bronze for tools and weapons. Gold was brought from the Land of Punt, probably Somalia, to Egypt, and was also found in the south of Egypt itself. Solomon's source, Ophir, is unidentified. Gold was also panned from rivers in western Turkey. The Dead Sea was a major provider of salt, essential for preserving fish. Along the Mediterranean coast, as well as fishing, there was an important industry in dyeing cloth, notably with the Tyrian purple. Spices and incense came from southern Arabia, the Yemen, although balsam grew in the Jordan valley. Ivory from African and Syrian elephants was beautifully carved to make veneers and inlays for wooden furniture. This luxurious fashion was harshly condemned by the prophet Amos (3:15; 6:4).

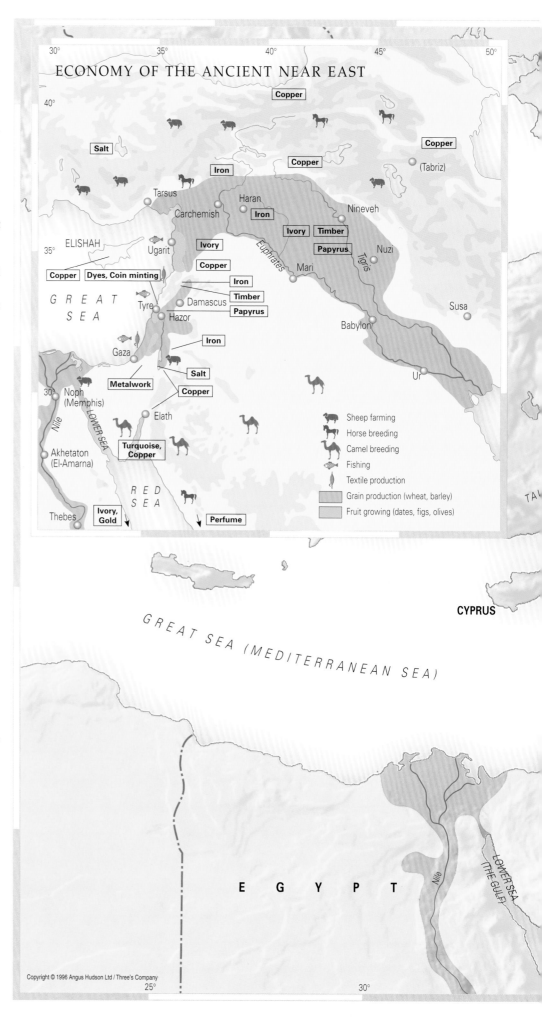

ECONOMY OF THE ANCIENT NEAR EAST

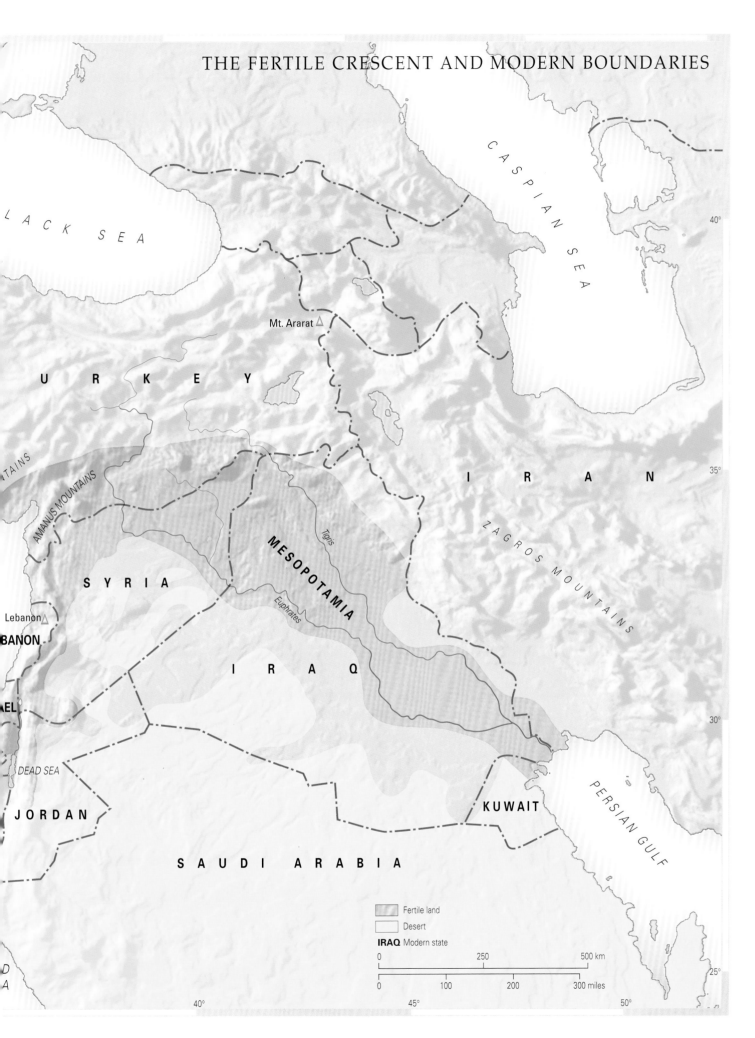

THE FERTILE CRESCENT AND MODERN BOUNDARIES

CASPIAN SEA

BLACK SEA

Mt. Ararat △

TURKEY

IRAN

TAINS

AMANUS MOUNTAINS

ZAGROS MOUNTAINS

MESOPOTAMIA

Tigris

SYRIA

Lebanon △

BANON

Euphrates

EL

IRAQ

DEAD SEA

JORDAN

KUWAIT

PERSIAN GULF

SAUDI ARABIA

Fertile land
Desert
IRAQ Modern state

0		250		500 km

0	100	200	300 miles

40°

45°

50°

40°

35°

30°

25°

D
A

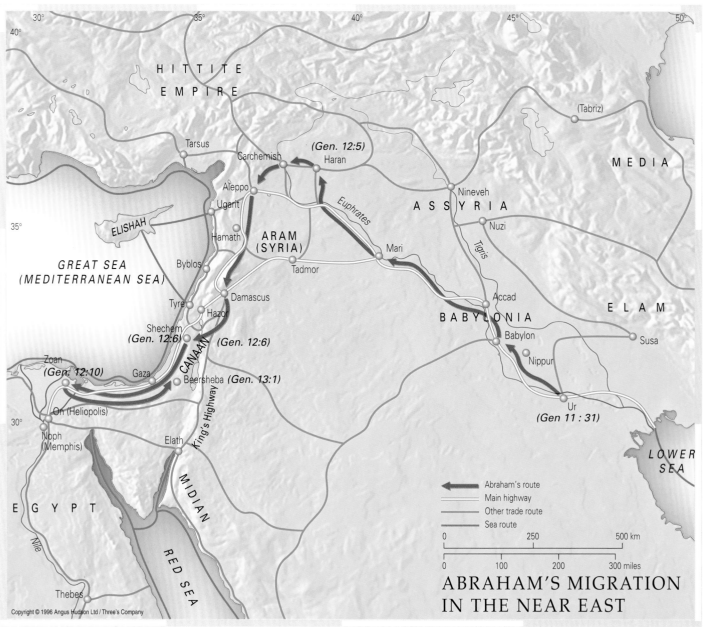

ABRAHAM'S MIGRATION IN THE NEAR EAST

Abraham's route
Main highway
Other trade route
Sea route

0 — 250 — 500 km
0 — 100 — 200 — 300 miles

Copyright © 1996 Angus Hudson Ltd / Three's Company

ABRAHAM'S JOURNEYS

Abraham's journeys began when his father took him from Ur of the Chaldees in southern Iraq. That was a major trading city and a centre for the worship of the moon-god Sin. The family made its home in Haran, another worship centre and city devoted to Sin. It was to this area that Abraham later sent Eliezer to find his son Isaac a wife, showing the importance of family ties for the Patriarchs.

By 2000 BCE there were both city-dwellers in Canaan and pastoralists who migrated in search of new pastures. Abraham never settled in a city, but by purchasing the Cave of Machpelah as a burial place he made a claim to the land. Various tribes lived there, called generally Canaanites. Among them were the Hittites who sold Abraham the cave. They may have been linked to the powerful Hittites ruling Anatolia from about 1800 to 1200 BCE, but they may have been a separate group.

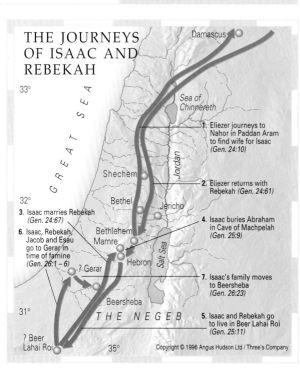

THE JOURNEYS OF ISAAC AND REBEKAH

1. Eliezer journeys to Nahor in Paddan Aram to find wife for Isaac (Gen. 24:10)
2. Eliezer returns with Rebekah (Gen. 24:61)
3. Isaac marries Rebekah (Gen. 24:67)
4. Isaac buries Abraham in Cave of Machpelah (Gen. 25:9)
5. Isaac and Rebekah go to live in Beer Lahai Roi (Gen. 25:11)
6. Isaac, Rebekah, Jacob and Esau go to Gerar in time of famine (Gen. 26:1–6)
7. Isaac's family moves to Beersheba (Gen. 26:23)

Copyright © 1996 Angus Hudson Ltd / Three's Company

16

THE JOURNEYS OF ABRAHAM IN CANAAN

ABRAHAM IN CANAAN

Abraham's career made another place in Canaan important to his descendants. The blessing King Melchizedek gave him at Salem, and the divine intervention as Abraham was about to sacrifice Isaac on Mount Moriah, point to the later importance of Jerusalem in Jewish history, for Salem is believed to be Jerusalem and Mount Moriah the hill there on which the Temple stood.

Although Abraham spent many years in Canaan and never returned to Mesopotamia, he made one further journey, following the road to Egypt which the caravans travelled bearing goods from Syria.

1. Journeys from Haran and builds altar at Shechem (*Gen. 12:6 – 7*)

4. Moves to Gerar of the Philistines (*Gen. 20:1*)

8. Buys Cave of Machpelah from Ephron the Hittite and buries Sarah (*Gen. 23:16–20*)

5. Makes treaty with Philistine King Abimelech at Beersheba (*Gen. 21:22*)

3. Returns from Egypt to settle at Mamre (*Gen. 13:18*)

2. Goes down to Egypt at time of famine (*Gen. 12:10*)

6. Journeys to Moriah to sacrifice Isaac (*Gen. 22:1–19*)

7. Returns to Beersheba (*Gen. 22:19*)

THE NEGEB

Copyright © 1996 Angus Hudson Ltd / Three's Company

The Cave of Machpelah, Hebron, traditionally the Patriarchs' burial place.

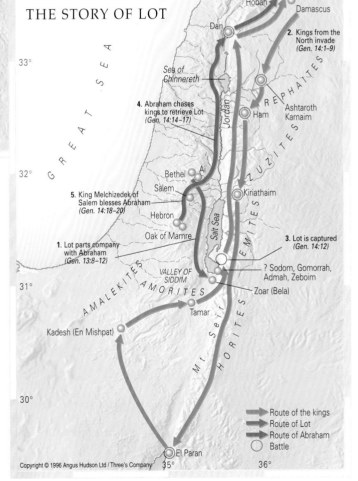

THE STORY OF LOT

4. Abraham chases kings to retrieve Lot (*Gen. 14:14–17*)

5. King Melchizedek of Salem blesses Abraham (*Gen. 14:18–20*)

1. Lot parts company with Abraham (*Gen. 13:8–12*)

2. Kings from the North invade (*Gen. 14:1–9*)

3. Lot is captured (*Gen. 14:12*)

? Sodom, Gomorrah, Admah, Zeboim

Zoar (Bela)

Route of the kings
Route of Lot
Route of Abraham
○ Battle

Copyright © 1996 Angus Hudson Ltd / Three's Company

THE PATRIARCHS

During the Patriarchal period we begin to see tribal associations with particular areas. Abraham and Isaac stayed in southern Canaan, in the area of Hebron, where the family burial place was, and near the Philistines of Gerar. Esau settled in southern Transjordan, in the Mount Seir region of Edom. Abraham, Isaac and Jacob all maintained links with Haran far to the north.

It was, however, the visits of Jacob's sons to Egypt, and eventually of the patriarch himself, that transplanted the family from Canaan. The stories of Joseph and his brothers agree with other evidence for Semitic people living in the Nile Delta area, especially between about 2000 and 1550 BCE. The circumstances of that period agree better than any other with the way of life and events the Patriarchal narratives describe.

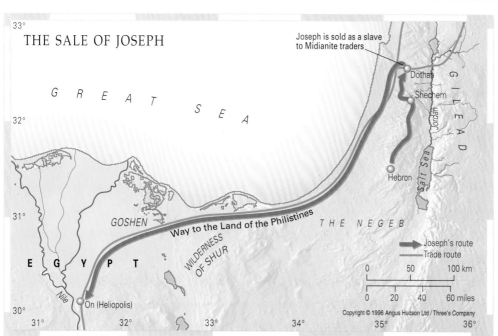

THE JOURNEYS OF JACOB AND RACHEL

Damascus

G R E A T   S E A

Sea of Chinnereth

Jordan

2. Jacob flees from Laban with Rachel, Leah and their family (Gen. 31:17)

4. Jacob's sons, Simeon and Levi, attack Shechem (Gen. 34:25)

Shechem
Succoth
Farah
Penuel   ? Mahanaim

Jabbok

Bethel (Luz)

5. Rachel dies giving birth to Benjamin (Gen. 35:18)

3. Esau comes from Seir to meet Jacob (Gen. 31:1)

Ephrath (Bethlehem)
Mamre

1. Jacob flees from Esau and works for Laban in Paddan Aram (Gen. 28:5, 29:15)

Hebron

Salt Sea

Beersheba

6. Jacob sees Isaac die (Gen. 35:29)

Mt. Seir   E D O M

| 0 | 25 | 50 km |
| 0 | 10 | 20 | 30 miles |

Copyright © 1996 Angus Hudson Ltd / Three's Company

33°
32°
31°
35°
36°

Orontes
Haran
PADDAN ARAM
Mount Lebanon
Euphrates
Damascus
Hebron
35°
30°
35°
40°

THE SALE OF JOSEPH

Joseph is sold as a slave to Midianite traders

G R E A T   S E A

Dothan
Shechem
GILEAD
Jordan
Hebron

Salt Sea

GOSHEN
Way to the Land of the Philistines
THE NEGEB
WILDERNESS OF SHUR

E G Y P T

Nile
On (Heliopolis)

→ Joseph's route
— Trade route

| 0 | 50 | 100 km |
| 0 | 20 | 40 | 60 miles |

Copyright © 1996 Angus Hudson Ltd / Three's Company

33°
32°
31°
30°
31°
32°
33°
34°
35°
36°

The Sphinx and the pyramids, Cairo, Egypt.

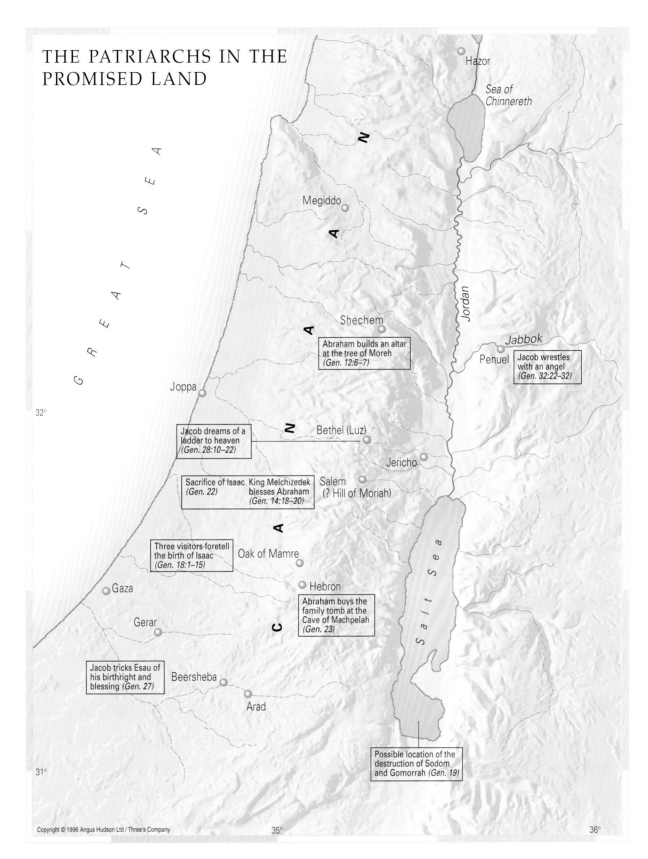

THE PATRIARCHS IN THE PROMISED LAND

Hazor

Sea of Chinnereth

G R E A T   S E A

Megiddo

N

A

Jordan

Shechem

A

Abraham builds an altar at the tree of Moreh
(Gen. 12:6–7)

Jabbok

Penuel

Jacob wrestles with an angel
(Gen. 32:22–32)

Joppa

32°

N

Bethel (Luz)

Jacob dreams of a ladder to heaven
(Gen. 28:10–22)

Jericho

Sacrifice of Isaac
(Gen. 22)

King Melchizedek blesses Abraham
(Gen. 14:18–20)

Salem
(? Hill of Moriah)

A

S a l t   S e a

Three visitors foretell the birth of Isaac
(Gen. 18:1–15)

Oak of Mamre

Gaza

Hebron

C

Abraham buys the family tomb at the Cave of Machpelah
(Gen. 23)

Gerar

Jacob tricks Esau of his birthright and blessing *(Gen. 27)*

Beersheba

Arad

Possible location of the destruction of Sodom and Gomorrah *(Gen. 19)*

31°

35°

36°

Mamre, where Isaac's birth was foretold.

Sheep in the Judean wilderness.

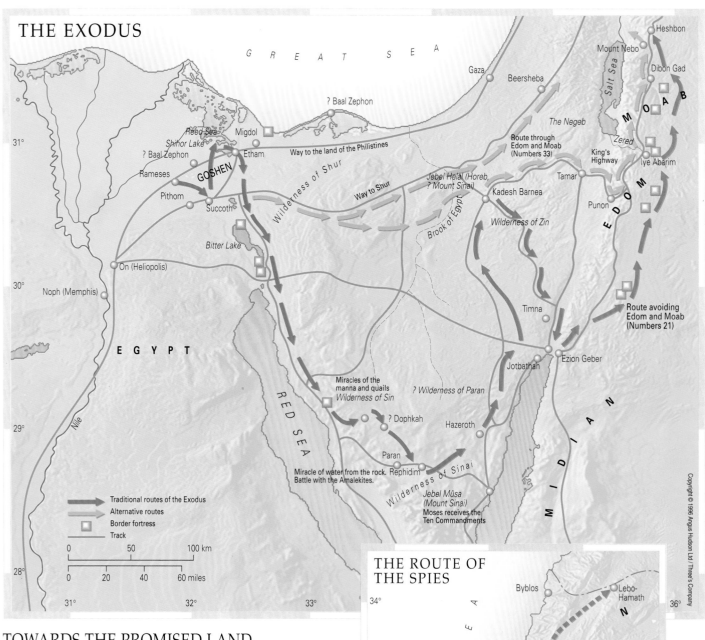

THE EXODUS

G R E A T   S E A

Gaza
Beersheba

? Baal Zephon

Reed Sea
Shihor Lake
? Baal Zephon
Migdol
Etham
Rameses
GOSHEN
Pithom
Succoth

The Negeb

Route through
Edom and Moab
(Numbers 33)

Heshbon
Mount Nebo
Dibon Gad
Salt Sea

Zered

M O A B

King's
Highway

Iye Abarim

Way to the land of the Philistines
Way to Shur
Wilderness of Shur

*Jebel Helal (Horeb,
? Mount Sinai)*
Kadesh Barnea
Tamar
Punon

E D O M

Bitter Lake

On (Heliopolis)

Wilderness of Zin

Brook of Egypt

Route avoiding
Edom and Moab
(Numbers 21)

Noph (Memphis)

E G Y P T

Timna
Jotbathah
Ezion Geber

Nile

R E D   S E A

Miracles of the
manna and quails
Wilderness of Sin

? *Wilderness of Paran*

M I D I A N

? Dophkah
Hazeroth
Paran

Miracle of water from the rock. Rephidim
Battle with the Amalekites.
Wilderness of Sinai

*Jebel Mûsa
(Mount Sinai)*
Moses receives the
Ten Commandments

Traditional routes of the Exodus
Alternative routes
Border fortress
Track

0   50   100 km
0   20   40   60 miles

31°   32°   33°

Copyright © 1996 Angus Hudson Ltd / Three's Company

TOWARDS THE PROMISED LAND

On his return to Egypt from Midian, Moses led the Israelites out of
captivity (Exodus 12–13). The route taken is debated. The traditional
route runs from Rameses to Succoth, and then turns northwards to cross
the Reed Sea, a marshy lake. It is stated in Exodus 13:17-18 that the
Israelites did not take the direct route to Canaan, the 'Way to the Land
of the Philistines', which was heavily fortified. Instead, they turned
south, taking the desert route.

The locations of some of the places visited by the Israelites during the
wilderness period are uncertain. The traditional site of Mount Sinai is
Jebel Musa. However, an alternative opinion places it at Jebel Helal in
north Sinai. If this were so, the Israelites would have taken the Way to
Shur, a much shorter journey to Canaan, via Beersheba. The route of the
Israelites' wandering in the desert has two apparently conflicting
traditions. Once the Israelites had reached Kadesh-barnea, according to
Numbers 21 they were refused permission by border guards to pass
through Edom and Moab. They had to retrace their steps to Ezion-geber
and skirt the eastern border of Edom and Moab to Heshbon. But
Numbers 33 lists towns in Edom and Moab through which the Israelites
passed on their way to Mount Nebo. Many scholars think that this list
records a migration of tribes at a different time.

THE ROUTE OF
THE SPIES

Byblos
Lebo-
Hamath

N

G R E A T   S E A

Damascus

Tyre

Amorites

Hazor
Sea of Chinnereth

C A N A A N

Shechem

Canaanites

Jordan

Amorites
Jebusites

? *Valley of Eshcol*
Jebus (Jerusalem)

Hittites

M O A B

Hebron

Salt Sea

C A N A A N

*THE
NEGEB*

Arad

E D O M

Brook of Egypt

Amalekites

Kadesh Barnea

Copyright © 1996 Angus Hudson Ltd / Three's Company

20

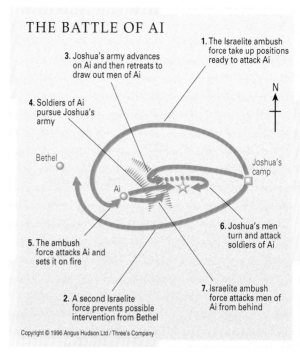

THE BATTLE OF AI

3. Joshua's army advances on Ai and then retreats to draw out men of Ai

1. The Israelite ambush force take up positions ready to attack Ai

4. Soldiers of Ai pursue Joshua's army

Bethel

Ai

Joshua's camp

N

6. Joshua's men turn and attack soldiers of Ai

5. The ambush force attacks Ai and sets it on fire

7. Israelite ambush force attacks men of Ai from behind

2. A second Israelite force prevents possible intervention from Bethel

Copyright © 1996 Angus Hudson Ltd / Three's Company

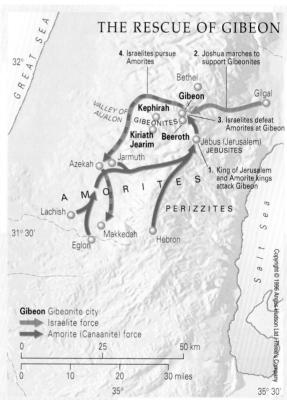

THE RESCUE OF GIBEON

4. Israelites pursue Amorites

2. Joshua marches to support Gibeonites

GREAT SEA

Bethel

Gibeon

Gilgal

Kephirah

VALLEY OF AIJALON

GIBEONITES

3. Israelites defeat Amorites at Gibeon

Kiriath Jearim

Beeroth

Jebus (Jerusalem)
JEBUSITES

Azekah

Jarmuth

1. King of Jerusalem and Amorite kings attack Gibeon

A M O R I T E S

PERIZZITES

Lachish

Salt Sea

Makkedah

Hebron

Eglon

Gibeon Gibeonite city
Israelite force
Amorite (Canaanite) force

0   25   50 km
0   10   20   30 miles

35°   35° 30'

Copyright © 1996 Angus Hudson Ltd / Three's Company

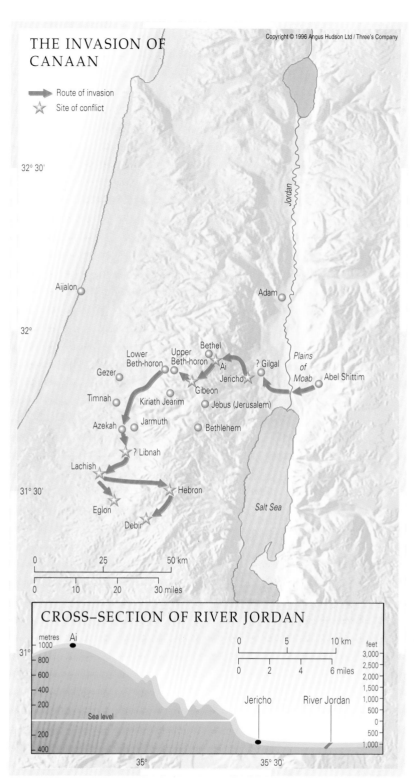

THE INVASION OF CANAAN

➤ Route of invasion
★ Site of conflict

Copyright © 1996 Angus Hudson Ltd / Three's Company

Jordan

32° 30'

32°

Aijalon

Adam

Bethel

Lower Beth-horon

Upper Beth-horon

Ai

? Gilgal

Plains of Moab

Abel Shittim

Gezer

Jericho

Timnah

Gibeon

Kiriath Jearim

Jebus (Jerusalem)

Azekah

Jarmuth

Bethlehem

31° 30'

? Libnah

Lachish

Hebron

Salt Sea

Eglon

Debir

0   25   50 km
0   10   20   30 miles

CROSS–SECTION OF RIVER JORDAN

metres
1000   Ai

800

600

400

200

Sea level

-200

-400

0   5   10 km
0   2   4   6 miles

feet
3,000
2,500
2,000
1,500
1,000
500
0
500
1,000

Jericho

River Jordan

35°   35° 30'

THE INVASION OF CANAAN

Jericho, the 'city of palms'.

Joshua led the Israelites across the River Jordan, opposite Abel-Shittim, and established camp at Gilgal (Joshua 4:19). From here, Joshua conducted his campaigns in the south of Canaan. After the capture of Jericho and Ai, the people of Gibeon signed a peace treaty with the Israelites. To counter this, the king of Jerusalem formed a coalition with the kings of Hebron, Jarmuth, Lachish and Eglon, and attacked Gibeon. Joshua's army supported Gibeon in the ensuing battle, and pursued the enemy as far as Makkedah. Many of the enemy soldiers were killed by huge hailstones, and after the battle the sun stood still in the middle of the sky for a full day (Joshua 10:1-15).

ISRAEL IN CANAAN

The most important battle in the conquest of northern Canaan was at Merom Waters (Joshua 11:1-11). A coalition of kings led by Jabin, the king of Hazor, was outwitted by Joshua's army; Hazor, the largest city in Canaan in this period, was burned.

The Israelites gradually took control of the highlands, and tended to settle there. The Canaanites, with their superior weaponry, especially the iron chariot, prevailed in the lowland areas. When the land was divided among the tribes of Israel, some towns remained unconquered, and the Israelites had to live alongside the Canaanites.

Part of the Israelite citadel at Hazor.

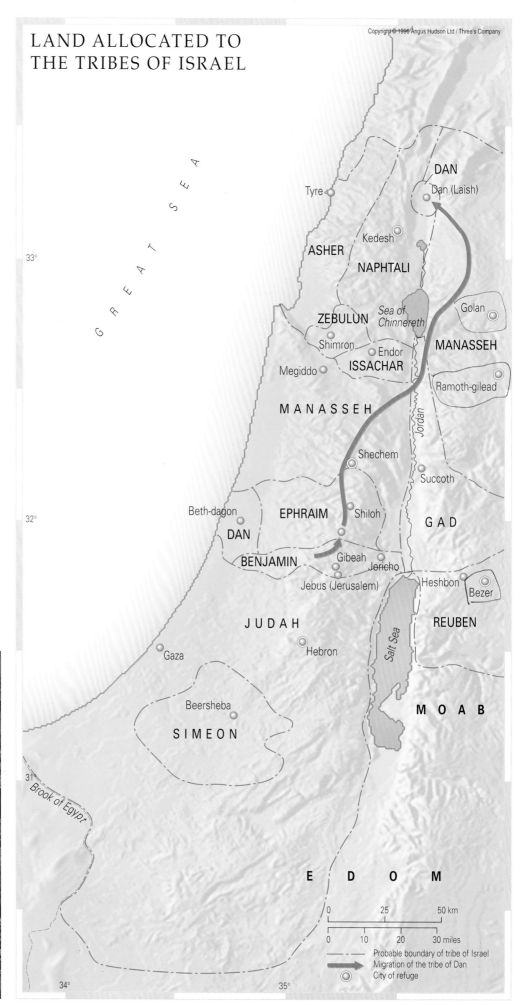

LAND ALLOCATED TO THE TRIBES OF ISRAEL

GREAT SEA

33°

32°

31°

34°

35°

DAN
Tyre
Dan (Laish)
Kedesh
ASHER
NAPHTALI
Golan
ZEBULUN
Sea of Chinnereth
MANASSEH
Shimron
Endor
ISSACHAR
Megiddo
Ramoth-gilead
MANASSEH
Jordan
Shechem
Succoth
Beth-dagon
EPHRAIM
Shiloh
GAD
DAN
BENJAMIN
Gibeah
Jericho
Jebus (Jerusalem)
Heshbon
Bezer
JUDAH
REUBEN
Gaza
Hebron
Salt Sea
Beersheba
MOAB
SIMEON
Brook of Egypt
E   D   O   M

| 0 | 25 | 50 km |
| 0 | 10 | 20 | 30 miles |

— · — Probable boundary of tribe of Israel
→ Migration of the tribe of Dan
◉ City of refuge

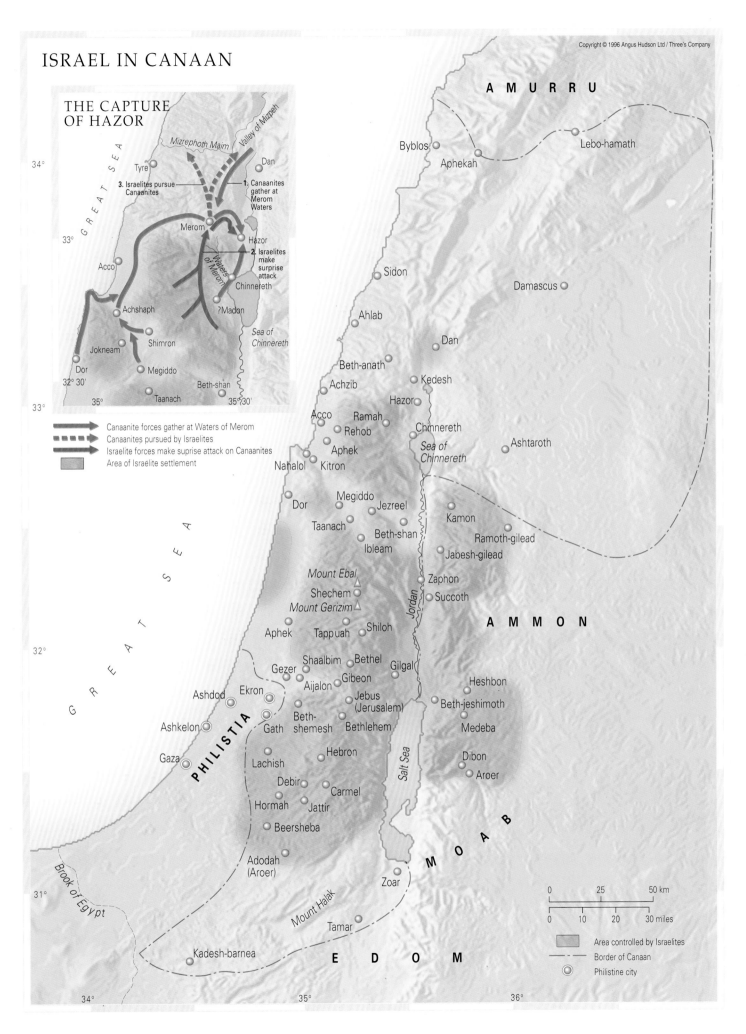

ISRAEL IN CANAAN

THE CAPTURE OF HAZOR

3. Israelites pursue Canaanites

1. Canaanites gather at Merom Waters

Mizrephoth Maim

Valley of Mizpeh

G R E A T   S E A

Tyre

Dan

Merom

Hazor

2. Israelites make surprise attack

Acco

Waters of Merom

Chinnereth

Achshaph

?Madon

Sea of Chinnereth

Jokneam

Shimron

Dor

Megiddo

Taanach

Beth-shan

→ Canaanite forces gather at Waters of Merom
┄┄► Canaanites pursued by Israelites
▬► Israelite forces make suprise attack on Canaanites
▨ Area of Israelite settlement

A M U R R U

Byblos

Aphekah

Lebo-hamath

Sidon

Damascus

Ahlab

Dan

Beth-anath

Kedesh

Achzib

Hazor

Acco

Ramah

Rehob

Chinnereth

Ashtaroth

Sea of Chinnereth

Aphek

Nahalol

Kitron

Dor

Megiddo

Jezreel

Kamon

Taanach

Beth-shan

Ramoth-gilead

Ibleam

Jabesh-gilead

Mount Ebal

Zaphon

Shechem

Succoth

Mount Gerizim

Jordan

A M M O N

Aphek

Tappuah

Shiloh

Shaalbim

Bethel

Gilgal

Gezer

Gibeon

Heshbon

Aijalon

Jebus
(Jerusalem)

Beth-jeshimoth

Ashdod

Ekron

Beth-
shemesh

Bethlehem

Medeba

Ashkelon

Gath

PHILISTIA

Dibon

Gaza

Hebron

Aroer

Lachish

Debir

Carmel

Salt Sea

Hormah

Jattir

Beersheba

M O A B

Adodah
(Aroer)

Zoar

G R E A T   S E A

Brook of Egypt

Mount Halak

Tamar

Kadesh-barnea

E D O M

Copyright © 1996 Angus Hudson Ltd / Three's Company

| 0 | 25 | 50 km |
| 0 | 10 | 20 | 30 miles |

▨ Area controlled by Israelites
─·─ Border of Canaan
◎ Philistine city

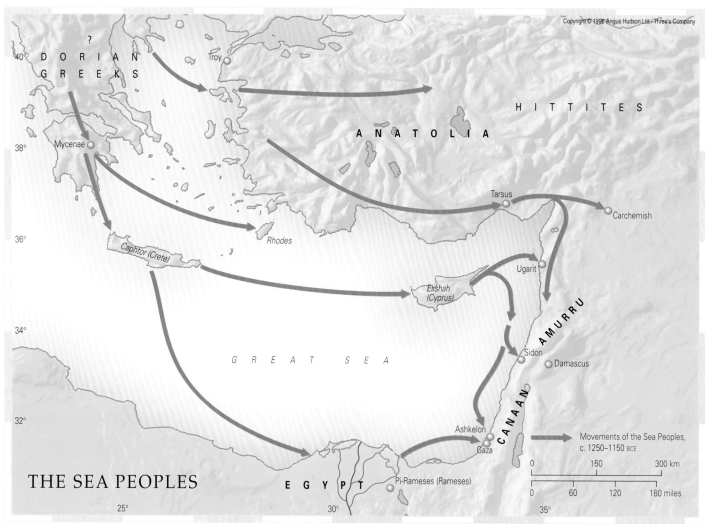

THE SEA PEOPLES

THE PHILISTINES

Large numbers of 'Sea Peoples', as the
Egyptians called them, including the
Philistines, migrated to the shores of
the eastern Mediterranean between
about 1250 and 1150 BCE. Ramesses III
tells how he repelled their forces from
the Nile delta in 1174 BCE and then they
settled along the coast of the southern
Levant, where they destroyed existing
Canaanite cities and built their own.

Archaeological finds include
distinctive Mycenaean-style pottery.
Indications of a well-organized
civilization support the Israelite notion
that the Philistines were powerful. Of
Israel's Judges, only Samson could
achieve temporary success against them
(Judges 13-16).

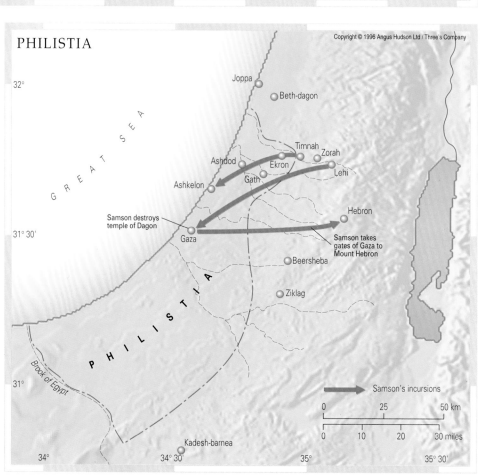

PHILISTIA

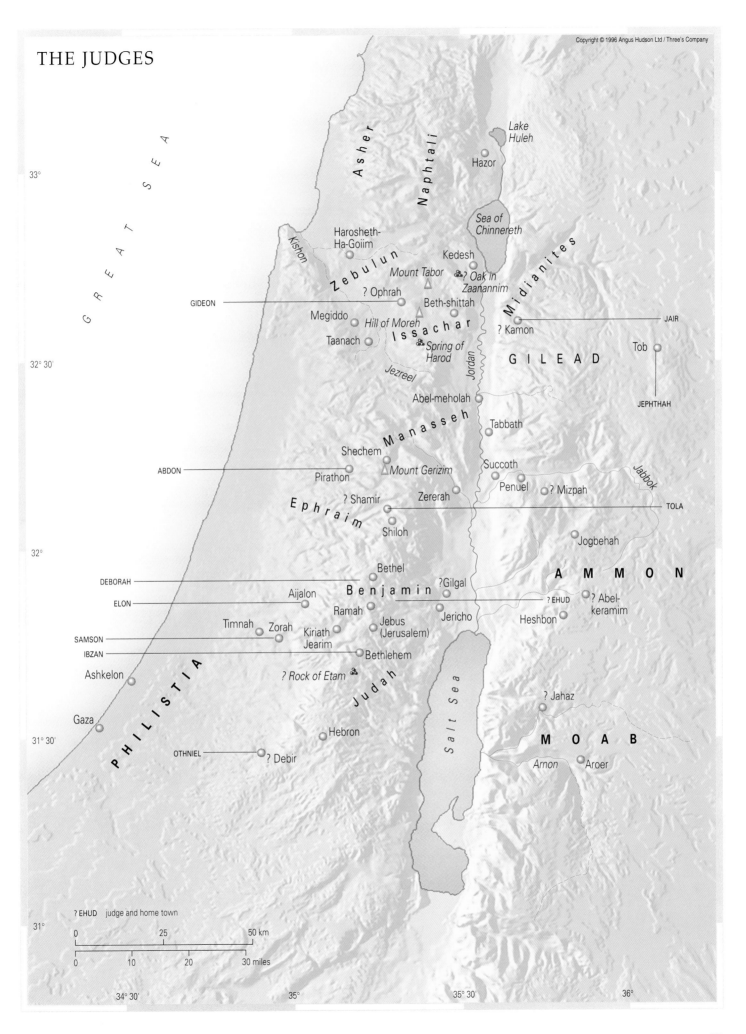

THE JUDGES

Lake Huleh

Hazor

G R E A T   S E A

A s h e r

N a p h t a l i

Sea of Chinnereth

Harosheth-Ha-Goiim

Kishon

Kedesh

? Oak in Zaanannim

Z e b u l u n

Mount Tabor

M i d i a n i t e s

? Ophrah

GIDEON

Beth-shittah

JAIR

Megiddo

Hill of Moreh

I s s a c h a r

? Kamon

G I L E A D

Tob

Taanach

Spring of Harod

Jezreel

Jordan

JEPHTHAH

Abel-meholah

Tabbath

M a n a s s e h

Shechem

Succoth

ABDON

△ *Mount Gerizim*

Jabbok

Pirathon

Penuel

? Mizpah

? Shamir

Zererah

TOLA

E p h r a i m

Shiloh

Jogbehah

Bethel

A M M O N

DEBORAH

?Gilgal

ELON

Aijalon

B e n j a m i n

? EHUD

? Abel-keramim

Ramah

Timnah

Zorah

Jebus (Jerusalem)

Jericho

Heshbon

SAMSON

Kiriath Jearim

IBZAN

Bethlehem

Ashkelon

? *Rock of Etam*

J u d a h

P H I L I S T I A

S a l t   S e a

? Jahaz

Gaza

M O A B

Hebron

Arnon

Aroer

OTHNIEL

? Debir

33°

32° 30'

32°

31° 30'

31°

34° 30'

35°

35° 30'

36°

? EHUD   judge and home town

0   25   50 km

0   10   20   30 miles

25

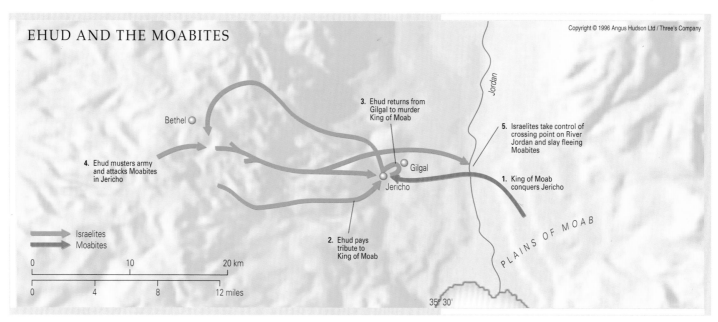

EHUD AND THE MOABITES

3. Ehud returns from Gilgal to murder King of Moab

5. Israelites take control of crossing point on River Jordan and slay fleeing Moabites

4. Ehud musters army and attacks Moabites in Jericho

Gilgal

Jericho

Bethel

1. King of Moab conquers Jericho

2. Ehud pays tribute to King of Moab

Jordan

PLAINS OF MOAB

→ Israelites
→ Moabites

0   10   20 km
0   4   8   12 miles

35° 30'

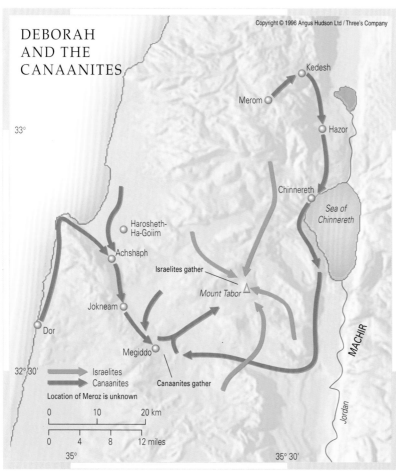

DEBORAH AND THE CANAANITES

Kedesh

Merom

Hazor

33°

Chinnereth

Sea of Chinnereth

Harosheth-Ha-Goiim

Achshaph

Israelites gather

Mount Tabor

Jokneam

MACHIR

Dor

Megiddo

Canaanites gather

→ Israelites
→ Canaanites

Location of Meroz is unknown

0   10   20 km
0   4   8   12 miles

32° 30'

35°

Jordan

35° 30'

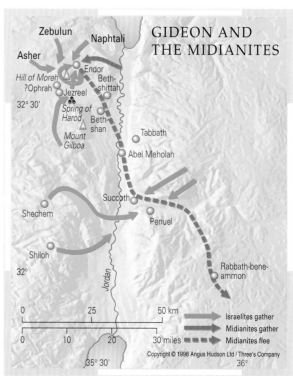

GIDEON AND THE MIDIANITES

Zebulun   Naphtali

Asher

Hill of Moreh
?Ophrah   Endor   Beth-shittah

Jezreel

32° 30'

Spring of Harod   Beth-shan

Mount Gilboa

Tabbath

Abel Meholah

Shechem   Succoth

Penuel

Shiloh

32°

Jordan

Rabbath-bene-ammon

0   25   50 km
0   10   20   30 miles

→ Israelites gather
⇢ Midianites gather
⇢ Midianites flee

35° 30'   36°

Mount Tabor stands out prominently in the landscape.

THE JUDGES

Israelite Judges were charismatic military leaders, who were considered to be chosen by God. It is likely that they operated at a local level in skirmishes with territorial rivals. The Judges spanned the period from Joshua's settlement to the monarchy. From time to time there were leagues of tribes (Judges 4:5; 6:35; 20:1), but there was little political unity between north and south.

JEPHTHAH AND THE AMMONITES

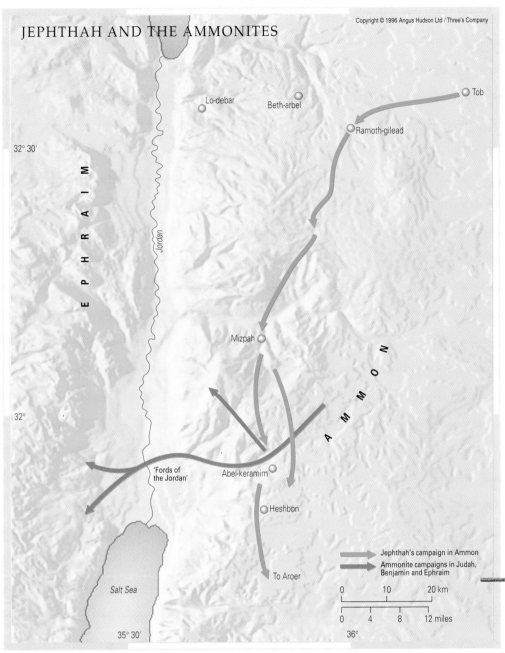

Copyright © 1996 Angus Hudson Ltd / Three's Company

E P H R A I M

Jordan

32° 30'

32°

Lo-debar

Beth-arbel

Tob

Ramoth-gilead

A M M O N

Mizpah

'Fords of the Jordan'

Abel-keramim

Heshbon

To Aroer

Salt Sea

35° 30'

36°

→ Jephthah's campaign in Ammon

→ Ammonite campaigns in Judah, Benjamin and Ephraim

| 0 | 10 | 20 km |
| 0 | 4 | 8 | 12 miles |

The Jordan Valley near Jericho.

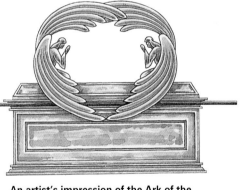

An artist's impression of the Ark of the Covenant.

CAPTURE OF THE ARK

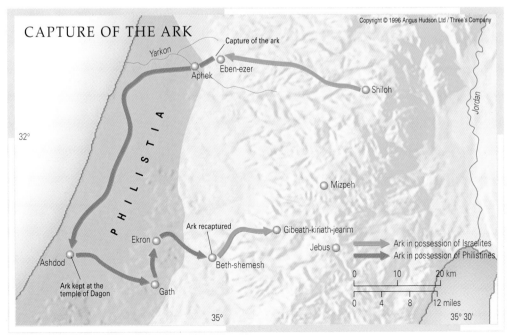

Copyright © 1996 Angus Hudson Ltd / Three's Company

Yarkon

Capture of the ark

Aphek

Eben-ezer

Shiloh

P H I L I S T I A

32°

Jordan

Mizpeh

Ekron

Ark recaptured

Gibeath-kiriath-jearim

Jebus

Ashdod

Beth-shemesh

Ark kept at the temple of Dagon

Gath

→ Ark in possession of Israelites

→ Ark in possession of Philistines

| 0 | 10 | 20 km |
| 0 | 4 | 8 | 12 miles |

35°

35° 30'

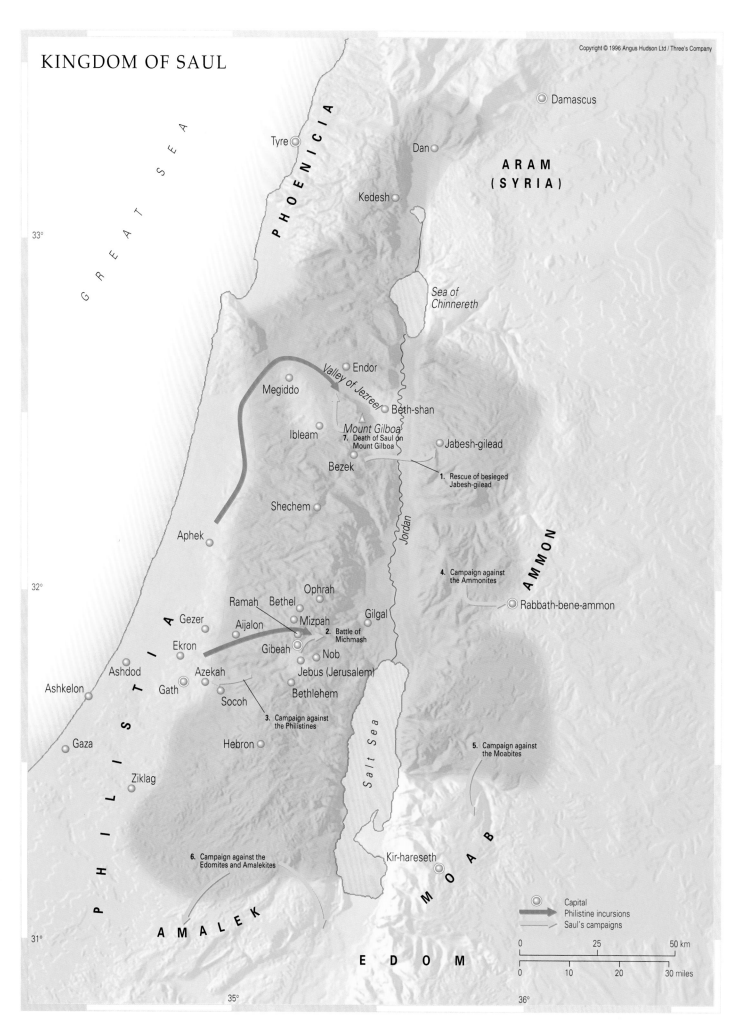

KINGDOM OF SAUL

Copyright © 1996 Angus Hudson Ltd / Three's Company

Damascus

GREAT SEA

Tyre

Dan

ARAM
(SYRIA)

PHOENICIA

Kedesh

33°

Sea of Chinnereth

Endor

Valley of Jezreel

Megiddo

Beth-shan

Ibleam

Mount Gilboa
7. Death of Saul on Mount Gilboa

Jabesh-gilead

Bezek

1. Rescue of besieged Jabesh-gilead

Shechem

Jordan

Aphek

AMMON

4. Campaign against the Ammonites

32°

Ophrah

Ramah   Bethel

Gezer   Mizpah   Gilgal

Aijalon

Rabbath-bene-ammon

Ekron   Gibeah

2. Battle of Michmash

Ashdod   Azekah   Nob

Ashkelon   Gath   Jebus (Jerusalem)

Socoh   Bethlehem

3. Campaign against the Philistines

Salt Sea

Gaza   Hebron

5. Campaign against the Moabites

Ziklag

MOAB

6. Campaign against the Edomites and Amalekites

Kir-hareseth

AMALEK

○ Capital
→ Philistine incursions
⌒ Saul's campaigns

0   25   50 km

0   10   20   30 miles

31°

EDOM

35°   36°

28

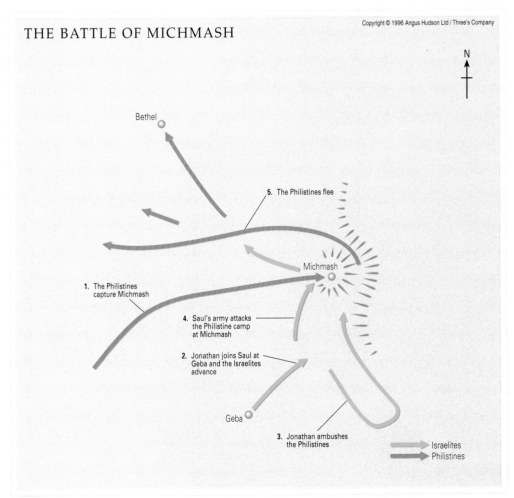

THE RESCUE OF JABESH-GILEAD

Copyright © 1996 Angus Hudson Ltd / Three's Company

32° 30'

3. Saul attacks Ammonites

2. Israelites assemble

1. King of Ammon attacks Jabesh-gilead

Bezek

Jabesh-gilead

Tirzah

Shechem

Jordan

Shiloh

32°

Rabbath-bene-ammon

Gibeah

→ Israelites
→ Ammonites

0   15   30 km

0   6   12   18 miles

Salt Sea

35°   35° 30'   36°

ISRAEL   GILEAD   AMMON

THE KINGDOM OF SAUL

Saul was made king of Israel by the prophet Samuel in response to popular clamour for a king (I Samuel 8:5). Neighbouring states were all kingdoms, and it was widely believed that Israel's military failures were due to her lack of leadership and unity.

Saul led Israel successfully against the Ammonites to relieve Jabesh-gilead, before being anointed king at Gilgal. In a concerted series of assaults on Philistine garrisons, the Israelites scored a number of victories over their old enemy 'from Michmash to Aijalon' (I Sam 14). With the help of his son Jonathan's ambush tactics, Saul recorded a famous victory at Michmash.

THE BATTLE OF MICHMASH

Copyright © 1996 Angus Hudson Ltd / Three's Company

N

Bethel

5. The Philistines flee

Michmash

1. The Philistines capture Michmash

4. Saul's army attacks the Philistine camp at Michmash

2. Jonathan joins Saul at Geba and the Israelites advance

Geba

3. Jonathan ambushes the Philistines

→ Israelites
→ Philistines

The hills near biblical Shiloh.

29

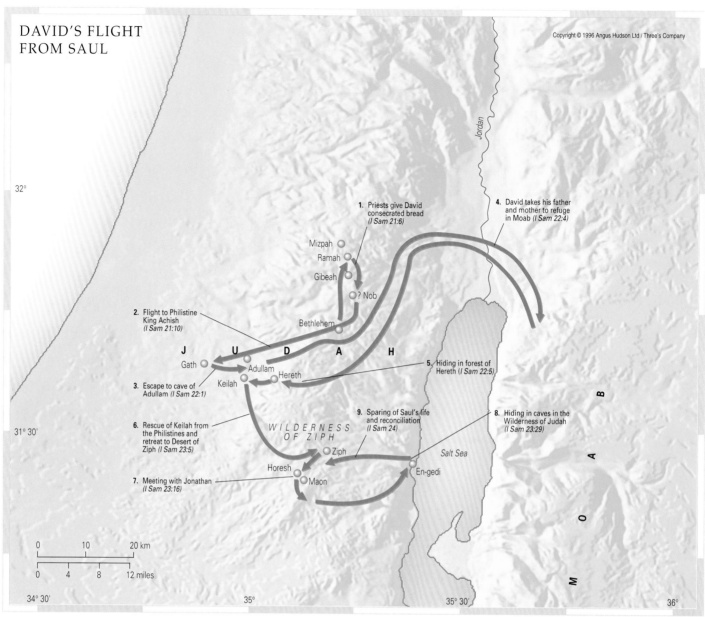

DAVID'S FLIGHT FROM SAUL

32°

1. Priests give David consecrated bread (I Sam 21:6)

4. David takes his father and mother to refuge in Moab (I Sam 22:4)

Mizpah
Ramah
Gibeah
? Nob

2. Flight to Philistine King Achish (I Sam 21:10)

Bethlehem

J U D A H

Gath
Adullam
Hereth

3. Escape to cave of Adullam (I Sam 22:1)

Keilah

5. Hiding in forest of Hereth (I Sam 22:5)

6. Rescue of Keilah from the Philistines and retreat to Desert of Ziph (I Sam 23:5)

9. Sparing of Saul's life and reconciliation (I Sam 24)

8. Hiding in caves in the Wilderness of Judah (I Sam 23:29)

WILDERNESS OF ZIPH

Ziph

Horesh

Maon

En-gedi

Salt Sea

7. Meeting with Jonathan (I Sam 23:16)

31° 30'

M O A B

0   10   20 km

0   4   8   12 miles

34° 30'   35°   35° 30'   36°

THE DEATH OF SAUL

Successful campaigns to the south of the kingdom prepared the way for Saul's successor, David, to enlarge the realm. However, Saul's jealousy of David, even to the point of trying to kill him, marks the turn in Saul's fortunes. After consulting a 'witch' (medium) at Endor, he and Jonathan died when the Israelites were defeated by the Philistines at the Battle of Gilboa (I Samuel 31:1-6).

David was forced to flee from the murderous Saul and he sought refuge in many places, including the court of a Philistine king. After Saul's death, David was first crowned King of Judah, and then of all Israel, at Hebron (II Sam 2).

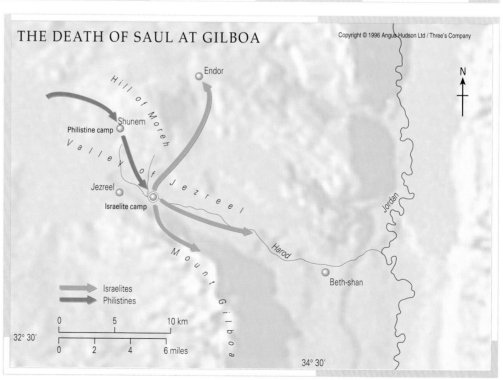

THE DEATH OF SAUL AT GILBOA

N

Endor

Hill of Moreh

Shunem
Philistine camp

Valley of Jezreel

Jezreel
Israelite camp

Harod

Mount Gilboa

Beth-shan

Jordan

→ Israelites
→ Philistines

0   5   10 km

0   2   4   6 miles

32° 30'

34° 30'

THE CAMPAIGNS OF DAVID

Damascus

ARAM
(SYRIA)

ZOBAH

Dan
Beth-rehob

8. Conquest of the
Arameans
(II Sam. 8:5–6)

Tyre

PHOENICIA

Acco

Helam

Sea of
Chinnereth

Edrei

Megiddo

Valley of
Jezreel

Beth-
shan

ISRAEL

4. Conquest of the
Plain of Sharon
and Valley of
Jezreel

Shechem

AMMON

7. War against Ammon
(II Sam. 8:12)

Yarkon

Gath
(Metheg-
ammah)

3. Conquest of the
Philistines
(II Sam. 5 & 8)

Rabbah

Gezer

Geba

Jericho

Heshbon

Ashdod

Sorek

Jerusalem

Jarmuth

Valley of
Rephaim

Kidron

Medeba

Valley of Elah

Bethlehem

JUDAH

Keilah

2. Capture of
Jerusalem
(II Sam. 5)

Salt
Sea

5. War against Moab
(II Sam. 8:12)

Gaza

PHILISTIA

Hebron

MOAB

Besor

Ziklag

Gath

Beersheba

THE NEGEB

1. Conquest of the
Negeb (I Sam. 30)

6. War against Edom
(II Sam. 8:13–14)

EDOM

Brook of Egypt

Kadesh-barnea

THE ARABAH

? Sela

Kir-hareseth

Jordan

G R E A T   S E A

Campaign of David
Campaign of the Philistines
Coalition forces of Aram and Ammon

0   25   50   75 km

0   15   30   45 miles

Ezion-geber

David set about consolidating what Saul had begun: uniting his people, breaking the power of the Philistines, and expanding the frontiers of his kingdom over the Edomites, Ammonites, Moabites and Arameans. His capture of Jerusalem from the Jebusites completed the conquest of Canaan. Then the Ark of the Covenant (a cultic chest containing the sacred tablets of Moses) was ceremoniously brought up to the city which David made his capital (II Samuel 6).

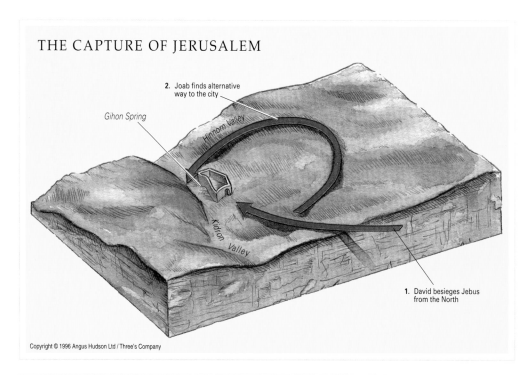

THE CAPTURE OF JERUSALEM

2. Joab finds alternative way to the city

Gihon Spring

Hinnom Valley

Kidron Valley

1. David besieges Jebus from the North

Copyright © 1996 Angus Hudson Ltd / Three's Company

The Gihon spring flows through the Kidron valley and was the main source of water for ancient Jerusalem. It is thought that David captured the city by making a surprise attack via the Gihon spring. The cross-section shows the possible route referred to in II Sam 5:8, 'Anyone who conquers the Jebusites will have to use the water shaft . . . '. The vertical shaft is about nine metres (37 feet) deep.

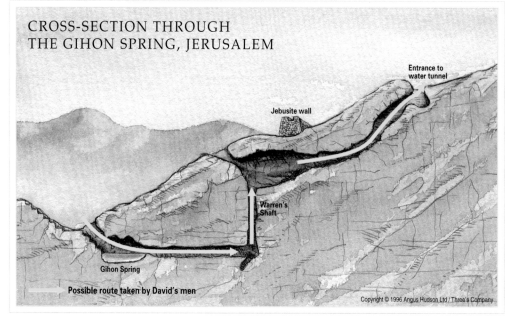

CROSS-SECTION THROUGH THE GIHON SPRING, JERUSALEM

Entrance to water tunnel

Jebusite wall

Warren's Shaft

Gihon Spring

Possible route taken by David's men

Copyright © 1996 Angus Hudson Ltd / Three's Company

Part of the Kidron valley, Jerusalem, site of the Gihon spring.

DAVID'S UNITED KINGDOM

Copyright © 1996 Angus Hudson Ltd / Three's Company

HAMATH

GREAT SEA

Cun
Lebo-hamath

PHOENICIA

Berothah

**A R A M
(S Y R I A)**

Sidon

Damascus

Ijon (Jaan)

Tyre

Dan

Usu

Kedesh

Acco

GESHUR

Chinnereth

Sea of
Chinnereth

Dor

Megiddo

Ramoth-gilead

Taanach

Beth-shan

I
S
R
A
E
L

Shechem

Jordan

Joppa

Jazer

A M M O N

Gezer

Rabbath-bene-
ammon

Ashdod

Jerusalem

Medeba

Ashkelon

Gath

P
H
I
L
I
S
T
I
A

Gaza

J
U
D
A
H

Hebron

Salt Sea

Aroer

Beersheba

King's Highway

Zoar

M O A B

J

Tamar

E
D
O
M

Kadesh-barnea

| 0 | 25 | 50 | 75 km |
| 0 | 15 | 30 | 45 miles |

Brook of Egypt

Territory of Judah and Israel
Vassal territory
Conquered territory
Route of Joab's census

Ezion-geber

34°   35°   36°

DAVID'S KINGDOM

David extended his kingdom to include lands from Dan to the Brook of Egypt. His empire stretched much farther, to the Euphrates in the north and Ezion-geber on the Gulf of Aqabah in the south. The peoples of Edom, Moab, Ammon and Aram became his vassal states, and were subjected to paying tribute (II Samuel 8:2-14). This, together with the tax levied on the huge volume of trade which passed through the Levant, brought in a healthy income for the treasury. David was able to commission buildings, such as his own palace in Jerusalem, for which he used craftsmen from neighbouring states (II Samuel 5:11). David was careful to maintain peace treaties with his allies, the Philistines and the people of Hamath.

David and his generals managed to hold together the hegemony they had imposed on the Levant, in spite of two rebellions within Israel (one by his son Absalom, the other by Sheba the Benjaminite). At his death, c. 970 BCE, David handed over to his son Solomon an empire which, fifty years earlier, would have been unimaginable, and the size of which would not be seen again under Israelite rule.

SOLOMON'S KINGDOM

After winning a difficult succession struggle, Solomon was to reign for some forty years (c. 970-930 BCE). His strengths were administration and diplomacy. He married the daughters of neighbouring kings as a means of sealing diplomatic relations, and entered joint commercial enterprises with Hiram, the king of the Phoenician city of Tyre. His own kingdom he divided into twelve administrative districts (I Kings 4:7-19). This facilitated a nationwide building programme. Each district had an administrator responsible for organizing the corvée (forced labour) needed to quarry the hill country and produce masonry for building. Administrators in the lowlands would collect the levy, mainly from Canaanites.

Solomon developed a trade monopoly and exploited the natural resources in his empire. He built the Temple and other public buildings in Jerusalem, and fortified the cities of Hazor, Megiddo, Gezer, Lower Beth-horon, Baalath and Tamar in the Arabah (I Kings 6, 7, 9:15-18). He constructed smelting furnaces for his iron and copper mining enterprises, and made a naval base at Ezion-geber.

However, the extravagance of some of his schemes and the forced labour policy sowed the seeds of discontent which would result in the break up of the realm during the reign of his successor.

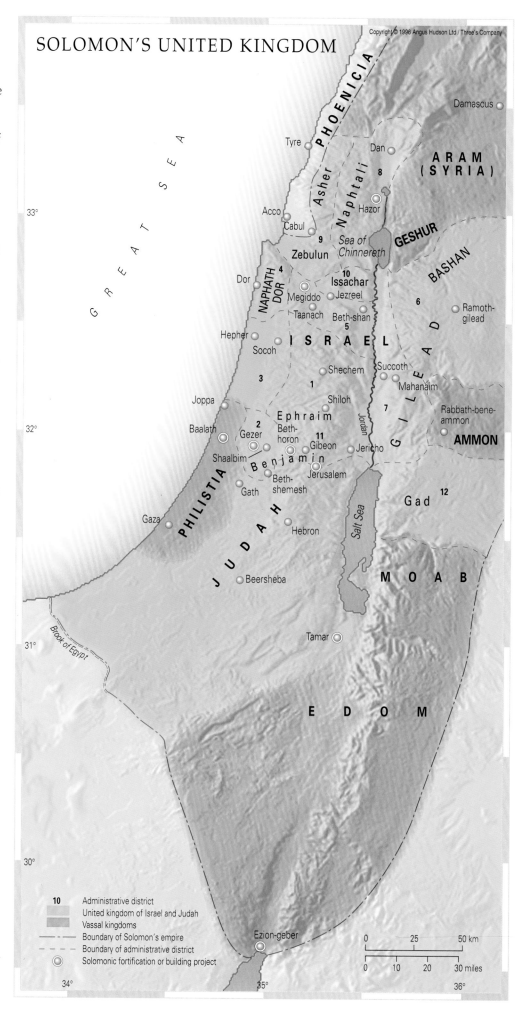

SOLOMON'S UNITED KINGDOM

Copyright © 1996 Angus Hudson Ltd / Three's Company

10	Administrative district
	United kingdom of Israel and Judah
	Vassal kingdoms
	Boundary of Solomon's empire
	Boundary of administrative district
	Solomonic fortification or building project

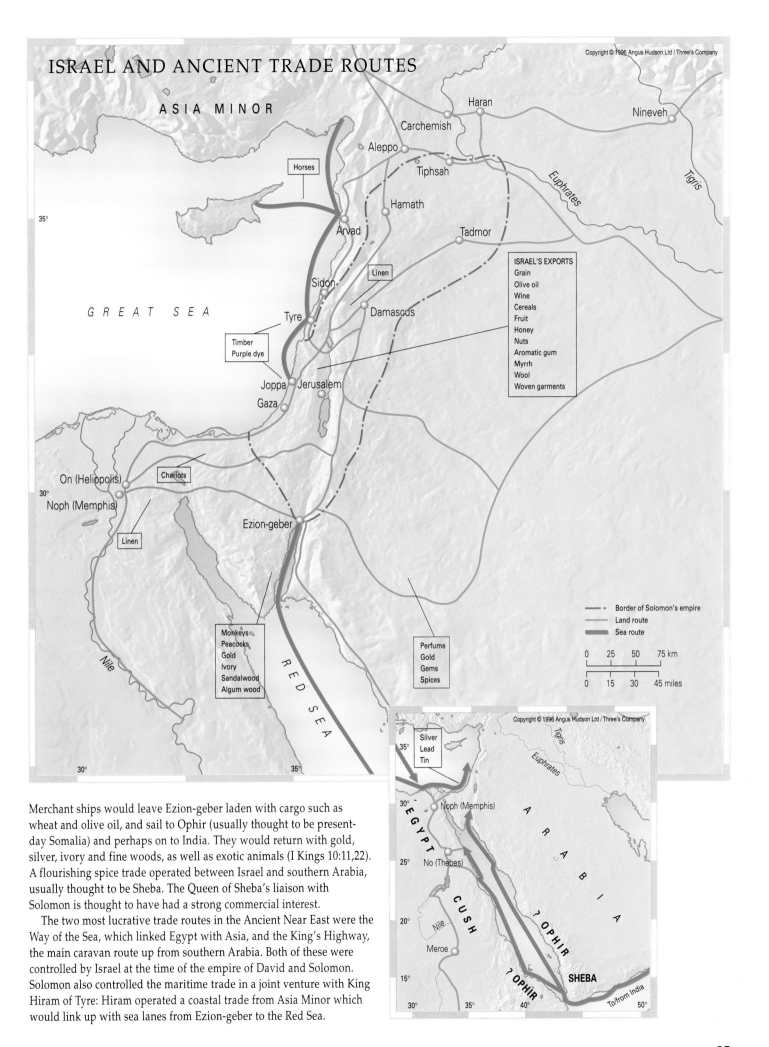

ISRAEL AND ANCIENT TRADE ROUTES

ASIA MINOR

Haran

Nineveh

Carchemish

Aleppo

Tiphsah

Euphrates

Tigris

Hamath

Horses

Arvad

Tadmor

Sidon

Linen

ISRAEL'S EXPORTS
Grain
Olive oil
Wine
Cereals
Fruit
Honey
Nuts
Aromatic gum
Myrrh
Wool
Woven garments

GREAT SEA

Tyre

Damascus

Timber
Purple dye

Joppa

Jerusalem

Gaza

On (Heliopolis)

Chariots

Noph (Memphis)

Ezion-geber

Linen

Nile

Monkeys
Peacocks
Gold
Ivory
Sandalwood
Algum wood

RED SEA

Perfume
Gold
Gems
Spices

-·-·- Border of Solomon's empire
——— Land route
——— Sea route

| 0 | 25 | 50 | 75 km |
| 0 | 15 | 30 | 45 miles |

35°

30°

30°

35°

Copyright © 1996 Angus Hudson Ltd / Three's Company

Silver
Lead
Tin

Copyright © 1996 Angus Hudson Ltd / Three's Company

Tigris

Euphrates

35°

30°

Noph (Memphis)

EGYPT

A R A B I A

25°

No (Thebes)

20°

CUSH

Nile

? OPHIR

Meroe

15°

? OPHIR

SHEBA

To/from India

30°

35°

40°

50°

Merchant ships would leave Ezion-geber laden with cargo such as wheat and olive oil, and sail to Ophir (usually thought to be present-day Somalia) and perhaps on to India. They would return with gold, silver, ivory and fine woods, as well as exotic animals (I Kings 10:11,22). A flourishing spice trade operated between Israel and southern Arabia, usually thought to be Sheba. The Queen of Sheba's liaison with Solomon is thought to have had a strong commercial interest.

The two most lucrative trade routes in the Ancient Near East were the Way of the Sea, which linked Egypt with Asia, and the King's Highway, the main caravan route up from southern Arabia. Both of these were controlled by Israel at the time of the empire of David and Solomon. Solomon also controlled the maritime trade in a joint venture with King Hiram of Tyre: Hiram operated a coastal trade from Asia Minor which would link up with sea lanes from Ezion-geber to the Red Sea.

JERUSALEM

The Jebusite city that David captured was built on a spur of a hill to the north. Apart from its good defensive position, with high surrounding walls, this site was also chosen for its water supply, which lay at the foot of the eastern slope, and was known as the Gihon spring. There was limited space, and many houses had to be built on stone terraces on the slopes. As the city expanded in Solomon's time, so the centre shifted northwards to the flatter top of the hill. David selected an old Jebusite threshing-floor, reputedly the site of Isaac's sacrifice on Mt Moriah, as the place for the altar (II Samuel 24:18). It was here that Solomon built his Temple. He built a magnificent palace too, made of cedars from Lebanon, which served as an armoury and treasury; and also a judgement hall, and a palace for one of his wives, the daughter of the Pharaoh of Egypt.

The Temple Mount area, reputedly the site of Mount Moriah.

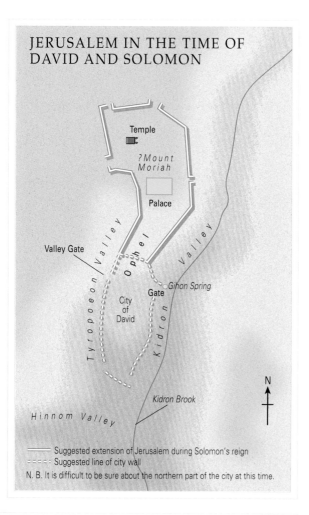

JERUSALEM IN THE TIME OF DAVID AND SOLOMON

Suggested extension of Jerusalem during Solomon's reign
Suggested line of city wall
N. B. It is difficult to be sure about the northern part of the city at this time.

MEGIDDO

Megiddo was a strategic city on the edge of the plain of Jezreel, guarding the Iron valley which passed through the Carmel range. The 'tell' (ruin mound) is some 20 metres (70 feet) high and the top covers more than 4 hectares (10 acres). Excavations have revealed that it was a Canaanite capital before Israelite settlement. Solomon fortified the gateway, but the stables were probably built in King Ahab's time.

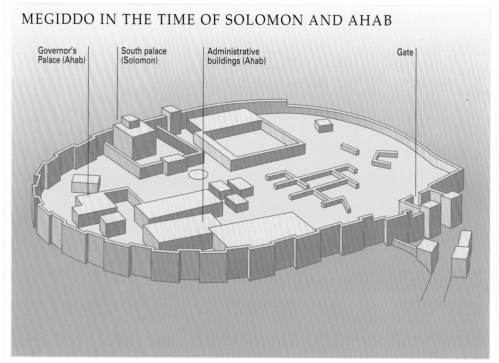

MEGIDDO IN THE TIME OF SOLOMON AND AHAB

Governor's Palace (Ahab) South palace (Solomon) Administrative buildings (Ahab) Gate

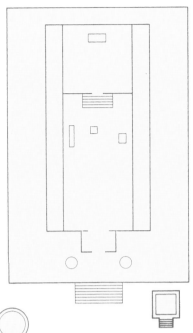

SOLOMON'S TEMPLE

Nothing remains of the Solomonic Temple. It is described in some detail in both I Kings and II Chronicles. Measurements are given and materials specified. Canaanite temple ruins have been excavated which are similar in style to the biblical description and may have provided a prototype for Solomon's Temple. The reconstruction (below) shows three main chambers – a porch, a main hall and the Holiest Place. The chief priest's ritual duties were performed in the main hall. The Holiest Place housed the Ark of the Covenant, which was guarded by two cherubim.

An artist's impression of Solomon's Temple.

Key to Plan

1 Holy Place
2 Ark of the Covenant
3 Altar of Sacrifice
4 Laver
5 Holiest Place
6 Jachin
7 Boaz

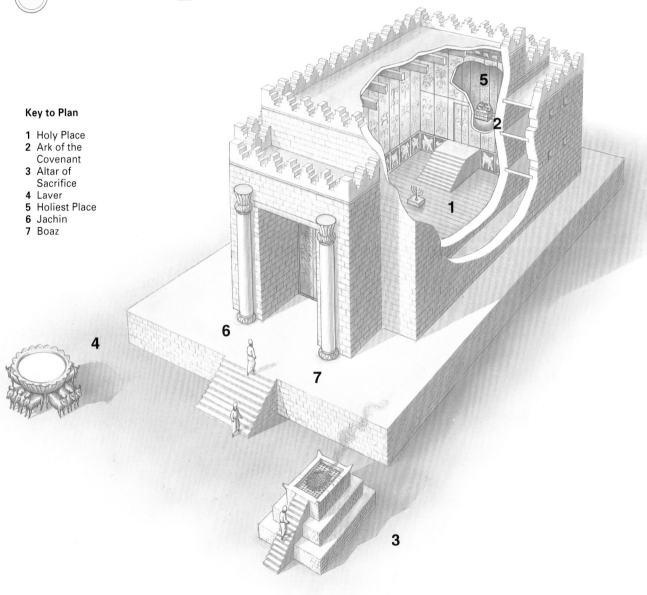

THE DIVISION OF THE KINGDOM

At Solomon's death, *c.* 930 BCE, his son Rehoboam was recognized as the new king in Judah, but was rejected by the elders of the northern tribes at the council of Shechem. They refused to accept him because he increased rather than lightened the taxation his father imposed. The northern tribes elected as their king Jeroboam, who had returned from Egypt, where he had found asylum in Solomon's reign.

Two kingdoms emerged, Israel in the north and Judah in the south, divided approximately along the traditional boundary between Ephraim and Benjamin (I Kings 12-13).

Conquered states broke away as civil war and diminishing control over trade routes weakened the two kingdoms. Syria, Ammon, Moab and the Philistines all reasserted their independence. Egypt, which for a long time had been unable to pursue her imperial ambitions into Asia, now took advantage of the situation and Pharaoh Shishak invaded Judah in the fifth year of Rehoboam's reign and his troops marched into Israel, in spite of Pharaoh's sheltering Jeroboam in his earlier exile.

An account of the invasion is recorded in the Temple at Karnak, in Egypt. More than 150 places were captured in Judah, the Negev, Israel and

The north gate of the excavated stronghold of Megiddo.

Transjordan. The speed and ferocity of Shishak's onslaught forced Rehoboam to surrender at Gibeon in order to prevent the inevitable destruction of Jerusalem. Shishak turned northwards and conquered Israel just as easily, Solomon's fortifications proving ineffective. One town after another was burned, including Megiddo.

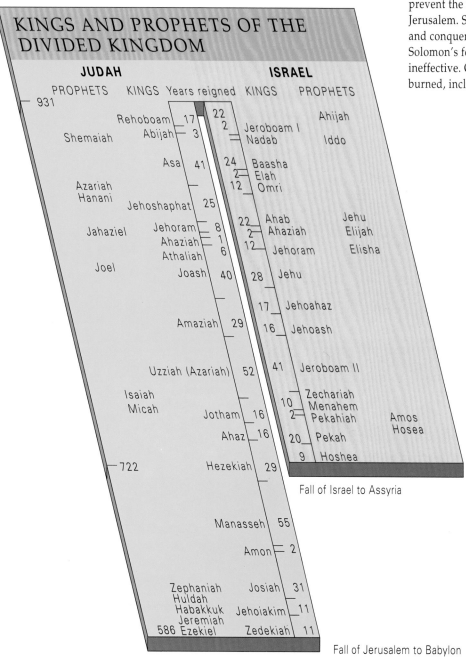

KINGS AND PROPHETS OF THE DIVIDED KINGDOM

JUDAH				ISRAEL	
PROPHETS	KINGS	Years reigned	KINGS	PROPHETS	
931					
	Rehoboam	17	22	Jeroboam I	Ahijah
Shemaiah	Abijah	3	2	Nadab	Iddo
	Asa	41	24	Baasha	
Azariah			2	Elah	
Hanani			12	Omri	
	Jehoshaphat	25	22	Ahab	Jehu
Jahaziel	Jehoram	8	2	Ahaziah	Elijah
	Ahaziah	1	12	Jehoram	Elisha
Joel	Athaliah	6			
	Joash	40	28	Jehu	
			17	Jehoahaz	
	Amaziah	29	16	Jehoash	
	Uzziah (Azariah)	52	41	Jeroboam II	
Isaiah				Zechariah	
Micah			10	Menahem	
	Jotham	16	2	Pekahiah	Amos
	Ahaz	16	20	Pekah	Hosea
722	Hezekiah	29	9	Hoshea	

Fall of Israel to Assyria

	Manasseh	55	
	Amon	2	
Zephaniah	Josiah	31	
Huldah			
Habakkuk	Jehoiakim	11	
Jeremiah			
586 Ezekiel	Zedekiah	11	

Fall of Jerusalem to Babylon

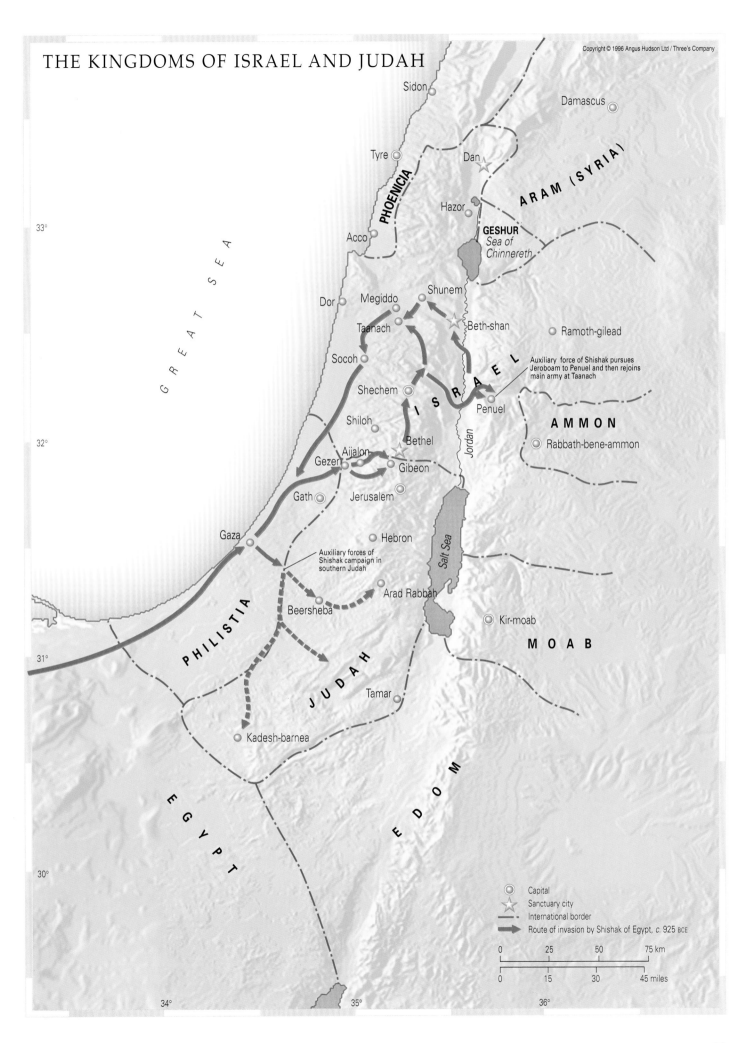

THE KINGDOMS OF ISRAEL AND JUDAH

Copyright © 1996 Angus Hudson Ltd / Three's Company

Sidon

Damascus

Tyre

Dan

ARAM (SYRIA)

Hazor

33°

PHOENICIA

Acco

GESHUR
Sea of Chinnereth

GREAT SEA

Dor

Shunem

Megiddo

Beth-shan

Ramoth-gilead

Taanach

Socoh

Auxiliary force of Shishak pursues
Jeroboam to Penuel and then rejoins
main army at Taanach

Shechem

I S R A E L

Jordan

Penuel

AMMON

Shiloh

32°

Bethel

Aijalon

Gezer

Gibeon

Rabbath-bene-ammon

Gath

Jerusalem

Hebron

Salt Sea

Gaza

Auxiliary forces of
Shishak campaign in
southern Judah

Arad Rabbah

Kir-moab

Beersheba

PHILISTIA

M O A B

J U D A H

Tamar

31°

Kadesh-barnea

E D O M

E G Y P T

30°

◎ Capital
☆ Sanctuary city
—··— International border
➤ Route of invasion by Shishak of Egypt, *c.* 925 BCE

0   25   50   75 km

0   15   30   45 miles

34°   35°   36°

39

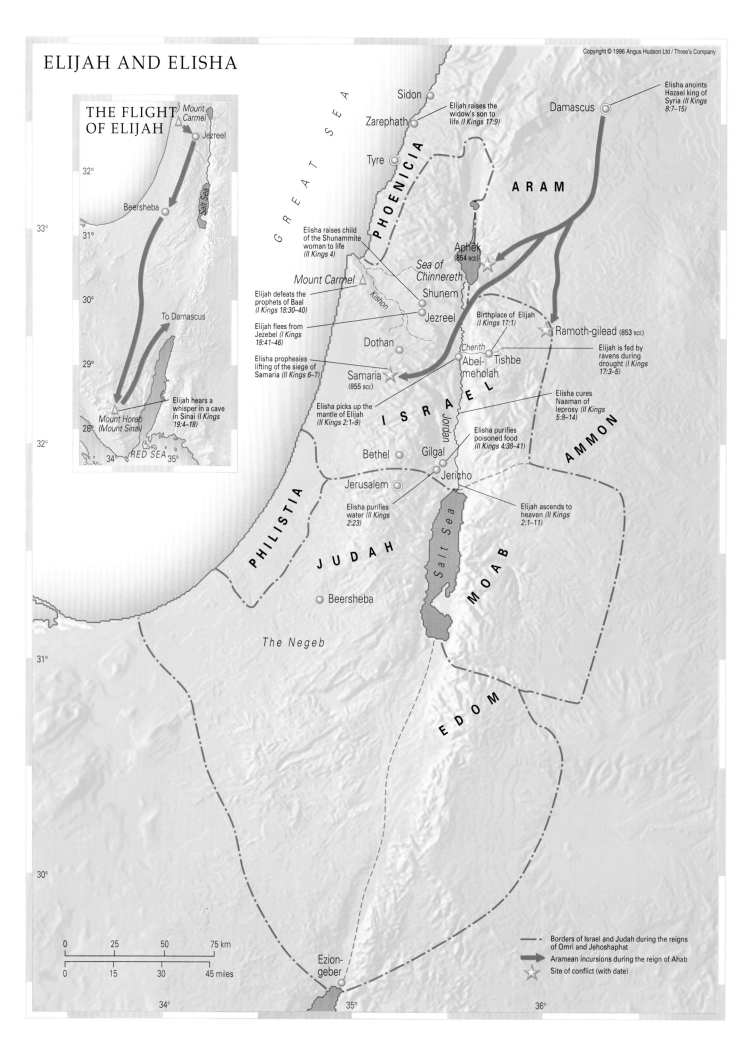

ELIJAH AND ELISHA

THE FLIGHT OF ELIJAH

Mount Carmel
Jezreel
32°
33°
31°
Beersheba
30°
To Damascus
29°
32°
28°
Mount Horeb
(Mount Sinai)
Elijah hears a whisper in a cave in Sinai (I Kings 19:4–18)
34°
RED SEA
35°
Salt Sea

Copyright © 1996 Angus Hudson Ltd / Three's Company

G R E A T   S E A

Sidon

Elijah raises the widow's son to life (I Kings 17:9)

Zarephath

Damascus

Elisha anoints Hazael king of Syria (II Kings 8:7–15)

Tyre

PHOENICIA

A R A M

Elisha raises child of the Shunammite woman to life (II Kings 4)

Aphek (854 BCE)

Sea of Chinnereth

Mount Carmel

Shunem

Elijah defeats the prophets of Baal (I Kings 18:30–40)

Kishon

Jezreel

Birthplace of Elijah (I Kings 17:1)

Ramoth-gilead (853 BCE)

Elijah flees from Jezebel (I Kings 18:41–46)

Dothan

Cherith

Tishbe

Elijah is fed by ravens during drought (I Kings 17:3–5)

Elisha prophesies lifting of the siege of Samaria (II Kings 6–7)

Samaria (855 BCE)

Abel-meholah

I S R A E L

Elisha cures Naaman of leprosy (II Kings 5:8–14)

Elisha picks up the mantle of Elijah (II Kings 2:1–9)

Jordan

Elisha purifies poisoned food (II Kings 4:38–41)

A M M O N

Bethel

Gilgal

Elisha purifies water (II Kings 2:23)

Jericho

Jerusalem

Elijah ascends to heaven (II Kings 2:1–11)

PHILISTIA

J U D A H

Salt Sea

M O A B

Beersheba

The Negeb

31°

30°

E D O M

0   25   50   75 km

0   15   30   45 miles

Ezion-geber

Borders of Israel and Judah during the reigns of Omri and Jehoshaphat

Aramean incursions during the reign of Ahab

Site of conflict (with date)

34°   35°   36°

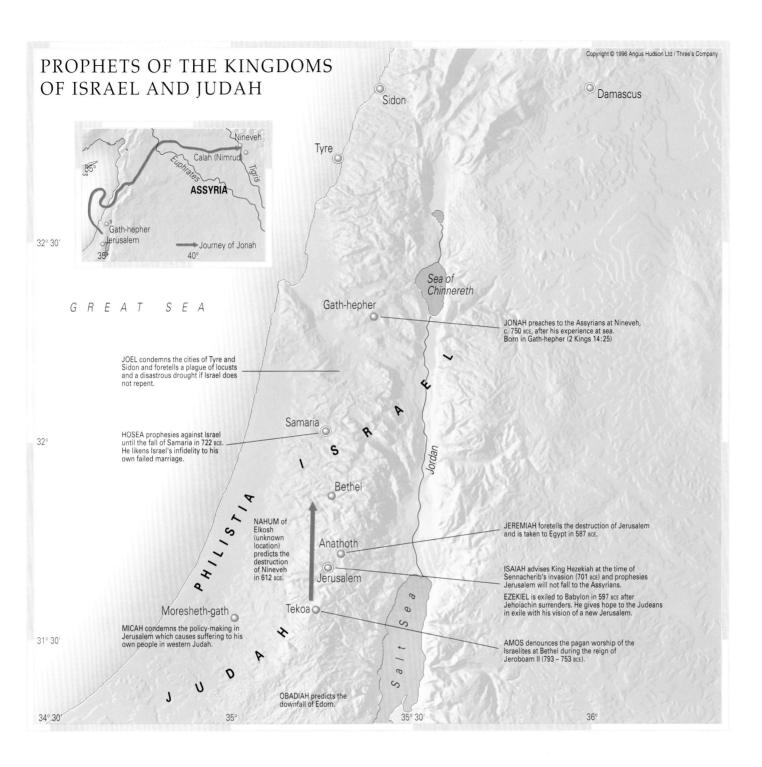

PROPHETS OF THE KINGDOMS
OF ISRAEL AND JUDAH

Sidon

Damascus

Nineveh

Calah (Nimrud)

ASSYRIA

Gath-hepher

Jerusalem

→ Journey of Jonah

Tyre

GREAT SEA

Sea of
Chinnereth

Gath-hepher

JONAH preaches to the Assyrians at Nineveh,
c. 750 BCE, after his experience at sea.
Born in Gath-hepher (2 Kings 14:25)

JOEL condemns the cities of Tyre and
Sidon and foretells a plague of locusts
and a disastrous drought if Israel does
not repent.

Samaria

HOSEA prophesies against Israel
until the fall of Samaria in 722 BCE.
He likens Israel's infidelity to his
own failed marriage.

ISRAEL

Jordan

Bethel

NAHUM of
Elkosh
(unknown
location)
predicts the
destruction
of Nineveh
in 612 BCE.

Anathoth

JEREMIAH foretells the destruction of Jerusalem
and is taken to Egypt in 587 BCE.

ISAIAH advises King Hezekiah at the time of
Sennacherib's invasion (701 BCE) and prophesies
Jerusalem will not fall to the Assyrians.

EZEKIEL is exiled to Babylon in 597 BCE after
Jehoiachin surrenders. He gives hope to the Judeans
in exile with his vision of a new Jerusalem.

Jerusalem

PHILISTIA

Salt Sea

Moresheth-gath

Tekoa

MICAH condemns the policy-making in
Jerusalem which causes suffering to his
own people in western Judah.

AMOS denounces the pagan worship of the
Israelites at Bethel during the reign of
Jeroboam II (793 – 753 BCE).

JUDAH

OBADIAH predicts the
downfall of Edom.

THE PROPHETS

Some fifty years after the separation of
Israel from Judah, in the early ninth
century BCE, Omri became king of
Israel. He moved the capital to Samaria,
and a period of relative peace and
prosperity began. His son Ahab married
Jezebel, the daughter of the king of
Tyre. As a result Israel became more
influenced by Phoenician culture,
including the cult of Baal. It was
Jezebel's sponsoring of Baal worship
over that of Yahweh, the God of Israel,

which invoked the wrath of Israel's
prophets, in particular Elijah (I Kings
18). Traditionally Israel's greatest
prophet, Elijah single-handedly
combatted the idolatry which
threatened Israel's religious integrity.

Elisha continued Elijah's policies and,
through his support for King Jehu,
brought about the downfall of the
House of Omri.

From the eighth century, the literary
prophets arose, whose works are
recorded in the Bible. They were
enlightened individuals, often from
within the priestly tradition, though not
afraid to criticize it. As divine

messengers, they could foresee
impending disasters, and counselled
their people and leaders to change their
ways in order to avoid the
consequences. The greatest of these
prophets were Isaiah, Jeremiah and
Ezekiel.

JEROBOAM II AND UZZIAH

Israel and Judah became powerful and wealthy nations during the reigns of Jeroboam II and Uzziah in the eighth century. Once again Israel and Judah gained control of the commercial highways in the region. Jeroboam reigned in Israel from *c.* 789 to 748 BCE. He recovered lands taken earlier by the Arameans of Damascus now that their power had been broken by the Assyrians. He established control over a large area of Aram (II Kings 14:25). The prophets Amos and Hosea condemned the internal moral and religious corruption and materialistic life-style.

Uzziah reigned in Judah from *c.* 785 to 734 BCE. He pushed back the frontier with the Philistines and recovered the territory of Edom which King David had conquered. The port of Ezion-geber was rebuilt, giving a renewed outlet to the Red Sea.

Assyrian spearmen, from an Assyrian relief.

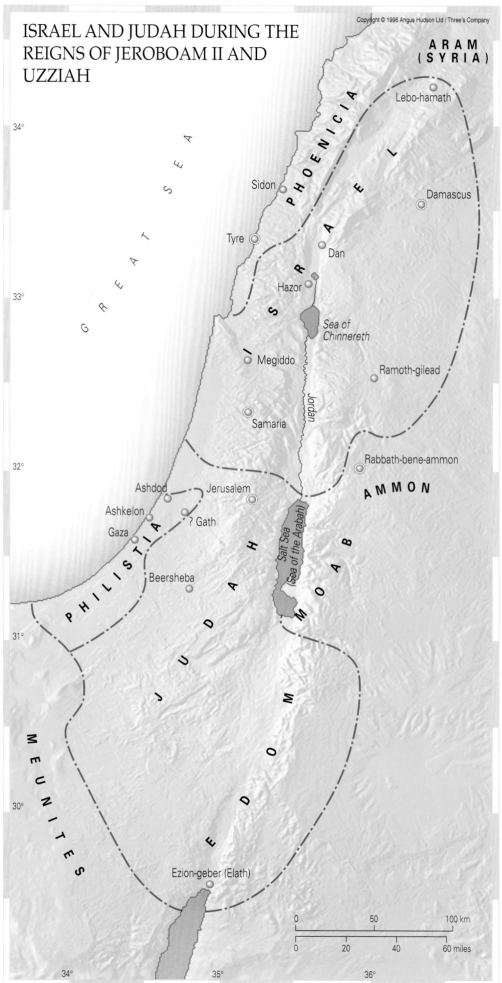

ISRAEL AND JUDAH DURING THE REIGNS OF JEROBOAM II AND UZZIAH

ARAM (SYRIA)

Lebo-hamath

PHOENICIA

Sidon

Damascus

Tyre

Dan

ISRAEL

Hazor

Sea of Chinnereth

Megiddo

Ramoth-gilead

Jordan

Samaria

Rabbath-bene-ammon

AMMON

Ashdod

Jerusalem

Ashkelon

? Gath

Gaza

PHILISTIA

JUDAH

Salt Sea (Sea of the Arabah)

MOAB

Beersheba

GREAT SEA

MEUNITES

EDOM

Ezion-geber (Elath)

0   50   100 km

0 20 40 60 miles

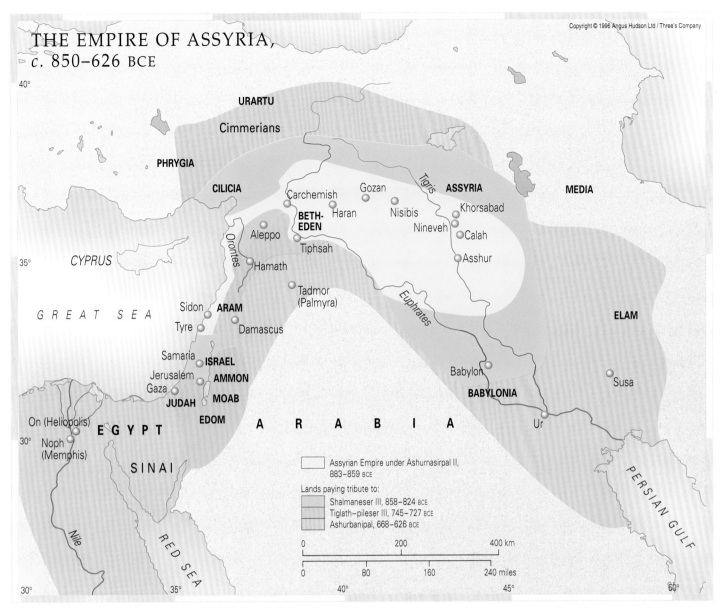

THE EMPIRE OF ASSYRIA, *c.* 850–626 BCE

URARTU

Cimmerians

PHRYGIA

CILICIA

Carchemish

Gozan

ASSYRIA

MEDIA

BETH-
EDEN

Haran

Nisibis

Khorsabad

Aleppo

Tiphsah

Nineveh

Calah

Orontes

Hamath

Asshur

CYPRUS

Tadmor
(Palmyra)

GREAT SEA

Sidon

ARAM

Tyre

Damascus

ELAM

Samaria

ISRAEL

Jerusalem

AMMON

Babylon

Gaza

JUDAH

MOAB

Susa

On (Heliopolis)

EGYPT

EDOM

ARABIA

BABYLONIA

Ur

Noph
(Memphis)

SINAI

Tigris

Euphrates

PERSIAN GULF

Nile

RED SEA

| | Assyrian Empire under Ashurnasirpal II, 883–859 BCE |

Lands paying tribute to:
Shalmaneser III, 858–824 BCE
Tiglath–pileser III, 745–727 BCE
Ashurbanipal, 668–626 BCE

0   200   400 km

0   80   160   240 miles

THE ASSYRIAN EMPIRE

Assyria had been a force in Mesopotamia since the fourteenth century BCE. By *c.* 900 BCE it was expanding into an empire which, over the next 250 years, was feared throughout the ancient Near East. At its maximum extent the empire stretched from Egypt to the Persian Gulf, though Egypt was controlled only briefly. The capital of the empire shifted in different periods: Ashurnasirpal (883-859) moved it from Assur to Calah (modern Nimrud); Khorsabad was made capital briefly by Sargon II (721-705); his son Sennacherib moved it again to Nineveh, where it remained until the fall of the empire.

The first military involvement Israel had with Assyria was at the Battle of

Detail from a relief at Nineveh: captured messengers from Urartu.

Qarqar, north of Hamath, when an alliance of twelve kings, including Ahab of Israel, checked the Assyrians' southward advance in 853 BCE. However, Assyria's victory at Damascus

in 796 BCE was a portent of the military power they would demonstrate through the next century.

43

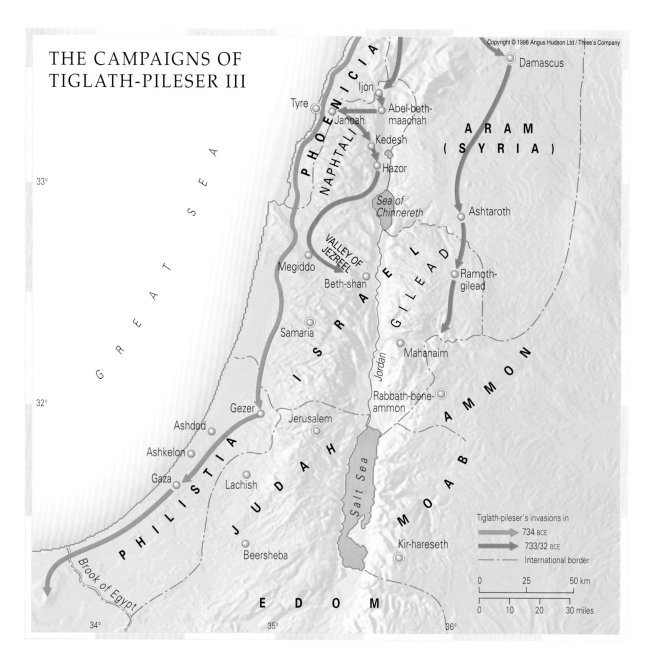

THE CAMPAIGNS OF TIGLATH-PILESER III

Copyright © 1996 Angus Hudson Ltd / Three's Company

Damascus

Ijon

Tyre

Abel-beth-maachah

Janoah

Kedesh

**A R A M
(S Y R I A)**

Hazor

Sea of Chinnereth

Ashtaroth

N A P H T A L I

P H O E N I C I A

VALLEY OF JEZREEL

Megiddo

Beth-shan

G I L E A D

Ramoth-gilead

I S R A E L

Samaria

Jordan

Mahanaim

G R E A T   S E A

Gezer

Jerusalem

Rabbath-bene-ammon

A M M O N

Ashdod

Ashkelon

J U D A H

Salt Sea

Gaza

Lachish

P H I L I S T I A

M O A B

Tiglath-pileser's invasions in

734 BCE

733/32 BCE

International border

Beersheba

Kir-hareseth

Brook of Egypt

E D O M

| 0 | 25 | 50 km |
| 0 | 10 | 20 | 30 miles |

33°

32°

34°

35°

36°

TIGLATH-PILESER III

From *c.* 740 BCE, the Assyrians put Israel and Judah under pressure. Until then the main purpose of Assyrian campaigns in the region had been to secure booty and tribute. With the accession of Tiglath-pileser III (745-727 BCE), Assyria began to assert more control over the states of the Levant, requiring regular tribute payments from loyal vassals; rebel kings were defeated and their realms often turned into Assyrian provinces.

Kings Pekah of Israel and Rezin of Damascus hoped to form a coalition against Assyria, but King Ahaz of Judah refused to join. They turned on Ahaz, who, against the advice of the prophet Isaiah, appealed to Tiglath-pileser for help (II Kings 16:7). At high speed Tiglath-pileser campaigned down the western flank of the Levant in 734, destroying the major cities of Philistia, as far as the Brook of Egypt. A year later he concentrated on Israel, and took all of Galilee as far south as the Valley of Jezreel. A third campaign crushed Damascus and penetrated as far as Gilead. Pekah was assassinated and his replacement, Hoshea, was obliged to pay a heavy tribute as a vassal king to Assyria (II Kings 17:3).

The Assyrian king Ashurbanipal, from an Assyrian relief.

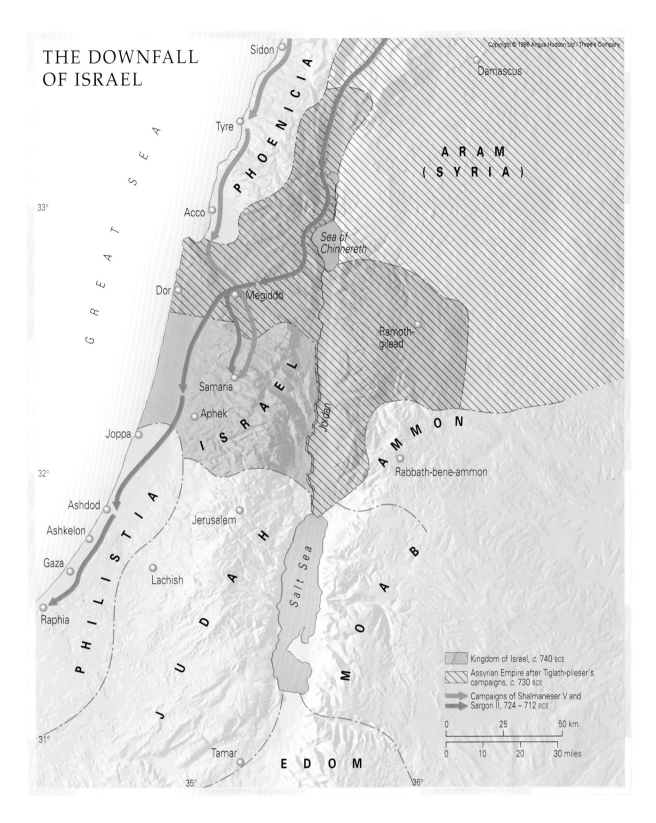

THE DOWNFALL OF ISRAEL

Damascus

Sidon

PHOENICIA

A R A M
(S Y R I A)

Tyre

33°

Acco

Sea of
Chinnereth

Dor

Megiddo

Ramoth-
gilead

ISRAEL

Samaria

Aphek

AMMON

Jordan

Joppa

32°

Rabbath-bene-ammon

Ashdod

Jerusalem

Ashkelon

PHILISTIA

JUDAH

Gaza

Salt Sea

B

Lachish

M O A B

Raphia

	Kingdom of Israel, c. 740 BCE
	Assyrian Empire after Tiglath-pileser's campaigns, c. 730 BCE
	Campaigns of Shalmaneser V and Sargon II, 724 – 712 BCE

0   25   50 km

0   10   20   30 miles

31°

Tamar

E D O M

35°

36°

THE FALL OF ISRAEL

Around 730 BCE, after Tiglath-pileser's campaigns, the administration of Israel was divided between Assyria and Israel. The northern and eastern parts conquered by Tiglath-pileser were made Assyrian provinces. Megiddo was rebuilt and became the administrative centre. Southern Israel was allowed to continue as a tribute-paying semi-autonomous state with its own king (at this time Hoshea), as long as it remained loyal to Assyria.

However, Hoshea tried to relieve his people of the heavy burden of tribute by turning to Egypt for military aid against Assyria. This prompted an attack from the new Assyrian king, Shalmaneser V, in 724 BCE. Hoshea was arrested and Samaria was besieged for three years before the city finally collapsed (II Kings 17:5-6). The inhabitants were deported to different parts of the Assyrian empire. A further campaign, under Sargon II, was launched in 720 BCE through the western region as far as Raphia, where the Assyrians were met by Egyptian forces.

SENNACHERIB

King Hezekiah of Judah saw the death of Sargon II (705 BCE) as an opportunity to rally potential allies against the mighty Assyria. He was promised support from the Cushites (Ethiopians) and Egyptians, though found only limited help in Philistia. He fortified some of the cities in western Judah and engineered underground water supplies in the event of siege. The Siloam tunnel into Jerusalem from the Gihon spring was one example.

The new Assyrian king, Sennacherib, invaded Phoenicia in 701 BCE and many city kings surrendered. The campaign continued southwards where Sennacherib defeated the Egyptian-Cushite force at Eltekeh. The chronology of events is uncertain, but at around the same time Sennacherib turned inland and, according to his Assyrian annals, sacked forty-six cities in western Judah, including the heavily fortified city of Lachish. The Assyrians marched on to Jerusalem. However, before the Assyrians could capture the city, their army was ravaged, perhaps by plague (the biblical author uses the term 'God's angel', II Kings 20:35), and they withdrew. Sennacherib did, though, extract a heavy tribute payment from Hezekiah.

The entrance to Hezekiah's Tunnel, which runs from the Gihon spring.

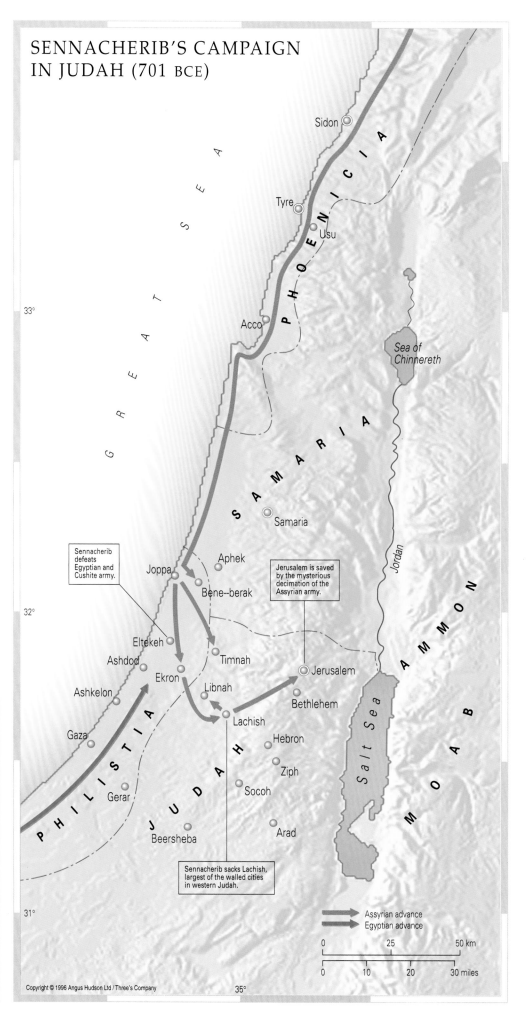

SENNACHERIB'S CAMPAIGN IN JUDAH (701 BCE)

Sennacherib defeats Egyptian and Cushite army.

Jerusalem is saved by the mysterious decimation of the Assyrian army.

Sennacherib sacks Lachish, largest of the walled cities in western Judah.

Assyrian advance
Egyptian advance

| 0 | 25 | 50 km |
| 0 | 10 | 20 | 30 miles |

Copyright © 1996 Angus Hudson Ltd / Three's Company

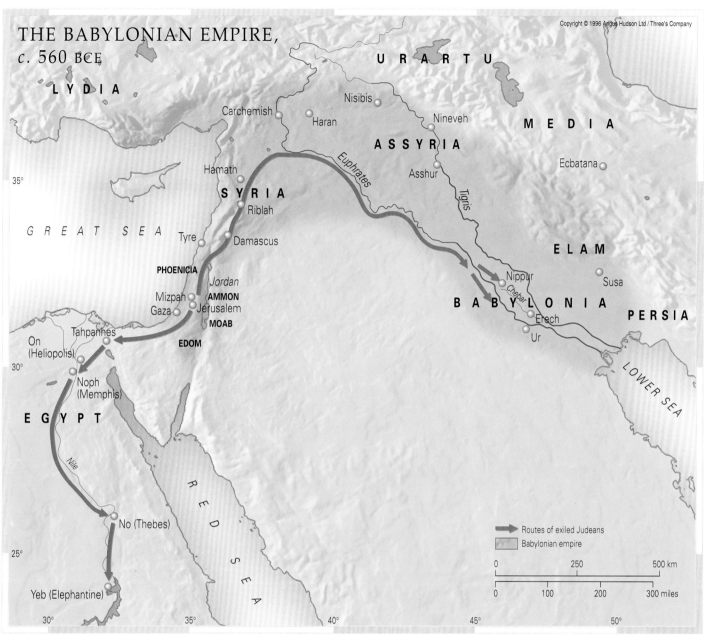

THE BABYLONIAN EMPIRE, c. 560 BCE

LYDIA

URARTU

Nisibis

Carchemish

Haran

Nineveh

ASSYRIA

MEDIA

Asshur

Ecbatana

Hamath

SYRIA

Euphrates

Tigris

Riblah

GREAT SEA

Tyre

Damascus

ELAM

PHOENICIA

Jordan

Nippur

Susa

Mizpah

AMMON

Chebar

BABYLONIA

PERSIA

Gaza

Jerusalem

Erech

MOAB

Ur

Tahpanhes

EDOM

On (Heliopolis)

Noph (Memphis)

LOWER SEA

EGYPT

Nile

RED SEA

No (Thebes)

Yeb (Elephantine)

Copyright © 1996 Angus Hudson Ltd / Three's Company

Routes of exiled Judeans

Babylonian empire

0   250   500 km

0   100   200   300 miles

35°

30°

25°

30°   35°   40°   45°   50°

THE BABYLONIAN EMPIRE

The Assyrians were gradually conquered by the Babylonians, with help from the Medes, over a period from 626 to 612 BCE, in which year the capital Nineveh finally fell. Babylonia became the new threat and the Egyptians, fearing the danger, went to Assyria's aid. They were defeated by the Babylonians at the decisive Battle of Carchemish in 605. Jehoiakim of Judah, who had been put on the throne by the Egyptians, now had to pay tribute to Nebuchadnezzar of Babylon (II Kings 24:1).

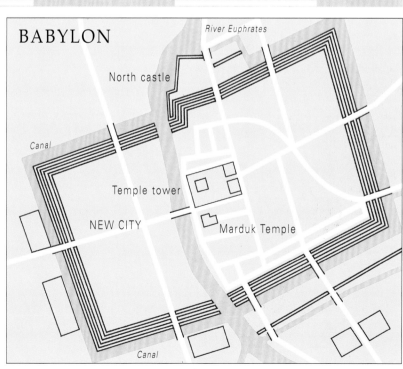

BABYLON

River Euphrates

North castle

Canal

Temple tower

NEW CITY

Marduk Temple

Canal

THE FALL OF JUDAH TO THE BABYLONIANS

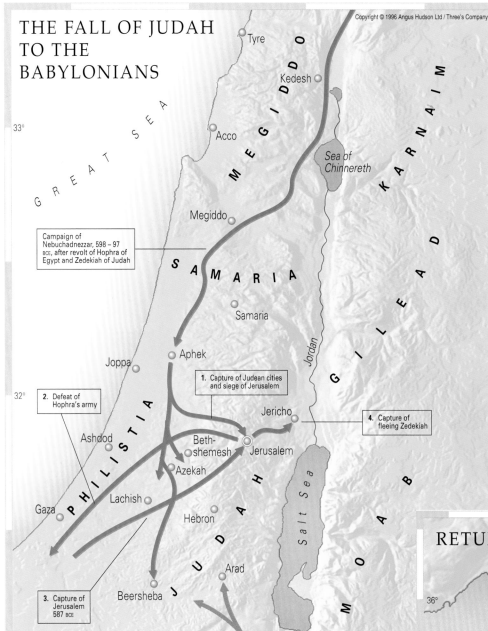

Campaign of Nebuchadnezzar, 598 – 97 BCE, after revolt of Hophra of Egypt and Zedekiah of Judah

2. Defeat of Hophra's army

1. Capture of Judean cities and siege of Jerusalem

4. Capture of fleeing Zedekiah

3. Capture of Jerusalem 587 BCE

Edomites make raids into south Judah

Tyre

Kedesh

Acco

Sea of Chinnereth

Megiddo

Samaria

Aphek

Joppa

Ashdod

Beth-shemesh

Jerusalem

Azekah

Jericho

Gaza

Lachish

Hebron

Arad

Beersheba

Salt Sea

GREAT SEA

MEGIDDO

KARNAIM

SAMARIA

GILEAD

PHILISTIA

JUDAH

MOAB

EDOM

Jordan

0   15   30   45 km
0   15   30 miles

Copyright © 1996 Angus Hudson Ltd / Three's Company

THE FALL OF JUDAH

The Egyptians and Babylonians struggled for supremacy in the Near East. Egypt encouraged Judah to rebel against Babylonian control, which Jehoiakim did in 600 BCE by withholding his tribute. This provoked a Babylonian invasion of Judah in 598, as well as invasions from Judah's neighbouring enemies, in particular the Edomites to the south. The young Jehoiachin succeeded to the throne of Judah on his father's death and was unable to resist the Babylonian pressure. He surrendered Jerusalem in 597. He and many fellow Judeans were deported to Babylon, while a new puppet king, Zedekiah, replaced him (II Kings 24:18).

Once again, Judah was persuaded to rebel and Jerusalem was quickly under siege again in 589. Hophra of Egypt engaged the Babylonians in the west but was defeated. The siege of Jerusalem was renewed. In spite of holding out for nearly two years the city was finally burned in 586, and its inhabitants taken into exile (II Kings 25:1-12).

RETURN OF THE EXILES

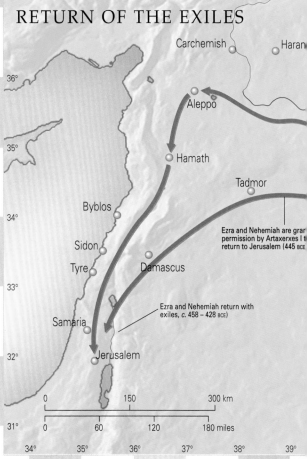

Carchemish

Haran

Aleppo

Hamath

Tadmor

Byblos

Ezra and Nehemiah are gran permission by Artaxerxes I t return to Jerusalem (445 BCE

Sidon

Tyre

Damascus

Ezra and Nehemiah return with exiles, c. 458 – 428 BCE)

Samaria

Jerusalem

0   150   300 km
0   60   120   180 miles

A mythical beast pictured on glazed tiles from the gate of ancient Babylon.

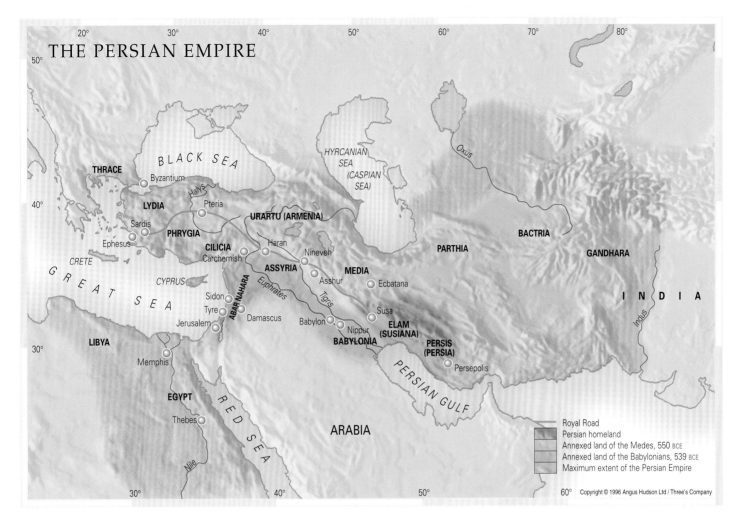

THE PERSIAN EMPIRE

THRACE
Byzantium
BLACK SEA
LYDIA
Halys
Pteria
Sardis
PHRYGIA
Ephesus
CRETE
URARTU (ARMENIA)
HYRCANIAN
SEA
(CASPIAN
SEA)
Oxus
BACTRIA
GANDHARA
CILICIA
Haran
Carchemish
Nineveh
ASSYRIA
MEDIA
PARTHIA
GREAT
SEA
CYPRUS
Asshur
Ecbatana
INDIA
Sidon
ABAR NAHARA
Euphrates
Tigris
Susa
Indus
Tyre
Jerusalem
Damascus
Babylon
Nippur
ELAM
(SUSIANA)
LIBYA
BABYLONIA
PERSIS
(PERSIA)
Memphis
Persepolis
PERSIAN GULF
EGYPT
Thebes
ARABIA
RED SEA
Nile

Royal Road
Persian homeland
Annexed land of the Medes, 550 BCE
Annexed land of the Babylonians, 539 BCE
Maximum extent of the Persian Empire

Copyright © 1996 Angus Hudson Ltd / Three's Company

Copyright © 1996 Angus Hudson Ltd / Three's Company

Tigris
Asshur
Euphrates
Zerubbabel leads main party of returning exiles, c. 538 BCE
Daniel foretells end of Babylonian Empire during banquet of Belshazzar, 539 BCE
Esther, Jewish queen to Xerxes I (Ahasuerus), saves Jewish community
Babylon
Deutero – Isaiah, an anonymous prophet, preaches during reign of Cyrus II
Susa
? Talabib
Nippur
Chebar
Ezekiel lives among exiled Judeans in Talabib on River Chebar

THE EXILE

The prophet Jeremiah records three occasions of deportation: in 597, 586 and again in 582. The people were taken to different parts of Babylonia but many seem to have settled by the River Chebar. Although Ezekiel and the Psalms record their misery and great sense of loss of homeland, conditions were not harsh. They developed their own farming communities and some Judeans rose to high rank in the Babylonian government. It was fifty years, though, before the more enlightened regime of the Persians conquered Babylon, as foreseen by the prophet Daniel at the banquet of Belshazzar. The return to Palestine happened in stages. The first, under Zerubbabel, was permitted by decree of the Persian emperor Cyrus the Great (reigned 559-529 BCE), shortly after the Persians took Babylon in 539 BCE. Later returns took place under Ezra and Nehemiah in the next century.

49

RETURN FROM EXILE

The initial enthusiasm of the returnees about rebuilding Jerusalem was gradually replaced by an anxiety over housing and feeding, and the hostility of neighbours who resented their immigration. The work of rebuilding the Temple lapsed. The prophets Haggai and Zechariah (*c.* 520 BCE) rebuked the Judeans for being more concerned about their own comfort than the restoration of their religious institutions. A spirited revival of interest brought completion of the Temple in 516 BCE.

Local opposition to the Judeans continued. Ezra travelled from Babylonia to Jerusalem in 458 to reinstate the Jewish Law, which was not being observed truly. In 445, Nehemiah was appointed governor of Judea by the Persian Emperor Artaxerxes I (464-423). His main task was to complete the rebuilding of Jerusalem's walls for greater protection against, among others, Sanballat, the governor of Samaria (Nehemiah 4). Most of the people of the Samaria region were brought there from other lands by the Assyrians after the fall of the northern kingdom in 721. They considered themselves Jews and the rightful inhabitants of all Palestine. Mutual resentment between the Jews from Babylon and the 'Samaritans' continued into New Testament times.

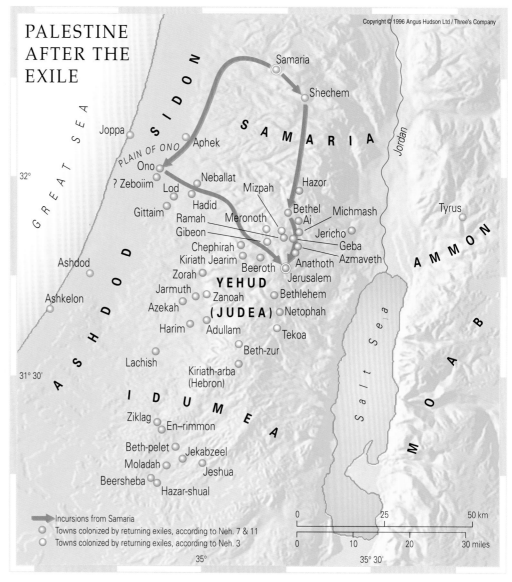

PALESTINE AFTER THE EXILE

Copyright © 1996 Angus Hudson Ltd / Three's Company

→ Incursions from Samaria
○ Towns colonized by returning exiles, according to Neh. 7 & 11
○ Towns colonized by returning exiles, according to Neh. 3

Section of the 'Broad Wall' in Jerusalem, possibly built in the late eighth century BCE.

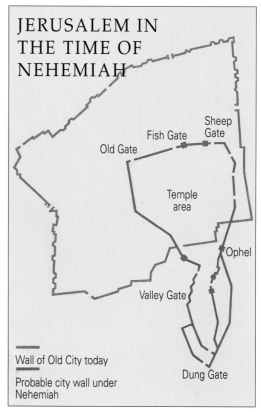

JERUSALEM IN THE TIME OF NEHEMIAH

Fish Gate · Sheep Gate · Old Gate · Temple area · Ophel · Valley Gate · Dung Gate

— Wall of Old City today
— Probable city wall under Nehemiah

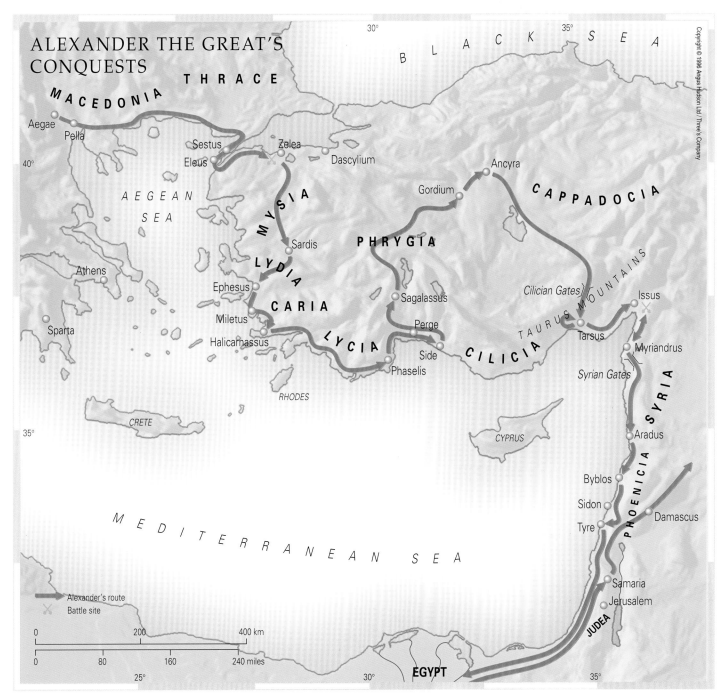

ALEXANDER THE GREAT'S CONQUESTS

THRACE

MACEDONIA

Aegae
Pella

Sestus
Eleus
Zelea
Dascylium

AEGEAN SEA

Athens

MYSIA

Sardis

PHRYGIA

Gordium

Ancyra

CAPPADOCIA

Ephesus

LYDIA

CARIA

Miletus

Halicarnassus

Sagalassus

Perge

LYCIA

Side

Phaselis

Sparta

RHODES

CRETE

CYPRUS

Cilician Gates

TAURUS MOUNTAINS

Tarsus

CILICIA

Issus

Myriandrus

Syrian Gates

Aradus

SYRIA

PHOENICIA

Byblos

Sidon

Tyre

Damascus

MEDITERRANEAN SEA

Samaria
Jerusalem

JUDEA

EGYPT

→ Alexander's route
✕ Battle site

| 0 | 200 | 400 km |
| 0 | 80 | 160 | 240 miles |

Copyright © 1996 Angus Hudson Ltd / Three's Company

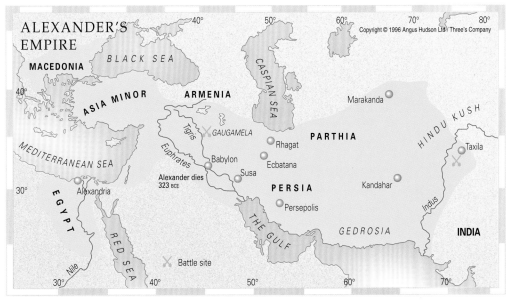

ALEXANDER'S EMPIRE

MACEDONIA

BLACK SEA

ASIA MINOR

ARMENIA

CASPIAN SEA

MEDITERRANEAN SEA

Tigris
✕ GAUGAMELA

Euphrates

Babylon

Alexander dies 323 BCE

Susa

PERSIA

Persepolis

Marakanda

PARTHIA

Rhagat

Ecbatana

HINDU KUSH

Taxila ✕

Kandahar

Indus

GEDROSIA

INDIA

EGYPT

Alexandria

Nile

RED SEA

THE GULF

✕ Battle site

Copyright © 1996 Angus Hudson Ltd / Three's Company

ALEXANDER THE GREAT

Alexander the Great conquered Palestine in 332 BCE. His vast and rapidly acquired empire was divided up among his generals on his death in 323 BCE. Two opposing empires emerged – the Seleucids of Greece and western Asia, and the Ptolemies of North Africa. Palestine, as a land bridge between the two, became their battleground, and in different times the vassal state of one or the other. In 198 BCE, it became part of the Seleucid Empire.

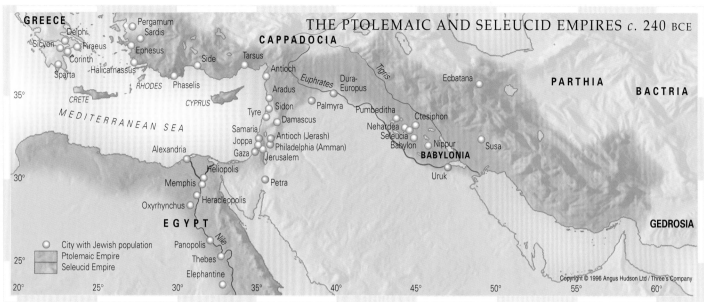

Copyright © 1996 Angus Hudson Ltd / Three's Company

○ City with Jewish population
Ptolemaic Empire
Seleucid Empire

THE MACCABEAN REVOLT

The Maccabean revolt broke out in 167 BCE when Mattathias openly rebelled against the Seleucid authorities by refusing to honour their pagan gods. Pagan worship had been instituted in Judea and Samaria as part of the process of hellenization that had crept through Jewish life ever since the Seleucids had come to power. Hellenized Jews from the high priestly families kowtowed to the excesses of the Seleucid ruler Antiochus IV Epiphanes, who even placed a statue of Zeus in the Temple and demanded sacrifices be made to it.

The Maccabee brothers led a series of campaigns against the Seleucid government which resulted in their eventual victory and establishment of the Hasmonean kingdom in 142 BCE (I Maccabees 13:41-42). This was an independent Jewish state. Traditional Jewish ritual was reinstated by descendants of the high-priestly family of Hashmon, who had always been critical of hellenizing tendencies in Judea. The kingdom reached its maximum extent under Alexander Janneus (103-76 BCE).

One of the reasons for the success of the Maccabees was the decline in power of the Seleucid Empire. The Parthians were hammering on their eastern front, while the Romans grew more powerful in the west. Athens fell in 86 BCE, and in 63 BCE the Roman general Pompey entered the Temple in Jerusalem and forced a settlement with the Hasmoneans by which Palestine became a Roman protectorate.

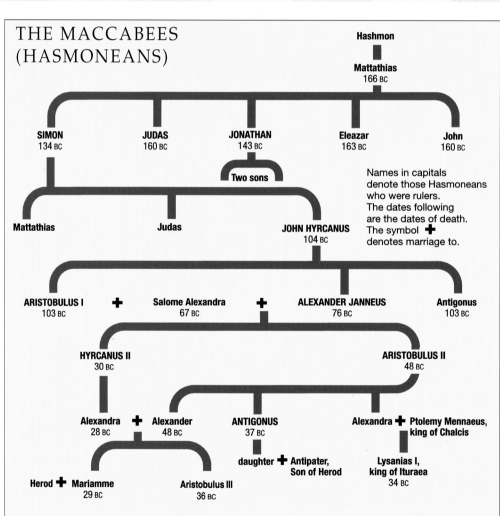

THE MACCABEES (HASMONEANS)

Hashmon
Mattathias 166 BC

SIMON 134 BC | JUDAS 160 BC | JONATHAN 143 BC | Eleazar 163 BC | John 160 BC

Two sons

Names in capitals denote those Hasmoneans who were rulers. The dates following are the dates of death. The symbol ✚ denotes marriage to.

Mattathias | Judas | JOHN HYRCANUS 104 BC

ARISTOBULUS I 103 BC ✚ Salome Alexandra 67 BC ✚ ALEXANDER JANNEUS 76 BC | Antigonus 103 BC

HYRCANUS II 30 BC | ARISTOBULUS II 48 BC

Alexandra 28 BC ✚ Alexander 48 BC | ANTIGONUS 37 BC | Alexandra ✚ Ptolemy Mennaeus, king of Chalcis

daughter ✚ Antipater, Son of Herod | Lysanias I, king of Ituraea 34 BC

Herod ✚ Mariamme 29 BC | Aristobulus III 36 BC

THE HASMONEAN KINGDOM

Copyright © 1996 Angus Hudson Ltd / Three's Company

PHOENICIA

M E D I T E R R A N E A N   S E A

Tyre

Antiochia

Gischala

Seleucia

Ptolemais

Sea of Galilee

Gabara

Sepphoris

Hippos

Dium

Geba

Mount Tabor △

Philoteria

Abila

GALILEE

Gadara

Dora

GILEAD

Strato's Tower

Scythopolis

Pella

SAMARIA

◎ Samaria

Mount Gerizim △

Shechem

Gerasa

Apollonia

Joppa

PEREA

Arimathea

JUDEA

Lydda

Philadelphia

Jamnia

Jericho

Emmaus

◎ Jerusalem

Samaga

Azotus

Medeba

Ascalon

Beth-zur

Anthedon

Marisa

Dead Sea

Gaza

Hebron

En-gedi

Orda

Gerar

IDUMEA

MOAB

Raphia

Beersheba

Malatha

◎ Rhinocorura

NABATAEA

Zoar

Jordan

P A R A L I A

33°

32°

31°

34°   35°   36°

Independent Judea after Jonathan's campaigns, 142 BCE
Land conquered by Simon, 142-135 BCE
John Hyrcanus I, 128-104 BCE
Aristobulus I, 104-103 BCE
Alexander Janneus, 103-76 BCE
Boundary of Hasmonean kingdom, 76 BCE
◎ Hellenistic city

0   25   50 km

0   10   20   30 miles

53

THE ECONOMY OF PALESTINE

Until Roman times Mediterranean trade had been controlled by the Phoenicians. But, with the Pax Romana, greater safety from pirates and bandits allowed more opportunities for commerce, both by sea and over land. The economy was still essentially agrarian: wheat was grown where possible in the valleys north of Jerusalem, giving way to barley in the south. The hill country provided pastureland for sheep and cattle. Vines, olives and dates were the main crops grown on the hillsides.

Metalwork in copper and iron thrived, and by this time there were organized potteries. Jerusalem was a major commercial centre, with 118 recorded luxury goods, such as jewellery and silk clothes. The Temple treasury drew annual tax payments from every Jew and was a source of great wealth. There was a system for banking, and money-changers would exchange foreign currencies for the shekel.

A half shekel coin struck during the Jewish Revolt, 66–70 CE.

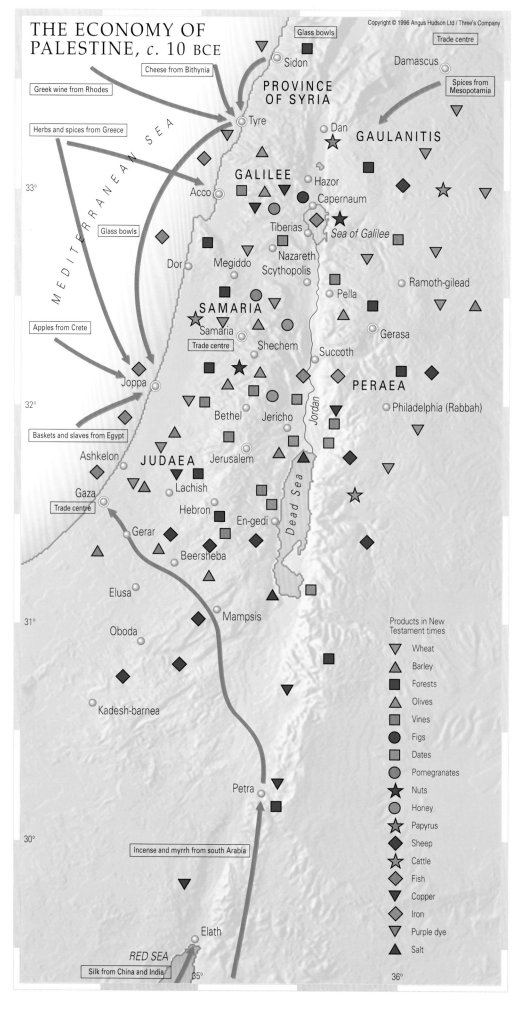

THE ECONOMY OF PALESTINE, *c.* 10 BCE

Copyright © 1996 Angus Hudson Ltd / Three's Company

Glass bowls

Trade centre

Cheese from Bithynia

Greek wine from Rhodes

Herbs and spices from Greece

Glass bowls

Apples from Crete

Baskets and slaves from Egypt

Trade centre

Trade centre

Spices from Mesopotamia

Incense and myrrh from south Arabia

Silk from China and India

MEDITERRANEAN SEA

PROVINCE OF SYRIA

GAULANITIS

GALILEE

SAMARIA

PERAEA

JUDAEA

Sea of Galilee

Jordan

Dead Sea

RED SEA

Sidon · Damascus · Tyre · Dan · Acco · Hazor · Capernaum · Tiberias · Nazareth · Scythopolis · Pella · Ramoth-gilead · Dor · Megiddo · Samaria · Shechem · Succoth · Gerasa · Joppa · Bethel · Jericho · Philadelphia (Rabbah) · Ashkelon · Jerusalem · Lachish · Gaza · Hebron · En-gedi · Gerar · Beersheba · Elusa · Mampsis · Oboda · Kadesh-barnea · Petra · Elath

Products in New Testament times

▽ Wheat
△ Barley
■ Forests
△ Olives
▢ Vines
● Figs
▢ Dates
● Pomegranates
★ Nuts
● Honey
☆ Papyrus
◆ Sheep
☆ Cattle
◆ Fish
▽ Copper
◇ Iron
▽ Purple dye
△ Salt

THE BAKER
atlas
of
CHRISTIAN
HISTORY

NEW TESTAMENT PERIOD

THE ROMAN EMPIRE

ATLANTIC

OCEAN

BRITANNIA

GERMANIA
INFERIOR

Rhine

LUGDUNENSIS

BELGICA

GERMANIA
SUPERIOR

RAETIA

NORICUM

AQUITANIA

Danube

PANNONIA

NARBONENSIS

ALPES POENINAE

DALMATIA

ALPES
COTTIAE

ALPES
MARITIMAE

Salonae

MOESIA

LUSITANIA

TARRACONENSIS

CORSICA

Rome

ITALIA

MACEDONIA

Thessa

BAETICA

SARDINIA

EPIRUS

Corinth

Carthage

SICILIA

MAURETANIA

Syracuse

ACHAE

AFRICA

M E D I T E R R A

Cyrene

CYRENAIC

THE ROMAN EMPIRE

The Emperor Augustus brought peace, prosperity and stability to the Roman Empire. By the time of his death in 14 CE, the frontiers of the empire had been made secure: the River Danube became the northern frontier and a series of buffer states protected Asia Minor and east Mediterranean from the Parthians in the east. Some of these states were 'client' kingdoms, which acknowledged Roman dominance in return for their protection.

Further conquests by the Emperor Trajan (Dacia, Arabia, Armenia and Mesopotamia) expanded the imperial boundary to its maximum extent in 116 CE. An extensive programme of road building enabled a Roman citizen to travel safely and quickly; from Britain to Mesopotamia he needed no languages other than Latin and Greek, no passport and only the Roman denarius for currency.

The remains of the Forum of ancient Rome, the administrative centre of the Roman Empire.

Map labels

30° 40° 50° 60°

55°

CASPIAN SEA

50°

BLACK SEA

45°

ACIA

BITHYNIA AND PONTUS

Nicomedia

ARMENIA

CAPPADOCIA

40°

ASSYRIA

Tigris

ASIA

GALATIA

MESOPOTAMIA

Ephesus

CILICIA

LYCIA AND PAMPHYLIA

Antioch

SYRIA

ETE

35°

CYPRUS

Euphrates

N SEA

JUDAEA

Jerusalem

30°

Alexandria

ARABIA/ NABATAEA

25°

AEGYPTUS

Nile

RED SEA

30° 40°

QUMRAN

The Qumran region at the north-west end of the Dead Sea has become famous for the discovery in 1947 of ancient manuscripts, known as the Dead Sea Scrolls. They contain sections of the Bible and rules of communal discipline. They probably belonged to a monastic community living at Qumran, widely believed to have been the Essenes. The Scrolls were found in caves among the hills overlooking Qumran, where they had been hidden from the Romans during the Jewish War of 66-70 CE.

The settlement at Qumran probably dates from about 145 BCE, after the demise of Antiochus Epiphanes IV. The group may have arisen in opposition to the hellenization of Judaism during his reign. The community practised strict self-discipline and interpreted the Old Testament prophecies as referring to current events. They expected the imminent advent of a messianic figure, and as they considered themselves the remnant of the true Israel they believed they alone would win God's salvation.

The barren Judean Hills at Qumran. It was in caves in these cliffs that the Dead Sea Scrolls were discovered.

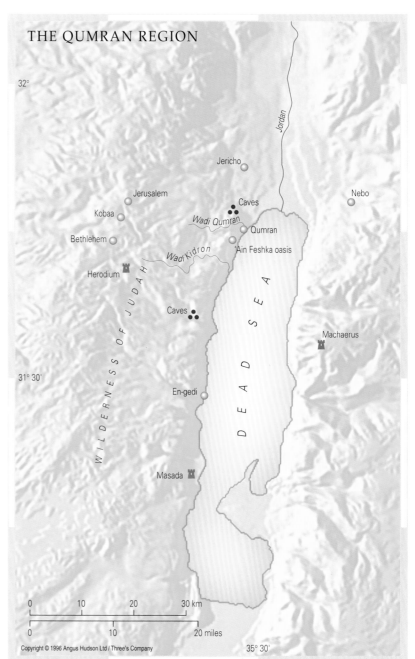

THE QUMRAN REGION

Copyright © 1996 Angus Hudson Ltd / Three's Company

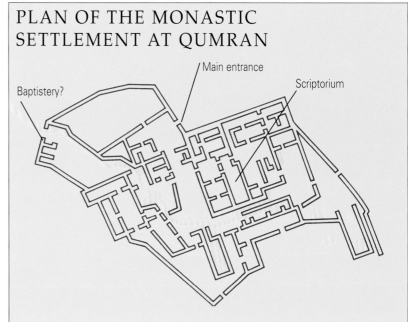

PLAN OF THE MONASTIC SETTLEMENT AT QUMRAN

Baptistery?

Main entrance

Scriptorium

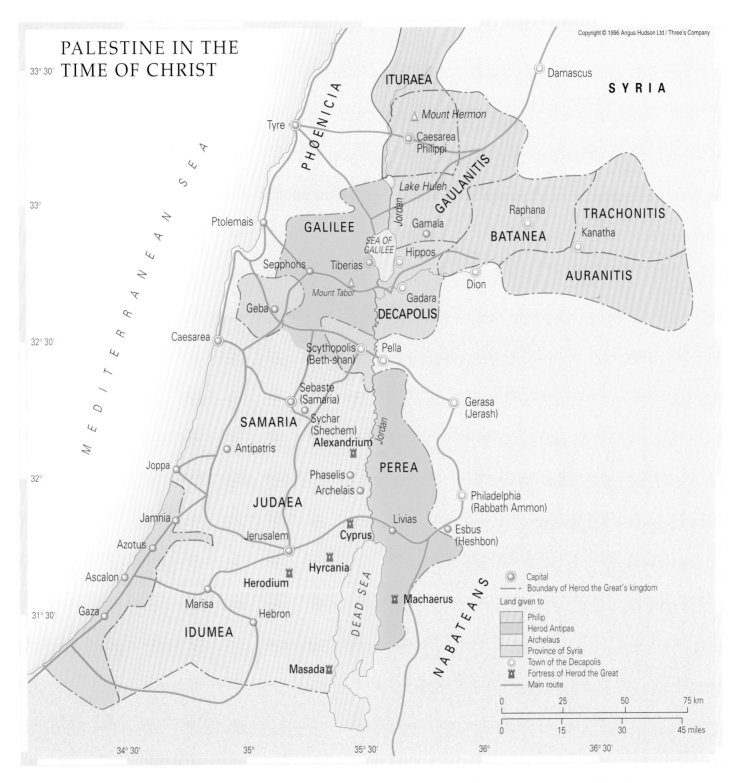

PALESTINE IN THE TIME OF CHRIST

33° 30'

SYRIA

ITURAEA

Damascus

PHOENICIA

△ *Mount Hermon*

Tyre

Caesarea
Philippi

GAULANITIS

33°

Lake Huleh

Jordan

TRACHONITIS

Raphana

Ptolemais

GALILEE

Gamala

BATANEA

Kanatha

*SEA OF
GALILEE*

Sepphoris

Tiberias

Hippos

AURANITIS

Mount Tabor

Gadara

Dion

Geba

DECAPOLIS

32° 30'

Caesarea

Scythopolis
(Beth-shan)

Pella

Sebaste
(Samaria)

Gerasa
(Jerash)

SAMARIA

Sychar
(Shechem)

Alexandrium

Antipatris

Jordan

32°

Joppa

Phaselis

PEREA

Archelais

Philadelphia
(Rabbath Ammon)

JUDAEA

Jamnia

Livias

Esbus
(Heshbon)

Azotus

Jerusalem

Cyprus

Ascalon

Hyrcania

Gaza

Herodium

31° 30'

Marisa

Hebron

DEAD SEA

Machaerus

IDUMEA

NABATEANS

Masada

◎	Capital
–·–·–	Boundary of Herod the Great's kingdom
	Land given to
	Philip
	Herod Antipas
	Archelaus
	Province of Syria
◎	Town of the Decapolis
🏰	Fortress of Herod the Great
——	Main route

0   25   50   75 km

0   15   30   45 miles

34° 30'   35°   35° 30'   36°   36° 30'

PALESTINE IN THE TIME OF CHRIST

Herod the Great was appointed King of Judaea by the Roman senate in 40 BCE. The Parthians then invaded Syria and Palestine and installed their own choice of king, the Hasmonean Mattathias Antigonus. By 37 BCE, however, Herod had secured the throne for himself and he continued to reign until his death in 4 BCE, whereupon the kingdom was

divided among his three sons. Herod was not popular with the Jews, despite his building of a new Temple in Jerusalem. His father was Idumaean (Edomite) and he was also very supportive of Roman policy, even erecting shrines to pagan gods.

Palestine now became a province ruled by tetrarchs (literally, ruler of a fourth part, but in practice a provincial ruler more subject to Rome than a king). Archelaus, called Herod the Ethnarch, ruled Judaea from 4 BCE to 6 CE. He was then sent into exile by the Romans after

complaints of his mismanagement. A Roman governor then ruled Judaea until 41 CE. Herod Antipas ruled Galilee and part of Transjordan from 4 BCE to 39 CE; and Herod Philip ruled the northern regions until 34 CE.

The Decapolis was a confederation of ten cities formed after Pompey's campaign (65-62 BCE). It gave protection to its Gentile citizens, who were mainly Greek-speaking Roman soldiers, against militant Jews and Arabian tribes.

JESUS' CHILDHOOD

According to Luke's Gospel, a Roman census was conducted by Quirinius, governor of Syria. Everyone had to go to their native town to register. Thus, Joseph took Mary to his native town of Bethlehem, where she went into labour and bore Jesus (Luke 2:1-7). According to Matthew, visiting Magi from the east, who had followed a portentous star, visited King Herod asking to see the child who would be king of the Jews. Anxious about this new rival, Herod ordered the killing of all babies in Bethlehem. Joseph and Mary fled to Egypt to escape the slaughter (Matthew 2:1-18).

After Herod's death they went to Nazareth, their hometown, which was under the milder rule of Herod Antipas. Following tradition, Jesus was presented in the Temple at the age of twelve. After setting off on the return trip, his parents discovered that Jesus was not with them (presumably they were among a crowd and had not noticed). They went back to Jerusalem to find him debating with the elders (Luke 2:41-52). Finally they headed back to Nazareth. Jews travelling between Nazareth and Jerusalem would normally cross to the other side of the River Jordan in order to avoid Samaria. What would be a three-day journey on foot via Samaria was made twice as long by going through Transjordan.

A statue of the Holy Family in Nazareth.

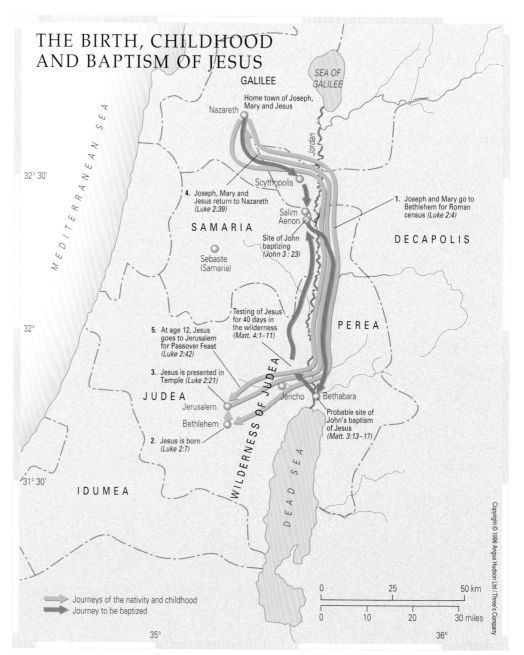

THE BIRTH, CHILDHOOD AND BAPTISM OF JESUS

GALILEE

SEA OF GALILEE

Home town of Joseph, Mary and Jesus

Nazareth

Scythopolis

4. Joseph, Mary and Jesus return to Nazareth (Luke 2:39)

1. Joseph and Mary go to Bethlehem for Roman census (Luke 2:4)

Salim Aenon

SAMARIA

Site of John baptizing (John 3 : 23)

DECAPOLIS

Sebaste (Samaria)

Testing of Jesus for 40 days in the wilderness (Matt. 4:1–11)

PEREA

5. At age 12, Jesus goes to Jerusalem for Passover Feast (Luke 2:42)

3. Jesus is presented in Temple (Luke 2:21)

JUDEA

Jerusalem

Jericho

Bethabara

Bethlehem

Probable site of John's baptism of Jesus (Matt. 3:13–17)

2. Jesus is born (Luke 2:7)

WILDERNESS OF JUDEA

DEAD SEA

IDUMEA

MEDITERRANEAN SEA

Jordan

Journeys of the nativity and childhood
Journey to be baptized

| 0 | 25 | 50 km |
| 0 | 10 | 20 | 30 miles |

35°   36°

32° 30'

32°

31° 30'

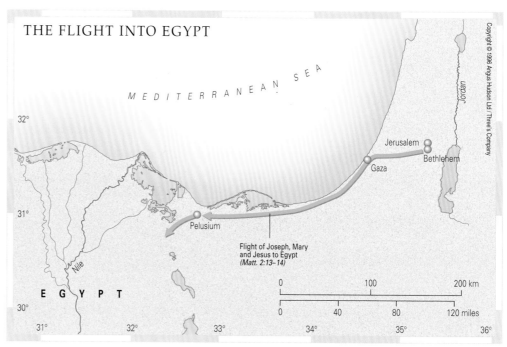

THE FLIGHT INTO EGYPT

MEDITERRANEAN SEA

Jordan

Jerusalem

Gaza

Bethlehem

Pelusium

EGYPT

Nile

Flight of Joseph, Mary and Jesus to Egypt (Matt. 2:13–14)

| 0 | 100 | 200 km |
| 0 | 40 | 80 | 120 miles |

32°

31°

30°

31°   32°   33°   34°   35°   36°

GALILEE IN THE TIME OF JESUS

? Transfiguration
(Matt. 17 : 1–13)

Mount Hermon

Tyre

T Y R E

Dan

Caesarea Philippi

Meeting the Syro-Phoenician
woman (Mark 7 : 24–30)

Peter's confession that
Jesus is the messiah
(Matt. 16 : 13–20)

U P P E R
G A L I L E E

Lake Huleh

Gischala

Cursing of the towns
(Matt. 11 : 20)

Chorazin

Bethsaida-Julias

Capernaum

Jesus settles here;
first disciples are called
(Matt. 4 : 13–22)

Ptolemais

L O W E R
G A L I L E E

Gennesaret

Jotapata

Cana

Arbela

Magdala

? Gergesa

*SEA OF
GALILEE*

Sycaminum

Water turned into wine
during a wedding
(John 2 : 1–11)

Sepphoris

Tiberias

Hippos

Jesus is rejected
in his home town
(Luke 4 : 28–30)

Nazareth

Sennabris

Yarmuk

Mount Carmel

Kishon

Geba

? Transfiguration
(Matt. 17 : 1–13)

Nain

Philoteria

*Mount
Tabor*

Raising of the widow's son
(Luke 7 : 11–17)

Gadara

Dora

VALLEY OF ESDRAELON

Jordan

32° 30'

Caesarea

Esdraelon

0   10   20 km

0   4   8   12 miles

Scythopolis

D E C A P O L I S

Healing of the
deaf and dumb
(Mark 7 : 31–37)

35°

35° 30'

33°

M E D I T E R R A N E A N   S E A

Copyright © 1996 Angus Hudson Ltd / Three's Company

GALILEE IN JESUS' TIME

Galilee was much more prosperous as a region than Judea, and supported a large population. Galileans were generally despised by the religious leaders in Jerusalem. Many were not Jews by descent; their forebears had been forcibly converted by Alexander Jannaeus. Galileans were, though, probably more in touch with the daily reality of the Roman Empire, as Galilee lay on the great trade routes which crossed the Near East, and many foreigners would have passed through the region.

Jesus grew up in Nazareth, which was an unimportant small town. Rejected by its people (Luke 4:16-30), he moved to the vicinity of Lake Galilee. Archaeological excavations have revealed that there were twelve towns on the shores of the lake. The preservation of fish by salting and its export across the Roman Empire was a major industry. The city of Tiberias, built by Herod Antipas (c. 18 CE) in commemoration of the Roman emperor, was one of the main fishing centres.

CHRIST'S MINISTRY IN GALILEE

Most of the ministry of Jesus took place around Lake Galilee. He sometimes taught in a boat while the crowds watched from the shore. Crossings were frequently made 'to the other side', and Jesus' first apostles were local fishermen (Mark 1:14-20). The lake was large and subject to sudden squalls, as winds would swoop across the valley, hence the unexpected 'storm at sea' (Mark 4:35-41).

The location of the drowning of the Gadarene swine is disputed (Mark 5:1-20). It may have been at the foot of the hill descending from the inland village of Gadara at the southern end of Lake Galilee, or it may have been the traditional site at Kursi (perhaps Gergesa) which lay on the eastern shore. The lake is 21 km (13 miles) long and 11 km (7 miles) wide.

A view of Lake Galilee from the shore near Capernaum.

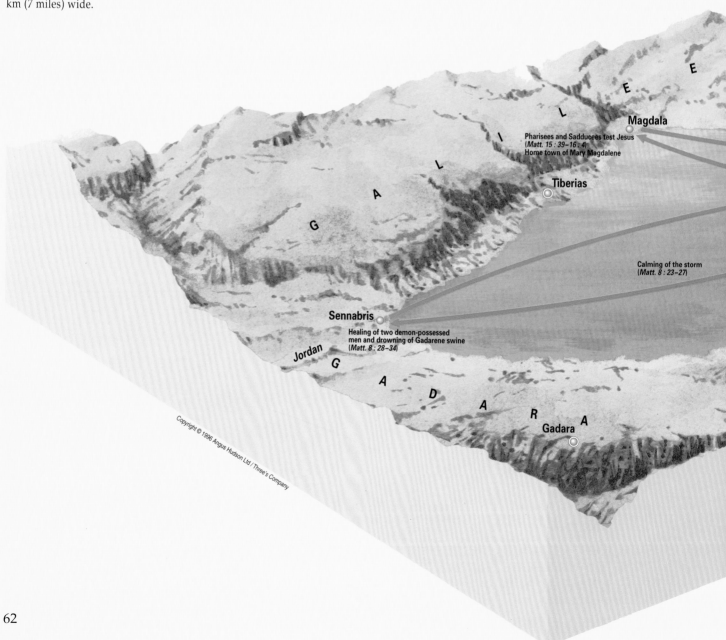

Magdala
Pharisees and Sadducees test Jesus
(*Matt. 15 : 39 – 16 : 4*)
Home town of Mary Magdalene

Tiberias

G A L I L E E

Calming of the storm
(*Matt. 8 : 23–27*)

Sennabris
Healing of two demon-possessed men and drowning of Gadarene swine
(*Matt. 8 : 28–34*)

Jordan

G A D A R A

Gadara

The partially reconstructed fourth-century synagogue at Capernaum.

The Mount of Beatitudes offers magnificent views over Lake Galilee.

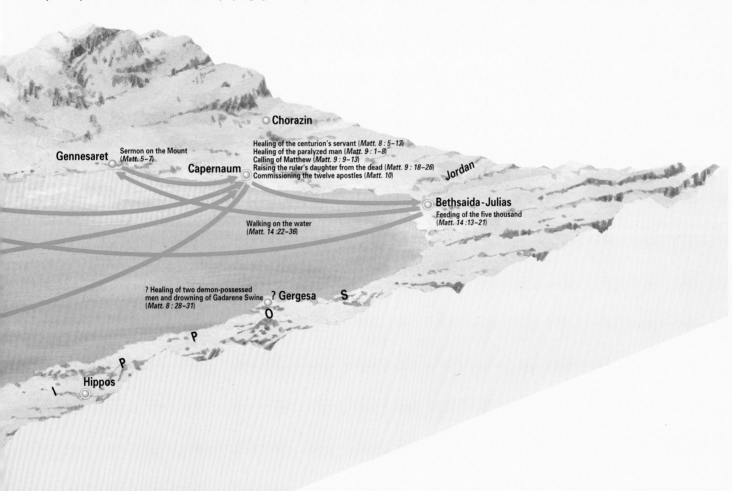

Chorazin

Healing of the centurion's servant (*Matt. 8 : 5–13*)
Healing of the paralyzed man (*Matt. 9 : 1–8*)
Calling of Matthew (*Matt. 9 : 9–13*)
Raising the ruler's daughter from the dead (*Matt. 9 : 18–26*)
Commissioning the twelve apostles (*Matt. 10*)

Gennesaret

Sermon on the Mount
(*Matt. 5–7*)

Capernaum

Jordan

Bethsaida-Julias

Feeding of the five thousand
(*Matt. 14 :13–21*)

Walking on the water
(*Matt. 14 :22–36*)

? Healing of two demon-possessed
men and drowning of Gadarene Swine
(*Matt. 8 : 28–31*)

? Gergesa

S

O

P

P

P

Hippos

I

JERUSALEM IN JESUS' TIME

Jesus visited Jerusalem several times during his three-year ministry, mainly to celebrate the festivals (John 2:13; 5:1; 7:10; 10:22-23). He stayed in Bethany at the house of Lazarus and his sisters, Mary and Martha (John 11).

As well as building cities and fortresses outside Jerusalem, Herod the Great made huge additions inside: the Temple Mount, the Antonia Fortress and the Upper Palace. The Upper City was the quarter of wealthy aristocrats. Herod's Palace was the residence of the Roman governors after Herod (6-41, 44-66 CE). It was most likely here, rather than at the Antonia Fortress, that Jesus was tried by Pontius Pilate (Matthew 27:11-26). It is also possible that he was tried at Herod Antipas' Palace.

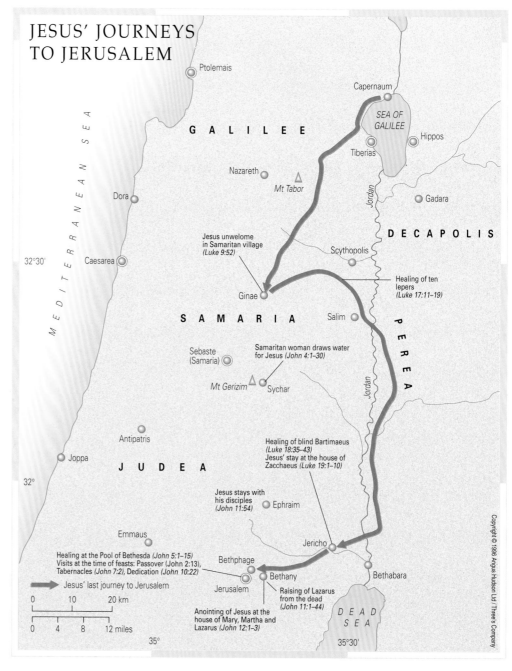

JESUS' JOURNEYS TO JERUSALEM

Ptolemais

Capernaum

GALILEE

SEA OF GALILEE

Hippos

Tiberias

Nazareth

Mt Tabor

Gadara

Dora

DECAPOLIS

Jesus unwelome in Samaritan village (Luke 9:52)

Scythopolis

32°30'

Caesarea

Healing of ten lepers (Luke 17:11–19)

Ginae

MEDITERRANEAN SEA

SAMARIA

Salim

PEREA

Sebaste (Samaria)

Samaritan woman draws water for Jesus (John 4:1–30)

Mt Gerizim   Sychar

Jordan

Antipatris

Healing of blind Bartimaeus (Luke 18:35–43)
Jesus' stay at the house of Zacchaeus (Luke 19:1–10)

Joppa

JUDEA

Jesus stays with his disciples (John 11:54)   Ephraim

32°

Jericho

Emmaus

Bethphage

Healing at the Pool of Bethesda (John 5:1–15)
Visits at the time of feasts: Passover (John 2:13), Tabernacles (John 7:2), Dedication (John 10:22)

Bethany

Bethabara

Jerusalem

Raising of Lazarus from the dead (John 11:1–44)

→ Jesus' last journey to Jerusalem

0   10   20 km

0   4   8   12 miles

Anointing of Jesus at the house of Mary, Martha and Lazarus (John 12:1–3)

DEAD SEA

35°

35°30'

Part of the Western Wall consists of masonry from Herod's Temple.

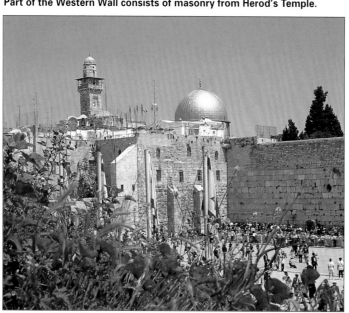

The Citadel, Jerusalem, is on the site of Herod's Palace.

JERUSALEM AT THE TIME OF CHRIST

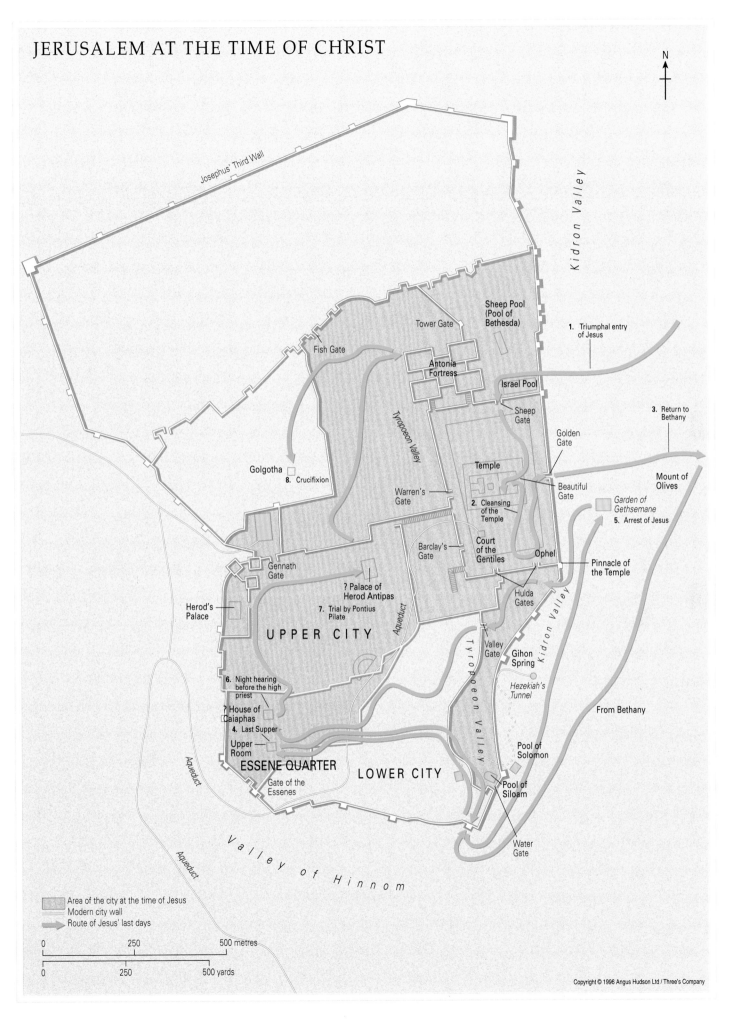

N

Josephus' Third Wall

Kidron Valley

Sheep Pool
(Pool of
Bethesda)

Tower Gate

1. Triumphal entry
of Jesus

Fish Gate

Antonia
Fortress

Israel Pool

Sheep
Gate

3. Return to
Bethany

Tyropoeon Valley

Golden
Gate

Temple

Mount of
Olives

Golgotha

8. Crucifixion

Warren's
Gate

Beautiful
Gate

2. Cleansing
of the
Temple

Garden of
Gethsemane

5. Arrest of Jesus

Barclay's
Gate

Court
of the
Gentiles

Ophel

Pinnacle of
the Temple

Gennath
Gate

? Palace of
Herod Antipas

Hulda
Gates

Herod's
Palace

7. Trial by Pontius
Pilate

Aqueduct

UPPER CITY

Tyropoeon Valley

Valley
Gate

Gihon
Spring

Kidron Valley

Hezekiah's
Tunnel

From Bethany

6. Night hearing
before the high
priest

? House of
Caiaphas

4. Last Supper

Upper
Room

Aqueduct

ESSENE QUARTER

LOWER CITY

Gate of the
Essenes

Pool of
Solomon

Pool of
Siloam

Aqueduct

Valley of Hinnom

Water
Gate

Area of the city at the time of Jesus
Modern city wall
Route of Jesus' last days

| 0 | 250 | 500 metres |
| 0 | 250 | 500 yards |

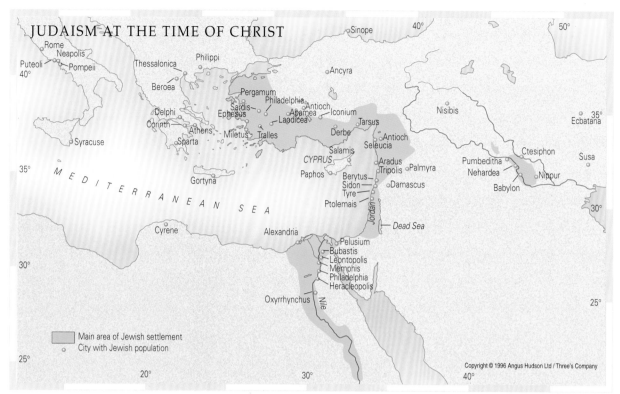

JUDAISM AT THE TIME OF CHRIST

With the coming of the Roman Empire and the Pax Romana, the movement of peoples across the Mediterranean world was made easier. Jews were beginning to spread to the west, beyond Italy. They were also able to spread eastwards through the Parthian Empire, and a sizeable community had established themselves in Babylonia. The main areas of concentration, though, remained in Judaea, Syria, western Asia Minor and Egypt, where Alexandria had become a major centre of Greco-Jewish culture.

JESUS' RESURRECTION

'Christ . . . was raised on the third day according to the Scriptures, and . . . he appeared to Peter, and then to the Twelve. After that, he appeared to more than five hundred of the brothers at the same time, most of whom are still living . . . Then he appeared to James, then to all the apostles, and last of all he appeared to me . . .'
(Paul: 1 Corinthians 15:4-8)

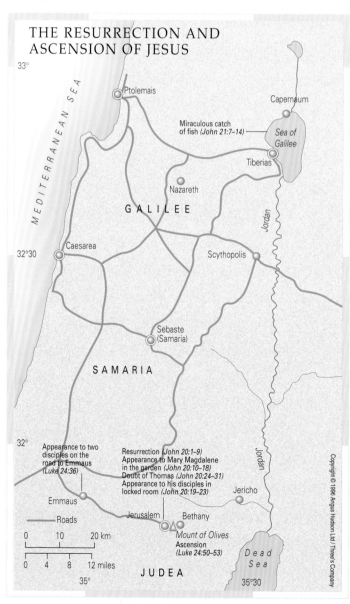

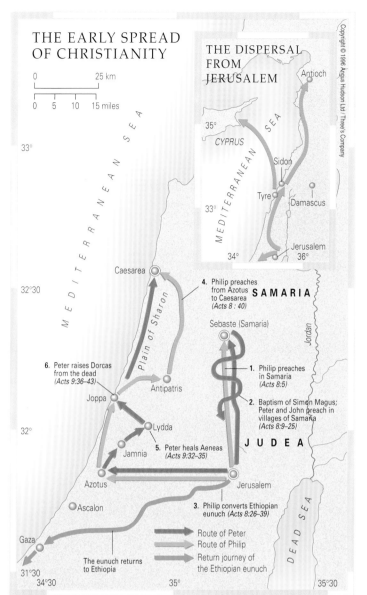

THE EARLY SPREAD OF CHRISTIANITY

THE DISPERSAL FROM JERUSALEM

0   25 km

0   5   10   15 miles

MEDITERRANEAN SEA

CYPRUS

33°

Antioch

Sidon

Tyre

Damascus

33°

34°

Jerusalem
36°

MEDITERRANEAN SEA

Caesarea

32°30

Plain of Sharon

4. Philip preaches from Azotus to Caesarea (Acts 8 : 40)

SAMARIA

Sebaste (Samaria)

Jordan

6. Peter raises Dorcas from the dead (Acts 9:36–43)

Antipatris

1. Philip preaches in Samaria (Acts 8:5)

Joppa

2. Baptism of Simon Magus; Peter and John preach in villages of Samaria (Acts 8:9–25)

Lydda

32°

Jamnia

5. Peter heals Aeneas (Acts 9:32–35)

JUDEA

Azotus

Jerusalem

Ascalon

3. Philip converts Ethiopian eunuch (Acts 8:26–39)

DEAD SEA

Gaza

The eunuch returns to Ethiopia

→ Route of Peter
→ Route of Philip
→ Return journey of the Ethiopian eunuch

31°30

34°30   35°   35°30

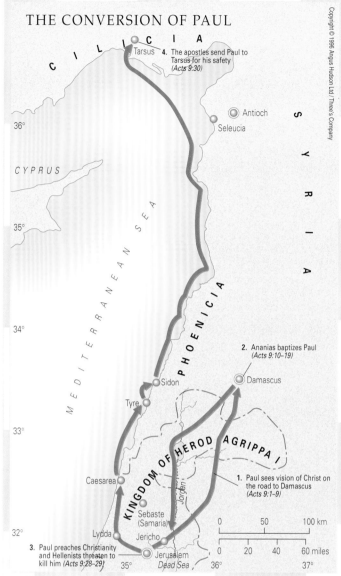

THE CONVERSION OF PAUL

CILICIA

Tarsus   4. The apostles send Paul to Tarsus for his safety (Acts 9:30)

36°

Antioch

Seleucia

S Y R I A

CYPRUS

35°

MEDITERRANEAN SEA

PHOENICIA

34°

2. Ananias baptizes Paul (Acts 9:10–19)

Sidon

Damascus

Tyre

KINGDOM OF HEROD AGRIPPA I

33°

Caesarea

1. Paul sees vision of Christ on the road to Damascus (Acts 9:1–9)

Sebaste (Samaria)

Jordan

32°

Lydda

Jericho

0   50   100 km

0   20   40   60 miles

3. Paul preaches Christianity and Hellenists threaten to kill him (Acts 9:28–29)

Jerusalem
Dead Sea
35°   36°   37°

By tradition, Stephen was martyred outside this gate into Jerusalem.

CHRISTIANITY BEFORE PAUL

After the martyrdom of Stephen on the charge of 'blasphemy' (Acts 6:11), many of the apostles left Jerusalem and preached elsewhere. Philip, Peter and John all made conversions in Samaria (Acts 8), a 'no-go' area for religious (or 'strict') Jews. The coastal plain of Judaea, as far as Caesarea, was also evangelized by Peter and Philip. As the persecution of Christians by Jews in Jerusalem became more evident, so Jewish Christians dispersed northwards. They had reached as far as Antioch, third largest city in the Roman Empire, by the time Paul embarked on his missionary journeys (Acts 13).

PAUL'S JOURNEY TO DAMASCUS

Some time after Stephen's death, while Paul (then Saul) was still a Pharisee, he got permission from the Temple authorities to go to Damascus to search out Christians (Acts 9:1-2). It was on the way there that he received his blinding vision of the risen Christ. After regaining his sight in Damascus with the help of Ananias in Straight Street, Paul became a Christian and was himself forced to flee for his life back to Jerusalem (Acts 9:23-26). He was soon in danger again, from Hellenistic Jews, and departed for his home town of Tarsus via Caesarea.

PAUL'S MISSIONARY JOURNEYS

Barnabas, who was preaching in Antioch, went to Tarsus and brought Paul back with him to Antioch. After a brief trip to Jerusalem they, together with Mark, set out on the first of three missionary journeys. Paul and his companions got a mixed reception. When they performed miracle cures they were sometimes treated as gods. At the other extreme, their preaching sometimes caused great offence to traditional Jews and on occasions they were thrown out of town.

The first journey established new churches in Galatia (Acts 13-14). It was probably to these communities that Paul addressed his Letter to the Galatians. The second journey took the gospel into Macedonia, and churches were founded at Philippi and Thessalonica (Acts 15:36 –18:22). Many women were baptized. Women in Greek society had greater freedom than they had in Palestine. They were allowed, for instance, to attend synagogue alongside the men, and so could have heard Paul's preaching. In Achaia, Paul founded the church at Corinth, which was to cause him so much trouble, and he presented his teaching at the highest philosophical court in the Western world: the Areopagus in Athens (Acts 17:19-34).

Roman corn ship from North Africa, on a coin of the Emperor Commodus.

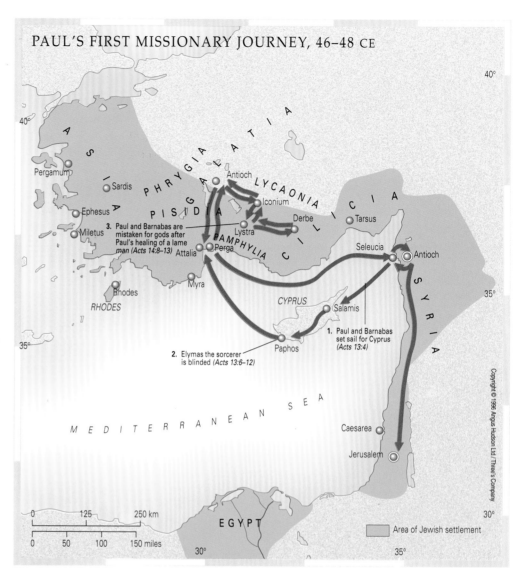

PAUL'S FIRST MISSIONARY JOURNEY, 46–48 CE

3. Paul and Barnabas are mistaken for gods after Paul's healing of a lame man (*Acts 14:8–13*)

1. Paul and Barnabas set sail for Cyprus (*Acts 13:4*)

2. Elymas the sorcerer is blinded (*Acts 13:6–12*)

Area of Jewish settlement

Copyright © 1996 Angus Hudson Ltd / Three's Company

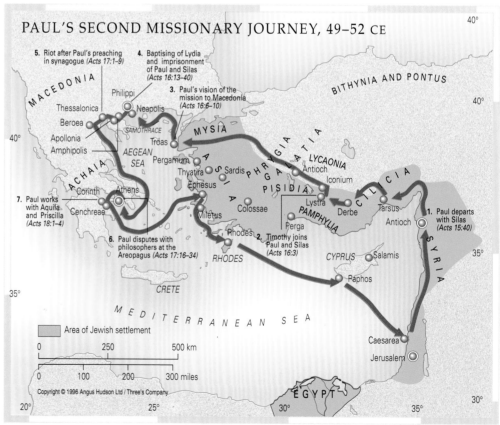

PAUL'S SECOND MISSIONARY JOURNEY, 49–52 CE

5. Riot after Paul's preaching in synagogue (*Acts 17:1–9*)

4. Baptising of Lydia and imprisonment of Paul and Silas (*Acts 16:13–40*)

3. Paul's vision of the mission to Macedonia (*Acts 16:6–10*)

7. Paul works with Aquila and Priscilla (*Acts 18:1–4*)

6. Paul disputes with philosophers at the Areopagus (*Acts 17:16–34*)

2. Timothy joins Paul and Silas (*Acts 16:3*)

1. Paul departs with Silas (*Acts 15:40*)

Area of Jewish settlement

Copyright © 1996 Angus Hudson Ltd / Three's Company

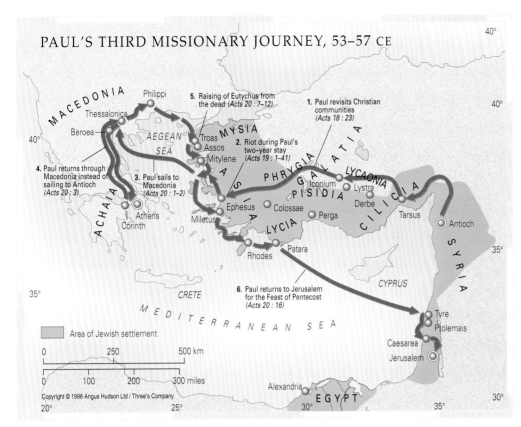

PAUL'S THIRD MISSIONARY JOURNEY, 53–57 CE

MACEDONIA

Philippi

Thessalonica

Beroea

5. Raising of Eutychus from the dead *(Acts 20 : 7–12)*

1. Paul revisits Christian communities *(Acts 18 : 23)*

AEGEAN SEA

MYSIA

Troas

Assos

Mitylene

2. Riot during Paul's two-year stay *(Acts 19 : 1–41)*

PHRYGIA

GALATIA

LYCAONIA

CILICIA

4. Paul returns through Macedonia instead of sailing to Antioch *(Acts 20 : 3)*

3. Paul sails to Macedonia *(Acts 20 : 1–2)*

ACHAIA

Athens

Corinth

A S I A

Ephesus

Miletus

Colossae

Perga

LYCIA

Iconium

PISIDIA

Lystra

Derbe

Tarsus

Antioch

SYRIA

Rhodes

Patara

6. Paul returns to Jerusalem for the Feast of Pentecost *(Acts 20 : 16)*

CRETE

M E D I T E R R A N E A N   S E A

CYPRUS

Tyre

Ptolemais

Caesarea

Jerusalem

Alexandria

EGYPT

Area of Jewish settlement

0   250   500 km

0   100   200   300 miles

Copyright © 1996 Angus Hudson Ltd / Three's Company

On the third journey, Paul stayed more than two years at Ephesus, building an important Christian community there (Acts 19). Christianity spread out generally in western Asia Minor, reaching Colossae and Laodicea. When he returned to Jerusalem his enemies provoked a riot in the Temple area, which brought about his arrest and trial in Caesarea before the Roman authorities (Acts 21-26).

The voyage to Rome undertaken by Paul in order to have his case heard by the Roman Emperor resulted in a period of house arrest of two years (Acts 28:30). According to tradition he was freed and he then visited Troas, Miletus and Corinth again. Further tradition maintains that he was executed in Rome during the Great Fire in 64 CE.

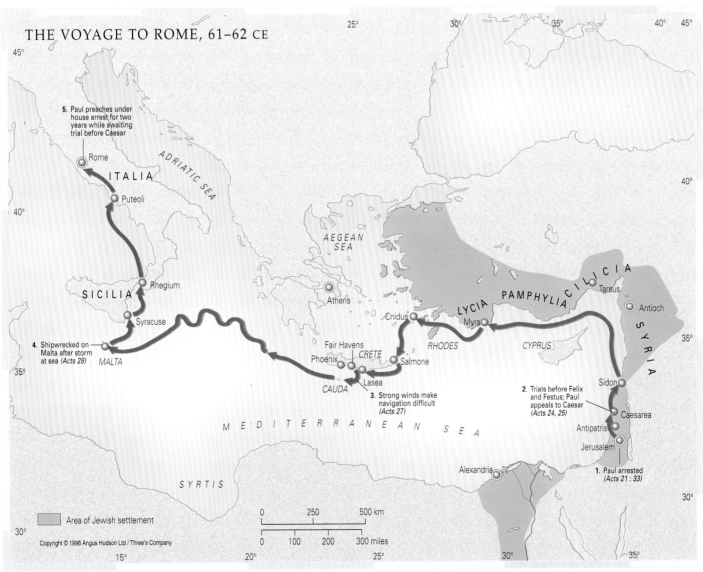

THE VOYAGE TO ROME, 61–62 CE

5. Paul preaches under house arrest for two years while awaiting trial before Caesar

Rome

ITALIA

ADRIATIC SEA

Puteoli

Rhegium

SICILIA

Syracuse

4. Shipwrecked on Malta after storm at sea *(Acts 28)*

MALTA

AEGEAN SEA

Athens

Cnidus

LYCIA

PAMPHYLIA

CILICIA

Tarsus

Myra

Antioch

RHODES

CYPRUS

SYRIA

Fair Havens

Phoenix

CRETE

Salmone

Lasea

CAUDA

3. Strong winds make navigation difficult *(Acts 27)*

Sidon

2. Trials before Felix and Festus; Paul appeals to Caesar *(Acts 24, 25)*

Caesarea

Antipatris

Jerusalem

1. Paul arrested *(Acts 21 : 33)*

M E D I T E R R A N E A N   S E A

Alexandria

S Y R T I S

Area of Jewish settlement

0   250   500 km

0   100   200   300 miles

Copyright © 1996 Angus Hudson Ltd / Three's Company

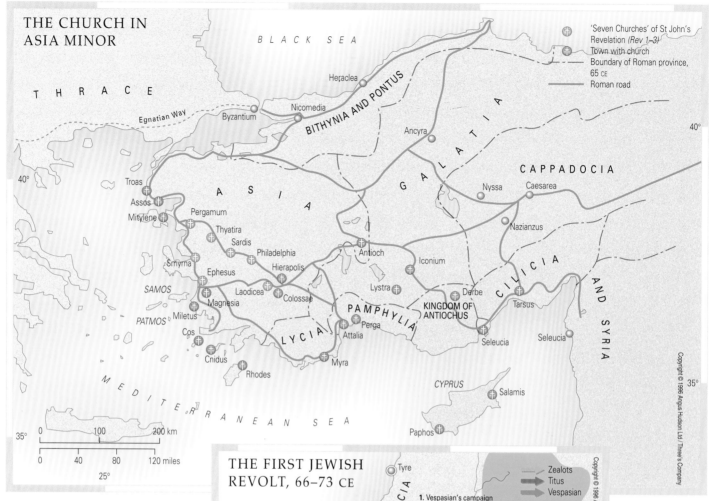

THE CHURCH IN ASIA MINOR

Asia Minor, with its large settled Jewish population, became the area of greatest growth for the church as Hellenistic Jews converted to Christianity. Many of the cities with large Jewish communities now had churches. John the Divine received his apocalyptic Revelation on the Isle of Patmos, off the west coast of Asia Minor. In it, 'seven churches' received messages of encouragement and condemnation (Revelation 1-3). They were all situated in western Asia Minor.

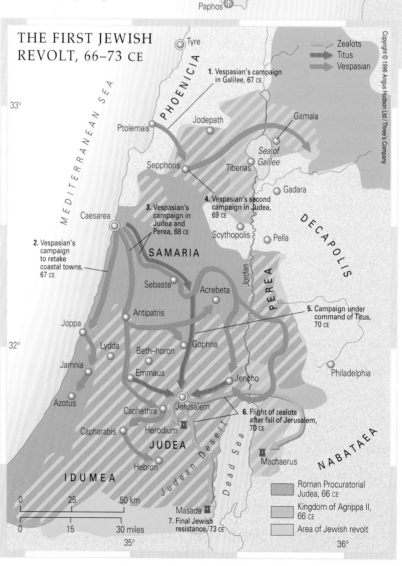

THE SIEGE OF JERUSALEM, 70 CE

Copyright © 1996 Angus Hudson Ltd / Three's Company

0   250   500 metres
0   250   500 yards

Titus with 12th and 15th legions

Third Wall

8. Romans renew attack and burn Antonia Fortress to the ground (20–22 July)

7. Titus builds siege wall to starve out Jews (early July)

3. Tenth Legion from Jericho camps at Mount of Olives

4. Romans breach third and then second walls (late May)

Second Wall

5. Titus sets up second camp inside third wall

Antonia Fortress

6. Romans besiege Antonia Fortress and Herod's towers, but suffer heavy losses (mid–June)

9. Temple porticoes are burned (15–17 August)

Temple

1. Titus makes first camp

Towers

Mount of Olives

2. Fifth Legion joins Titus from Emmaus

Herod's Palace

UPPER CITY

10. Temple is burned (28 August)

12. Romans capture Upper City and Herod's Palace (30 August)

Siege Wall

LOWER CITY   11. Romans capture Lower City (30 August)

N

Route of Titus and Fifth Legion
Route of Tenth Legion

THE FIRST JEWISH REVOLT

From 44 CE, Judaea was under the control of Roman procurators. Since the days of Herod, the Zealot party had been in revolt against Rome. Now, with increasing intolerance towards the Jews, the Roman authorities had caused the Pharisees to join ranks with the Zealots.

Once the revolt had sparked, it spread quickly through most of Judea and Galilee. The Roman general Vespasian arrived in Caesarea and set up his base at Ptolemais. He soon recaptured Galilee and the Golan in 67 CE, before turning south. In spite of the Jews' general hatred of the Romans, the war occasioned a good deal of factional fighting, which the Romans were able to exploit. The Jews' lack of unity resulted in the relentless re-occupation by the Romans of Samaria, Peraea and Judaea.

In spite of some fierce defence by the Zealots, Titus, Vespasian's son, did not take long to capture Jerusalem. He built a siege wall in order to starve out the inhabitants. Within three months of the beginning of the siege, the Temple had been burned and the other buildings destroyed.

Relief of the Romans in procession; another part shows them carrying the sacred vessels of the Temple in triumph after the destruction of Jerusalem, from Titus' Arch, Rome.

THE FALL OF MASADA

Masada is a massive outcrop of rock in the Judaean Desert. Herod the Great built a palace complex on the top. After the fall of Jerusalem a Zealot group under Eleazar took refuge there. With plenty of food and water, they were able to withstand the Roman offensive until 73 CE.

The Romans first built a siege wall around the rock to prevent the supply of more rations. They then built an earthen ramp up to the west side of the rock. On that, a base of wood and iron supported a siege tower. The Romans then had a vantage point from which to breach, with a battering ram, the main wall that surrounded the summit of the rock. Realising their hopeless plight, the 960 refugee Jews committed suicide overnight while waiting for the final assault.

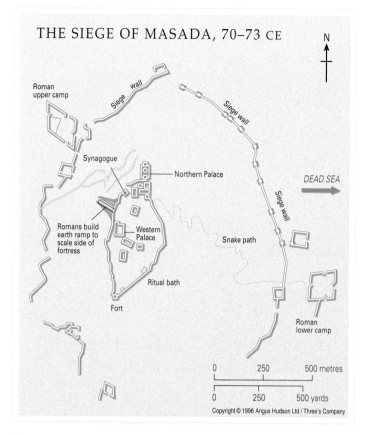

THE SIEGE OF MASADA, 70–73 CE

N

Roman upper camp

Siege wall

Siege wall

DEAD SEA

Synagogue

Northern Palace

Siege wall

Romans build earth ramp to scale side of fortress

Western Palace

Ritual bath

Snake path

Fort

Roman lower camp

| 0 | 250 | 500 metres |
| 0 | 250 | 500 yards |

Copyright © 1996 Angus Hudson Ltd / Three's Company

Replica of a Roman siege-engine, designed to catapult stones into a besieged stronghold such as Masada.

This view of Herod's Masada stronghold shows clearly the ramp constructed by the Romans to force their way in.

THE BAKER
atlas
of
CHRISTIAN
HISTORY

THE EARLY CHURCH

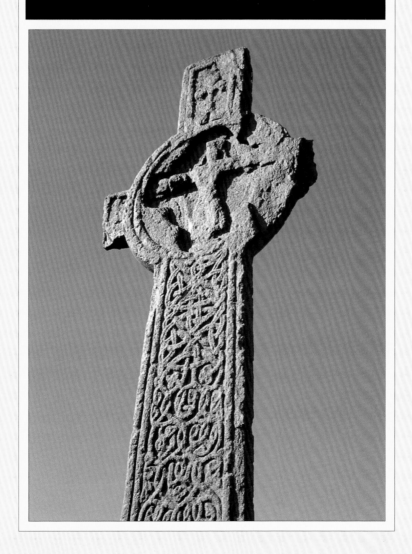

THE EXTENT OF CHRISTIANITY BY 100 CE

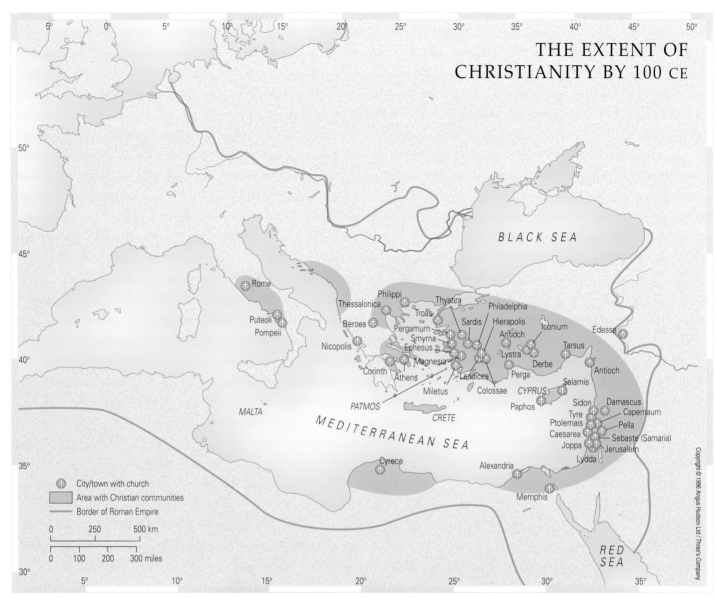

THE SPREAD OF CHRISTIANITY BY 100 CE

Patmos, the Aegean island to which John the Divine was exiled.

Paul and his fellow Jewish apostles carried the gospel to regions beyond Palestine. With the express purpose of evangelizing the Gentiles, they travelled extensively in Asia Minor and Greece. They visited synagogues in the Jewish Diaspora and talked with Gentiles in the marketplaces. Behind them they left small, uncertain groups of Christians whose faith was nurtured in subsequent visits and in the letters we know from the New Testament.

By the end of the first century Christianity was still virtually confined to the eastern Roman Empire, except for the communities in Rome, Puteoli and those around the Bay of Naples. The only possible church known outside the empire was at Edessa. Names of cities with Christians are known from the New Testament, such as the seven churches of Revelation, and from contemporary correspondence. Ignatius tells of churches in Magnesia and Tralles, and later writers of Alexandria, the home of Paul's helper, Apollos.

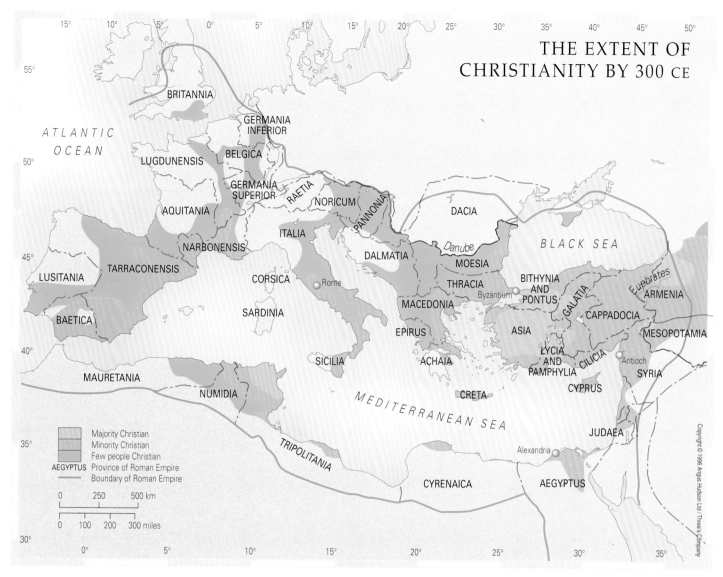

THE EXTENT OF CHRISTIANITY BY 300 CE

ATLANTIC OCEAN

BRITANNIA

GERMANIA INFERIOR

LUGDUNENSIS

BELGICA

GERMANIA SUPERIOR

RAETIA

NORICUM

PANNONIA

DACIA

AQUITANIA

ITALIA

NARBONENSIS

DALMATIA

MOESIA

BLACK SEA

Danube

TARRACONENSIS

CORSICA

Rome

THRACIA

Byzantium

BITHYNIA AND PONTUS

ARMENIA

Euphrates

LUSITANIA

SARDINIA

MACEDONIA

GALATIA

CAPPADOCIA

MESOPOTAMIA

BAETICA

EPIRUS

ASIA

LYCIA AND PAMPHYLIA

CILICIA

Antioch

SICILIA

ACHAIA

CYPRUS

SYRIA

MAURETANIA

NUMIDIA

CRETA

MEDITERRANEAN SEA

JUDAEA

Alexandria

Majority Christian
Minority Christian
Few people Christian
AEGYPTUS Province of Roman Empire
Boundary of Roman Empire

TRIPOLITANIA

0   250   500 km
0 100 200 300 miles

CYRENAICA

AEGYPTUS

Copyright © 1996 Angus Hudson Ltd / Three's Company

THE SPREAD OF CHRISTIANITY BY 300 CE

By the end of the third century the complexion of the Christian world was quite different. In the changes following the failure of the Jewish revolts, the Church and Judaism had increasingly gone their separate ways, and Christianity had become largely a religion of the Gentiles. With the expansion of the Church westwards as far as Roman Britain, its informal centre had shifted from Jerusalem to Rome. The scene was set for the Emperor Constantine to embrace Christianity around 312 CE. By the end of the fourth century it would be the official religion of the empire.

The view from the great theatre at Ephesus, an important Christian centre.

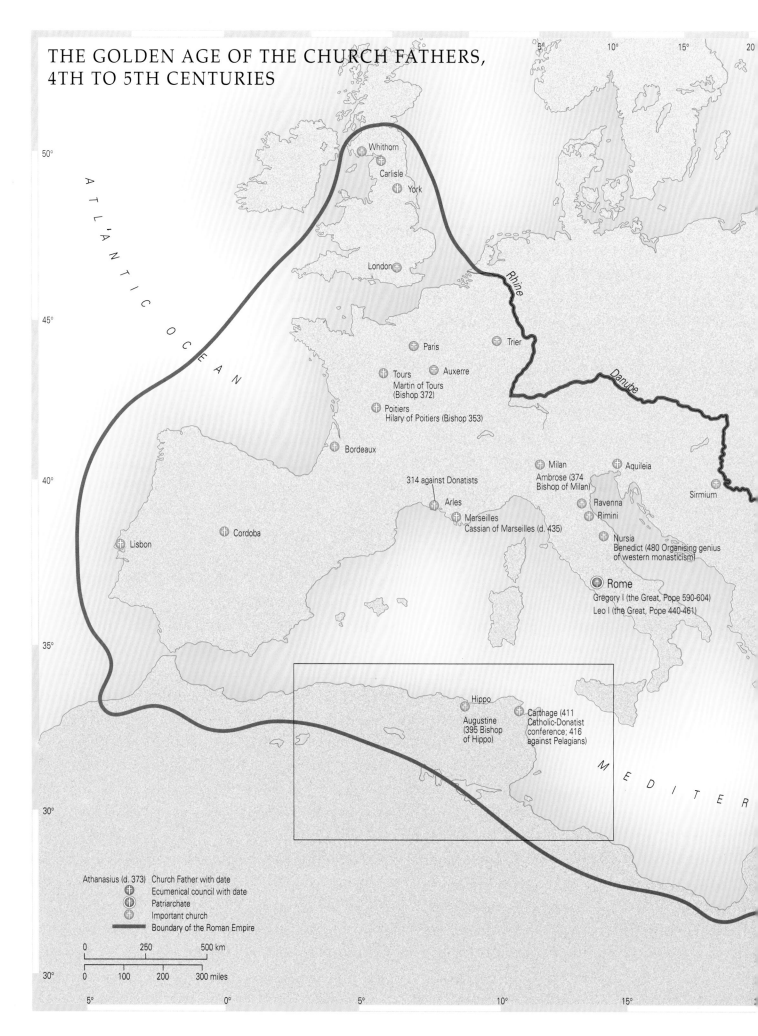

THE GOLDEN AGE OF THE CHURCH FATHERS, 4TH TO 5TH CENTURIES

Whithorn

Carlisle

York

London

Rhine

Paris

Trier

Tours
Auxerre

Martin of Tours
(Bishop 372)

Danube

Poitiers
Hilary of Poitiers (Bishop 353)

Bordeaux

Milan
Aquileia

Ambrose (374
Bishop of Milan)

314 against Donatists

Sirmium

Arles

Ravenna

Marseilles
Cassian of Marseilles (d. 435)

Rimini

Cordoba

Nursia

Lisbon

Benedict (480 Organising genius
of western monasticism)

Rome

Gregory I (the Great, Pope 590-604)
Leo I (the Great, Pope 440-461)

A T L A N T I C   O C E A N

Hippo

Augustine
(395 Bishop
of Hippo)

Carthage (411
Catholic-Donatist
conference; 416
against Pelagians)

M E D I T E R R

Athanasius (d. 373) Church Father with date

Ecumenical council with date

Patriarchate

Important church

Boundary of the Roman Empire

0   250   500 km

0   100   200   300 miles

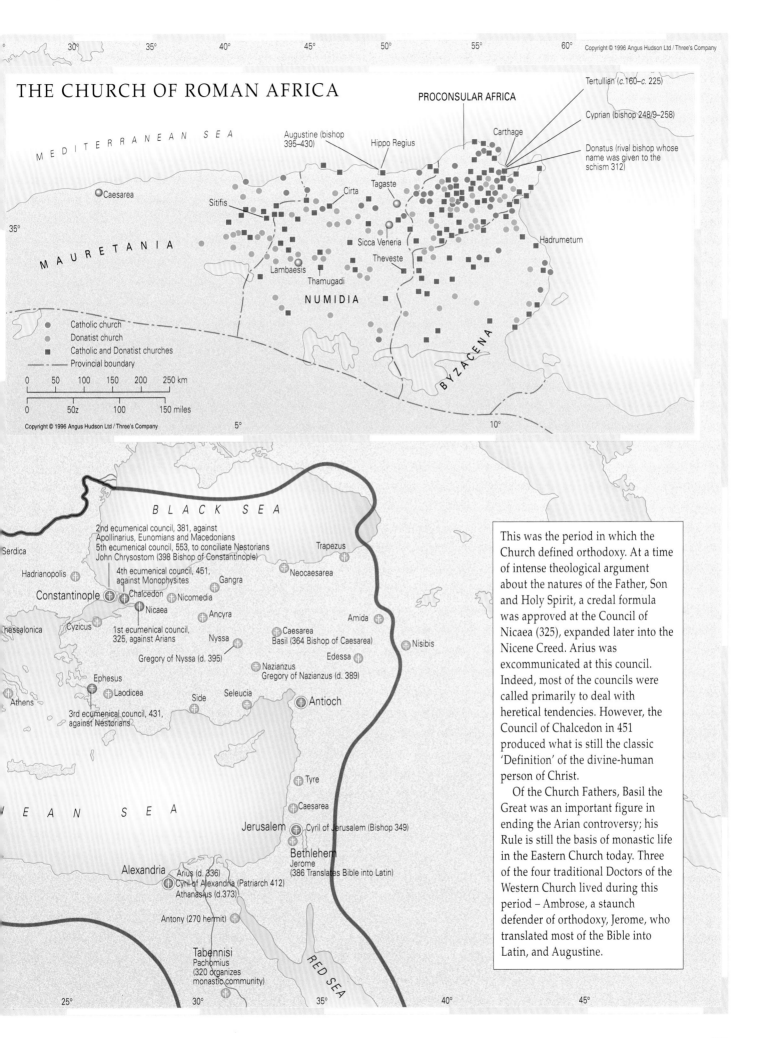

THE CHURCH OF ROMAN AFRICA

MEDITERRANEAN SEA

PROCONSULAR AFRICA

Tertullian (c.160–c. 225)

Cyprian (bishop 248/9–258)

Donatus (rival bishop whose name was given to the schism 312)

Carthage

Augustine (bishop 395–430)

Hippo Regius

Caesarea

Sitifis

Cirta

Tagaste

MAURETANIA

35°

Sicca Veneria

Hadrumetum

Lambaesis

Theveste

Thamugadi

NUMIDIA

BYZACENA

Catholic church

Donatist church

Catholic and Donatist churches

Provincial boundary

0   50   100   150   200   250 km

0   50z   100   150 miles

Copyright © 1996 Angus Hudson Ltd / Three's Company

Copyright © 1996 Angus Hudson Ltd / Three's Company

BLACK SEA

2nd ecumenical council, 381, against Apollinarius, Eunomians and Macedonians
5th ecumenical council, 553, to conciliate Nestorians
John Chrysostom (398 Bishop of Constantinople)

Serdica

Trapezus

Hadrianopolis

Neocaesarea

4th ecumenical council, 451, against Monophysites

Gangra

Constantinople

Chalcedon

Nicomedia

Nicaea

Ancyra

Amida

Thessalonica

Cyzicus

1st ecumenical council, 325, against Arians

Nyssa

Caesarea
Basil (364 Bishop of Caesarea)

Nisibis

Gregory of Nyssa (d. 395)

Edessa

Nazianzus
Gregory of Nazianzus (d. 389)

Ephesus

Laodicea

Side

Seleucia

Antioch

Athens

3rd ecumenical council, 431, against Nestorians

EAN SEA

Tyre

Caesarea

Jerusalem

Cyril of Jerusalem (Bishop 349)

Bethlehem
Jerome
(386 Translates Bible into Latin)

Alexandria

Arius (d. 336)

Cyril of Alexandria (Patriarch 412)

Athanasius (d.373)

Antony (270 hermit)

RED SEA

Tabennisi
Pachomius
(320 organizes monastic community)

This was the period in which the Church defined orthodoxy. At a time of intense theological argument about the natures of the Father, Son and Holy Spirit, a credal formula was approved at the Council of Nicaea (325), expanded later into the Nicene Creed. Arius was excommunicated at this council. Indeed, most of the councils were called primarily to deal with heretical tendencies. However, the Council of Chalcedon in 451 produced what is still the classic 'Definition' of the divine-human person of Christ.

Of the Church Fathers, Basil the Great was an important figure in ending the Arian controversy; his Rule is still the basis of monastic life in the Eastern Church today. Three of the four traditional Doctors of the Western Church lived during this period – Ambrose, a staunch defender of orthodoxy, Jerome, who translated most of the Bible into Latin, and Augustine.

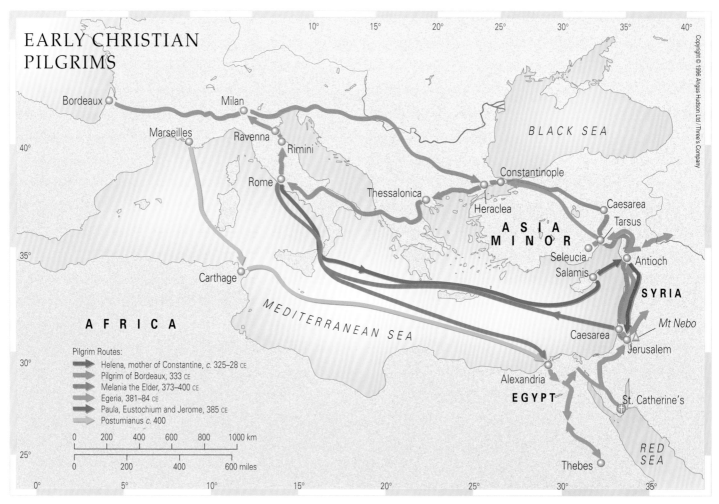

EARLY CHRISTIAN PILGRIMS

Pilgrim Routes:

➤ Helena, mother of Constantine, c. 325–28 CE
➤ Pilgrim of Bordeaux, 333 CE
➤ Melania the Elder, 373–400 CE
➤ Egeria, 381–84 CE
➤ Paula, Eustochium and Jerome, 385 CE
➤ Postumianus c. 400

THE CHURCH OF ROMAN NORTH AFRICA

By the end of the second century the African Church was a theological force in Catholicism. Tertullian and Cyprian of Carthage laid the groundwork of major Christian doctrines, including the Trinity and Original Sin. Augustine of Hippo developed these doctrines when he expounded his teachings on the church and sacraments, and predestination and grace, during the controversies with the Donatists and the Pelagians.

One of the most bitter controversies of the Early Church was the Donatist schism. Many bishops from Numidia refused to accept Caecilian as the bishop of Carthage because he was consecrated by one who had 'lapsed' during the Great Persecution of Diocletian (303-313). Known from their first great leader as Donatists, they formed the 'true', or pure, church.

Donatism remained the stronger church until the influential ministry of Augustine gave Catholicism the upper hand. However, the Catholic Church suffered a setback when the Vandals, mainly Arian, invaded in 429. Despite a revival under Justinian (534), further expansion of the African Church was halted by the Arab conquest in the seventh century.

The Emperor Diocletian (303-313) initiated the Great Persecution of the church, which affected Africa more severely than elsewhere.

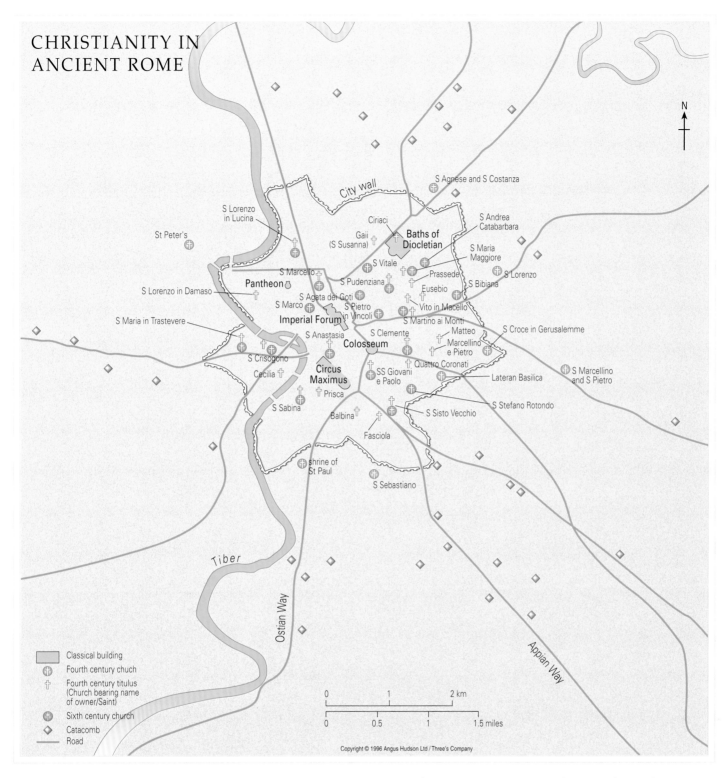

CHRISTIANITY IN ANCIENT ROME

St Peter's

S Lorenzo in Lucina

City wall

Ciriaci

Gaii (S Susanna)

Baths of Diocletian

S Andrea Catabarbara

S Agnese and S Costanza

N

S Vitale

S Maria Maggiore

S Marcello

Pantheon

S Lorenzo in Damaso

S Pudenziana

Prassede

S Lorenzo

S Agata dei Goti

Eusebio

S Bibiana

S Marco

S Pietro in Vincoli

Vito in Macello

Imperial Forum

S Maria in Trastevere

S Martino ai Monti

S Croce in Gerusalemme

S Anastasia

Colosseum

S Clemente

Matteo

S Crisogono

Marcellino e Pietro

S Marcellino and S Pietro

Cecilia

Circus Maximus

SS Giovani e Paolo

Quattro Coronati

Lateran Basilica

Prisca

S Sabina

S Sisto Vecchio

S Stefano Rotondo

Balbina

Fasciola

shrine of St Paul

S Sebastiano

Tiber

Ostian Way

Appian Way

Classical building

Fourth century chuch

Fourth century titulus (Church bearing name of owner/Saint)

Sixth century church

Catacomb

Road

0   1   2 km

0   0.5   1   1.5 miles

Copyright © 1996 Angus Hudson Ltd / Three's Company

CHRISTIANS IN ANCIENT ROME

The first known Christian community in Rome was that to which Paul addressed his Letter to the Romans, *c.* 58 CE. Both Paul and Peter were martyred, according to tradition, after the fire of Rome (64 CE) during Nero's reign. Christians were often, as then, scapegoats and suffered periodic persecution. During the Decian Persecution (249-51), Fabian, bishop of Rome, was martyred. The Christians built distinctive burial-places, the catacombs, which by Roman law were inviolable but had to be built outside the city wall.

After the toleration of the Edict of Milan (313), the church in Rome grew. The authority of the popes increased and many churches were built under Pope Sylvester I (314-35) and his successors. Christianity appealed to men and women of every class. Marcella (325-410) is famous for using her palace on the Aventine Hill as a Christian centre at which Jerome taught. She, along with many other Christians, died when the Visigoths sacked Rome in 410.

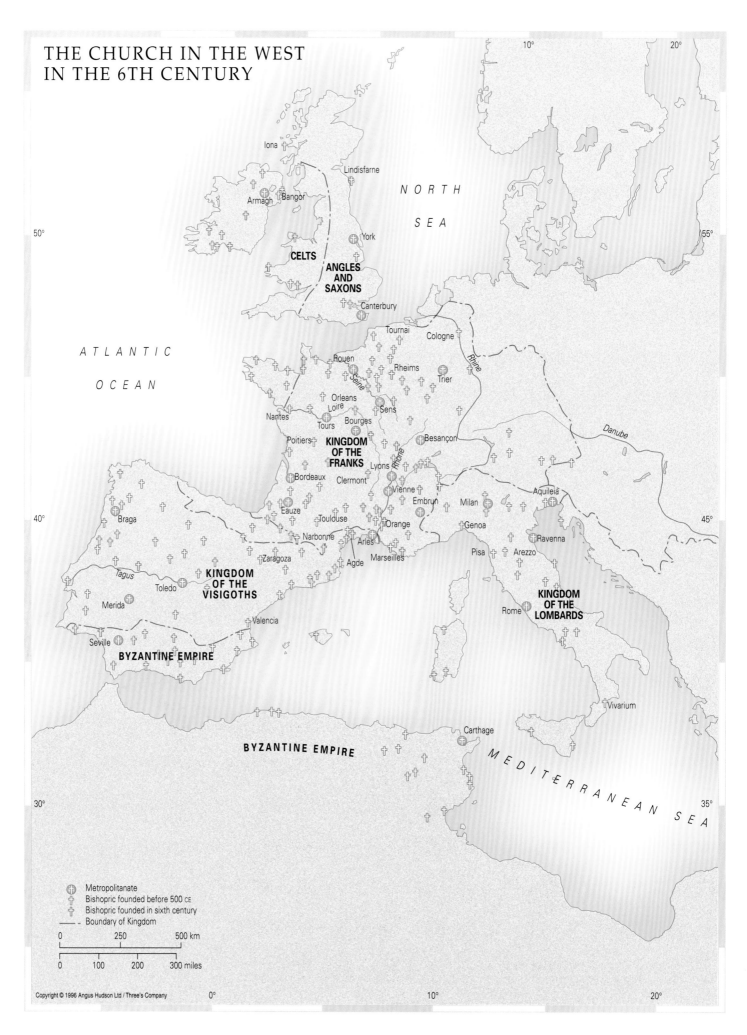

THE CHURCH IN THE WEST
IN THE 6TH CENTURY

NORTH SEA

Iona

Lindisfarne

Armagh Bangor

CELTS

York

**ANGLES
AND
SAXONS**

Canterbury

*ATLANTIC
OCEAN*

Tournai Cologne

Rouen
Seine Rheims Trier *Rhine*

Orleans
Loire Sens
Nantes
Tours Bourges

Poitiers **KINGDOM
OF THE
FRANKS** Besançon

Bordeaux Clermont Lyons *Rhône*

Vienne Embrun Milan Aquileia

Eauze Orange Genoa
Braga Toulouse Ravenna

Narbonne Arles Pisa Arezzo
Zaragoza Agde Marseilles

Tagus
Toledo **KINGDOM
OF THE
VISIGOTHS** **KINGDOM
OF THE
LOMBARDS**
Merida Rome

Valencia
Seville
BYZANTINE EMPIRE *Danube*

Vivarium

Carthage

BYZANTINE EMPIRE *MEDITERRANEAN SEA*

⊕ Metropolitanate
✝ Bishopric founded before 500 CE
✝ Bishopric founded in sixth century
— Boundary of Kingdom

0   250   500 km

0   100   200   300 miles

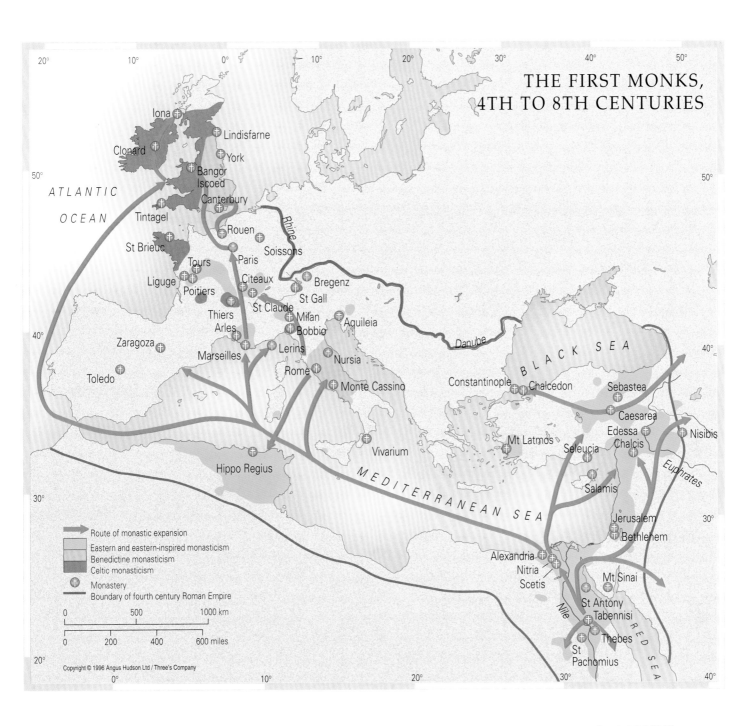

THE FIRST MONKS, 4TH TO 8TH CENTURIES

Route of monastic expansion
Eastern and eastern-inspired monasticism
Benedictine monasticism
Celtic monasticism
Monastery
Boundary of fourth century Roman Empire

| 0 | 500 | 1000 km |
| 0 | 200 | 400 | 600 miles |

Copyright © 1996 Angus Hudson Ltd / Three's Company

THE CHURCH IN THE WEST IN THE SIXTH CENTURY

The most influential figure in the sixth-century Western Church was Pope Gregory I, 'the Great' (c. 540-604). He set his sights on the northern frontiers of Christendom, and his attempts to gather in the pagan tribes of England and Germany signalled the gradual turning of Christianity from a Mediterranean to a European religion. Church leaders encouraged popular forms of Christian piety which appealed to the pagan mind. Miraculous cures associated with shrines and holy relics, and the protection of patron saints became more prevalent.

As the authority of the papacy grew, so did its estates. Known later as the Patrimony of St Peter, they grew from Constantine's reign, when the churches could own property without restriction. The Ostrogothic Kingdom was supplanted by Lombard invaders from Germany who formed a kingdom in 584.

THE FIRST MONKS

From the middle of the third century Christian hermits led ascetic lives in the Egyptian and Syrian deserts. St Antony (251?-356) attracted a large community of hermits, c. 305; St Pachomius (c. 290-346) initiated the communal style of living with his first monastery at Tabennisi. Monasticism spread out from Egypt and Syria in the fourth century. Basil of Caesarea wrote a less extreme Rule for the Eastern Church, and Benedict of Nursia formulated a Rule which was adopted in the West. Benedictine monasticism was slow to catch on, but from the eighth century until the twelfth became virtually the sole form of religious life.

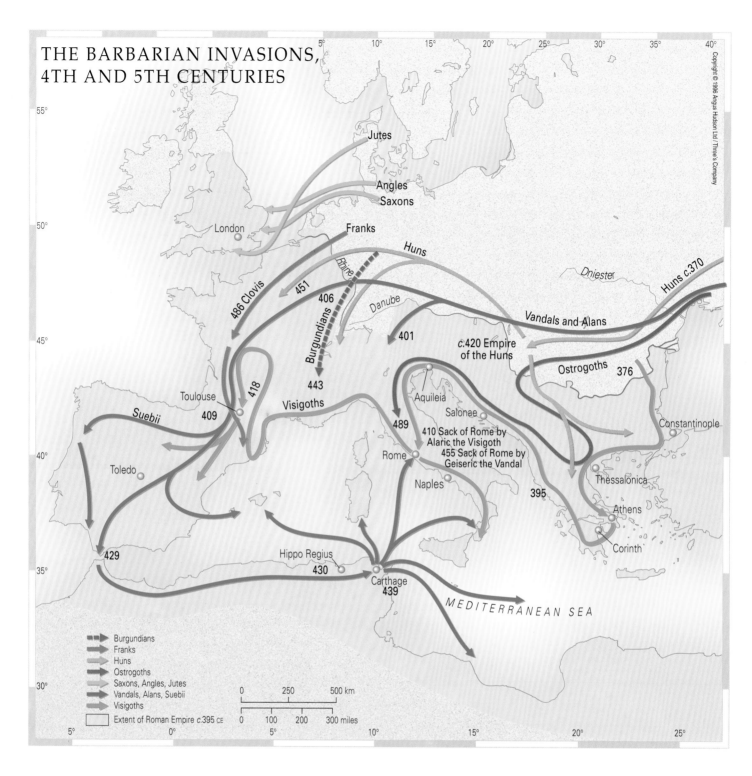

Jutes

Angles
Saxons

Franks

Huns

Rhine

Dniester

486 Clovis

451

406

Burgundians

Danube

Huns c.370

Vandals and Alans

401

c.420 Empire
of the Huns

Ostrogoths 376

418

443

Toulouse

Visigoths

Aquileia

Suebii

409

489

Salonae

Constantinople

410 Sack of Rome by
Alaric the Visigoth
455 Sack of Rome by
Geiseric the Vandal

Toledo

Rome

Thessalonica

395

Naples

Athens

429

Hippo Regius

Corinth

430

Carthage
439

MEDITERRANEAN SEA

London

Burgundians
Franks
Huns
Ostrogoths
Saxons, Angles, Jutes
Vandals, Alans, Suebii
Visigoths
Extent of Roman Empire c.395 CE

0   250   500 km

0   100   200   300 miles

THE BARBARIAN INVASIONS

Ever since the third century the Goths had been making raids on the Danube frontier of the Roman Empire. In the fourth century the Goths divided into the Visigoths (west of the River Dniester) and the Ostrogoths (east of the River Dniester), and both were forced southwards and westwards after 376 by the Huns. The Visigoths were

allowed to settle in the Balkans, but only under a huge tax burden. Their rebellion eventually brought about the sack of Rome in 410.

In the fifth century, massive population movements threw Western Europe into political turmoil. When the menace of the Huns diminished after the death of Attila in 453, other Barbarian peoples asserted claims to territories. The Frankish leader Clovis took advantage of the disintegrating Roman Empire and united northern Gaul under himself in 494. His adoption of Christianity brought the mass

conversion of Franks to the Catholic Church. Clovis' successors formed the successful Merovingian dynasty, who ruled the Frankish Kingdom until the Carolingians emerged in the eighth century. The Visigoths maintained a strong kingdom in Spain and southern Gaul. The Vandals established a kingdom in North Africa.

Wulfila the Goth converted most of his people to Arian Christianity around 350. In turn, many of the Germanic tribes who came into contact with the Goths, such as the Vandals, also adopted Arianism. The threat to

THE BARBARIAN KINGDOMS, *c.* 530

JUTES

ANGLES

SAXONS

CELTS

SAXONS

London

JUTES

ATLANTIC OCEAN

Rhine

THURINGIANS

Trier

Paris

LOMBARDS

FRANKS

Danube

ALAMANNI

SLAVS

BURGUNDIANS

OSTROGOTHS

Geneva

Milan

Sirmium

Ravenna

ROMAN EMPIRE

SUEBII

BASQUES

Toulouse

Narbonne

Constantinople

CORSICA

Rome

Thessalonica

Toledo

SARDINIA

VISIGOTHS

BALEARICS

Athens

Cordoba

SICILY

Carthage

CRETE

Hippo Regius

MEDITERRANEAN SEA

VANDALS

Catholic orthodoxy was compounded when the Arian Ostrogoths ruled in Italy (493-553).

The Anglo-Saxon invasions of Britain pushed back the Celtic Church and left the field clear for the Roman Christianity of Augustine to take new hold in England after 597.

Canterbury Cathedral, Kent.

83

JUSTINIAN'S EMPIRE

When Justinian I became Byzantine emperor in 527, Italy, western North Africa and southern Spain were in the hands of Germanic tribes. By the end of his reign in 565 he had conquered all these lands and at Ravenna instituted an 'Exarchate' government over Italy. This extension of the Byzantine Empire over lands of the West helped to strengthen Catholicism as the Arian leadership of the Vandals in North Africa and the Ostrogoths in Italy disappeared.

Justinian strove in vain to unite opposing factions in the Church. At the Council of Chalcedon in 451 the Monophysites and Nestorians had been declared heretics. However, the Monophysites remained strong in the Middle East, giving rise to the Coptic Church in Egypt and, in time, the Syrian Orthodox Church. Nestorianism took root in the Persian Empire and gradually expanded eastwards.

Justinian is credited with building a number of churches, including the reconstruction of Hagia Sophia after its burning during riots in Constantinople, and developing St Catherine's Monastery at the foot of Mt Sinai.

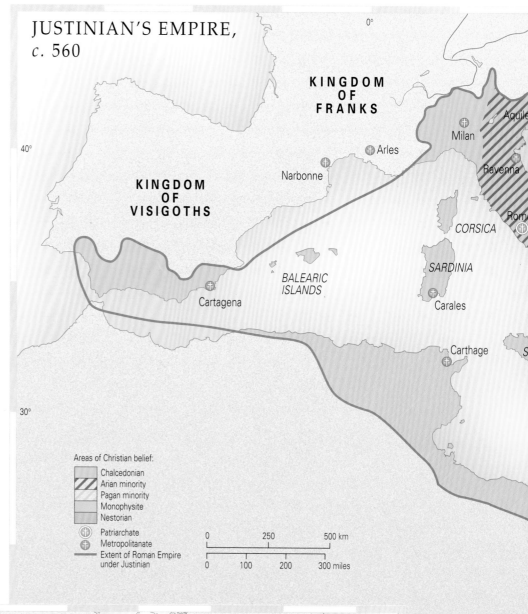

JUSTINIAN'S EMPIRE, *c.* 560

KINGDOM OF FRANKS

KINGDOM OF VISIGOTHS

Narbonne

Arles

Milan

Aquile

Ravenna

Rom

CORSICA

SARDINIA

Carales

BALEARIC ISLANDS

Cartagena

Carthage

Areas of Christian belief:
- Chalcedonian
- Arian minority
- Pagan minority
- Monophysite
- Nestorian
- ⊕ Patriarchate
- ⊕ Metropolitanate
- —— Extent of Roman Empire under Justinian

| 0 | 250 | 500 km |
| 0 100 | 200 | 300 miles |

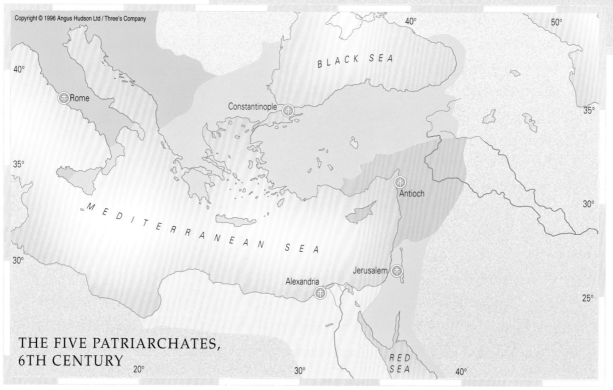

BLACK SEA

Rome

Constantinople

Antioch

M E D I T E R R A N E A N   S E A

Jerusalem

Alexandria

RED SEA

THE FIVE PATRIARCHATES, 6TH CENTURY

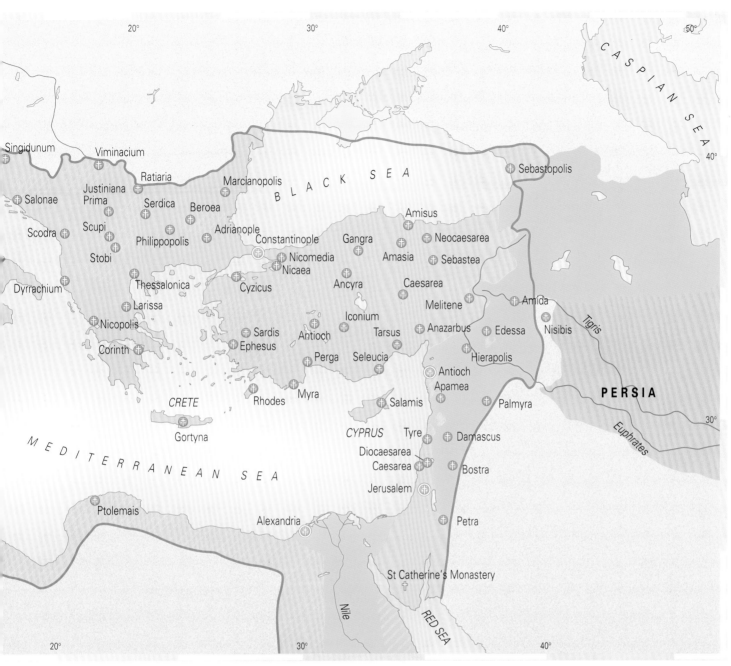

Singidunum
Viminacium
Ratiaria
Justiniana Prima
Salonae
Serdica
Beroea
Scupi
Scodra
Philippopolis
Stobi
Dyrrachium
Thessalonica
Larissa
Nicopolis
Corinth
Sardis
Ephesus
Perga
Rhodes
Myra

BLACK SEA
Marcianopolis
Adrianople
Constantinople
Nicomedia
Nicaea
Cyzicus
Iconium
Antioch
Seleucia
Salamis

Amisus
Gangra
Amasia
Ancyra
Tarsus
Perga

Neocaesarea
Sebastopolis
Neocaesarea
Sebastea
Caesarea
Melitene
Anazarbus
Edessa
Hierapolis
Antioch
Apamea
Palmyra
Damascus
Bostra

Amida
Nisibis
Tigris
Euphrates
PERSIA

CASPIAN SEA

CRETE
Gortyna

MEDITERRANEAN SEA

CYPRUS
Tyre
Diocaesarea
Caesarea
Jerusalem
Petra

Ptolemais
Alexandria

St Catherine's Monastery

Nile
RED SEA

THE PATRIARCHATES

At the beginning of the fourth century, Rome, Alexandria and Antioch were the primary sees of the Church. The later rise in importance of the sees at Constantinople and Jerusalem meant that by the sixth century there were five pre-eminent bishops who were titled 'Patriarchs', with jurisdiction over their associated lands.

St Catherine's Monastery, at the foot of Mount Sinai, was probably developed by Justinian.

85

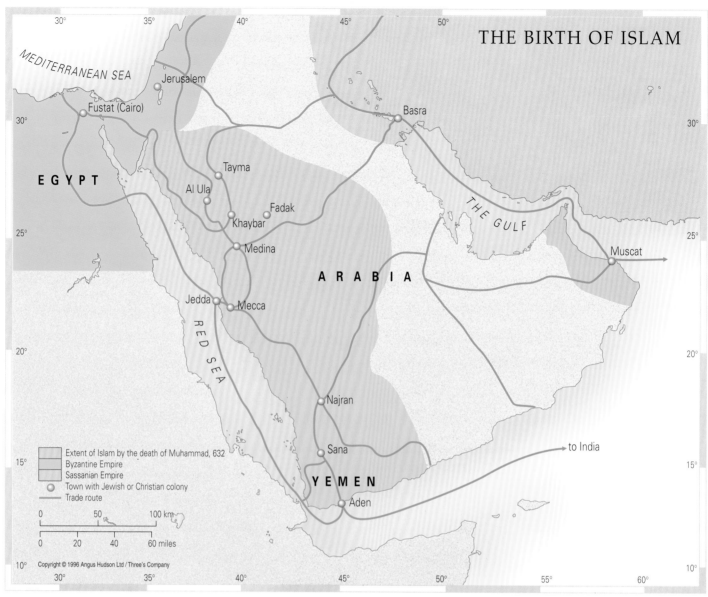

THE BIRTH OF ISLAM

The '*hijra*' or 'emigration' of the Prophet Muhammad from Mecca to Medina in 622 CE marks the beginning of the Islamic calendar. The people of Medina were sympathetic to his teachings about the oneness of God and the wickedness of materialism. As an outsider, Muhammad was also able to arbitrate in tribal quarrels and soon established an authority as a leader. His successes on the battlefield meant that, by his death in 632, most of western Arabia had turned to follow his new religion, Islam.

Muhammad saw Judaism and Christianity as precursors of Islam. He regarded himself as the 'seal' of a line of prophets which began with Abraham and included Jesus. He was therefore friendly to Jewish and Christian populations of the towns he converted to Islam. The rapidity with which Islam swept through North Africa and the Middle East in the early years is an indicator partly of how tolerant Islam was as a society allowing the practice of other monotheistic religions, and partly of how receptive those 'conquered' peoples were to Islam. In only one or two generations most Christians had converted to Islam, after some six centuries of Roman and Byzantine rule.

The Monophysite and Nestorian churches of Egypt, Ethiopia and the Middle East not only survived Islam but had a common enemy with it: Byzantium. An Arab Christian culture had developed since the fifth century and it came to reside more easily in an Islamic community than in a Byzantine one which was dominated by Chalcedonian orthodoxy. The successor to Muhammad, Abu Bakr (632-34), took Islam to the frontier of Byzantium in Syria and his successor, Umar (634-44), provoked a counter-offensive. The ensuing battle at Yarmuk (*c.* 636) resulted in a Muslim victory and opened the door to further conquests in northern Syria and Iraq.

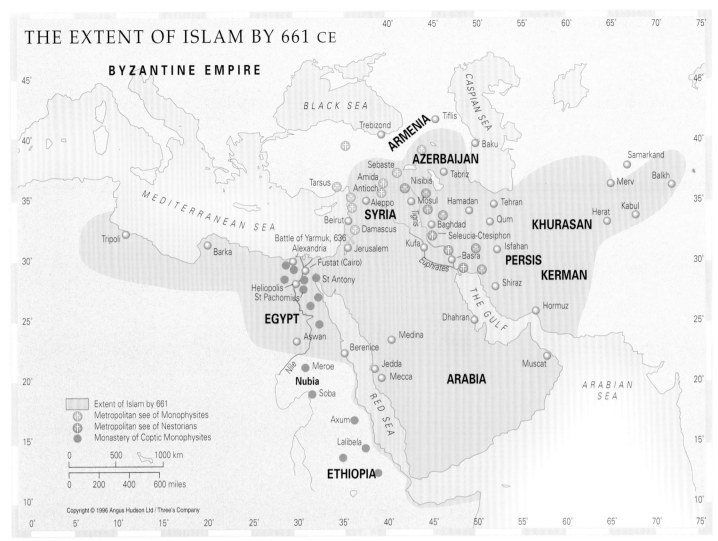

THE EXTENT OF ISLAM BY 661 CE

BYZANTINE EMPIRE

BLACK SEA

Trebizond

ARMENIA · Tiflis

CASPIAN SEA

Baku

AZERBAIJAN

Sebaste · Tabriz

Samarkand

Tarsus · Amida · Nisibis

Merv · Balkh

Antioch · Mosul · Hamadan · Tehran

Herat · Kabul

Aleppo

SYRIA · Baghdad · Qum

KHURASAN

Beirut · Seleucia-Ctesiphon

Damascus · Isfahan

Kufa · Basra

PERSIS

MEDITERRANEAN SEA

Tripoli

Battle of Yarmuk, 636

Alexandria · Jerusalem

KERMAN

Barka · Fustat (Cairo)

Shiraz

St Antony

THE GULF

Heliopolis

St Pachomius

Hormuz

Dhahran

EGYPT

Aswan

Medina

Muscat

Berenice

ARABIAN SEA

Nile · Meroe

Jedda

Nubia · Soba

Mecca

ARABIA

Axum

Lalibela

ETHIOPIA

RED SEA

Tigris

Euphrates

Legend:
- Extent of Islam by 661
- ⊕ Metropolitan see of Monophysites
- ⊕ Metropolitan see of Nestorians
- ● Monastery of Coptic Monophysites

Scale: 0 — 500 — 1000 km
0 — 200 — 400 — 600 miles

The Dome of the Rock, Jerusalem, is a major Islamic shrine.

Islam spread to Egypt too at this time.

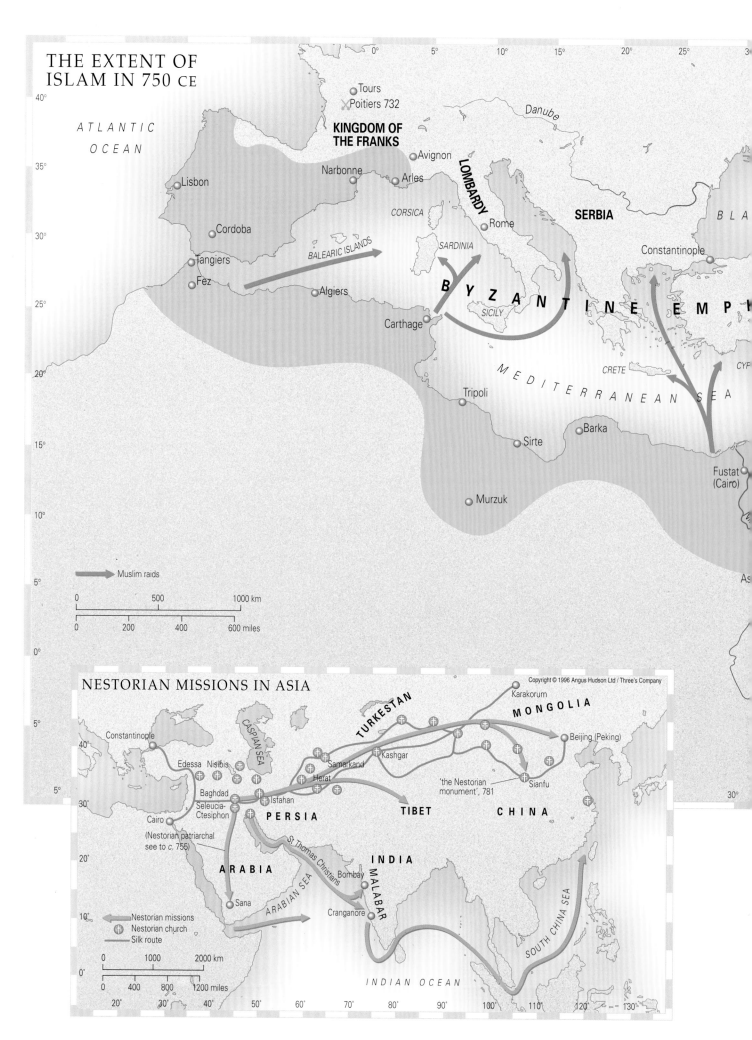

THE EXTENT OF ISLAM IN 750 CE

ATLANTIC
OCEAN

Tours
Poitiers 732

**KINGDOM OF
THE FRANKS**

Avignon
Narbonne
Arles

LOMBARDY

SERBIA

Danube

Lisbon

Cordoba

Tangiers
Fez

BALEARIC ISLANDS

CORSICA

SARDINIA

Rome

Constantinople

B L A

B Y Z A N T I N E   E M P I

Algiers

Carthage

SICILY

CRETE

CYP

M E D I T E R R A N E A N   S E A

Tripoli

Sirte

Barka

Fustat
(Cairo)

Murzuk

As

→ Muslim raids

0   500   1000 km

0   200   400   600 miles

NESTORIAN MISSIONS IN ASIA

Copyright © 1996 Angus Hudson Ltd / Three's Company

Karakorum

TURKESTAN

M O N G O L I A

CASPIAN SEA

Constantinople

Edessa Nisibis

Kashgar

Samarkand

Beijing (Peking)

Herat

'the Nestorian
monument', 781

Sianfu

Baghdad

Isfahan

PERSIA

TIBET

C H I N A

Seleucia-
Ctesiphon

Cairo

(Nestorian patriarchal
see to c. 755)

St Thomas Christians

I N D I A

Bombay

MALABAR

A R A B I A

ARABIAN SEA

Cranganore

Sana

SOUTH CHINA SEA

← Nestorian missions
⊕ Nestorian church
— Silk route

0   1000   2000 km

0   400   800   1200 miles

INDIAN OCEAN

20°   30°   40°   50°   60°   70°   80°   90°   100°   110°   120°   130°

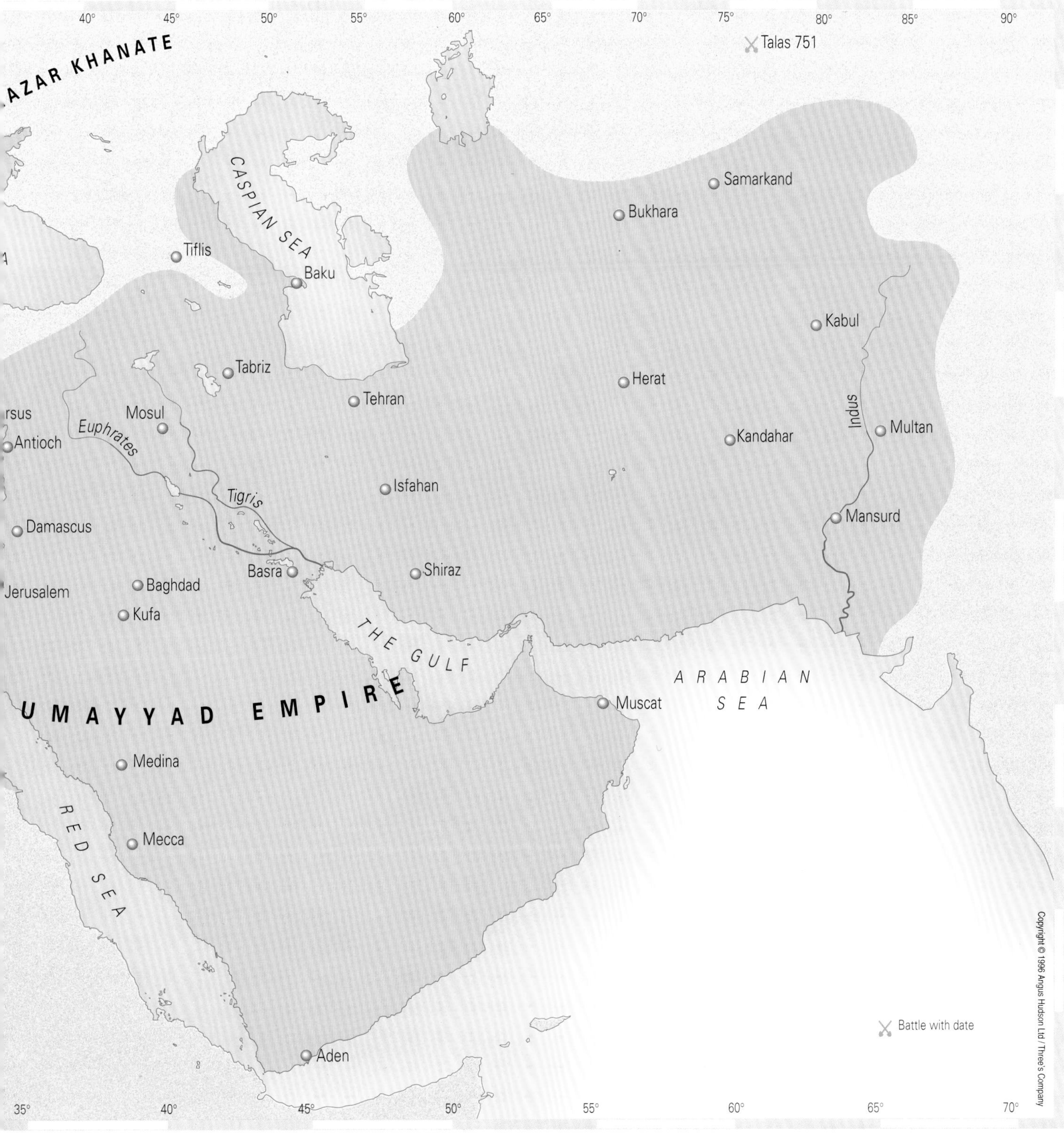
KHAZAR KHANATE
CASPIAN SEA
Talas 751
Samarkand
Bukhara
Tiflis
Baku
Kabul
Tabriz
Herat
Tehran
Tarsus
Mosul
Euphrates
Antioch
Indus
Multan
Kandahar
Isfahan
Tigris
Damascus
Mansurd
Basra
Shiraz
Jerusalem
Baghdad
Kufa
THE GULF
ARABIAN SEA
UMAYYAD EMPIRE
Muscat
Medina
RED SEA
Mecca
Battle with date
Aden
Copyright © 1996 Angus Hudson Ltd / Three's Company

ISLAM TO 750 CE

After the death of Ali, the fourth caliph (leader of Islam), the Islamic community became split into the majority orthodox Sunni and the Shiites, who followed the descendants of Ali. The first Sunni caliphate was the Umayyad dynasty, ruling from Damascus, which lasted until 750 CE. It was a dynamic period of expansion.

Within a century of its foundation Islam had overrun more than half of Christendom. The relentless advance was finally halted in the West at Poitiers by the Franks in 732, after which Islam retreated behind the Pyrenees to establish itself in Spain.

To the peoples of the conquered countries, Islamic supremacy meant little more than a change of masters. The embracing nature of Islam allowed native cultures to continue and there was no attempt at religious conversion. Jews and Christians were allowed to practise their own faiths as long as they paid the *jizya*, or poll tax.

One result of tolerant Islam was the flourishing of Nestorian churches in the east and their proliferation along the Silk Road into China.

THE EMPIRE OF CHARLEMAGNE

N O R T H

S E A

York

BRITAIN

Hamburg

SAXONY

Corvey

Cologne THURINGIA Mainz Fulda

St Riquier Echternach Aachen

St Wandrille Laon Rheims Prum BOHEMIA

Corbie Soissons Trier Lorsch BAVARIA

Rouen Paris Metz Hirsau Kremsmunster

Chartres Auxerre Strasbourg Salzburg

BRITTANY Le Mans Orleans Sens Reichenau

Angers Tours Luxeuil St Gallen CARINTHIA

Noirmoutier Bourges Besançon ALAMANNIA

ATLANTIC Poitiers Ferrières LOMBARDY Aquileia

OCEAN AQUITANIA BURGUNDY Venice

Limoges Lyons Tarentaise Milan Brescia

Bordeaux Vienne Pavia Ravenna

Embrun Bobbio

GASCONY Toulouse Arles PROVENCE Aix-en-Provence

Narbonne Marseilles CORSICA Rome

UMAYYAD CALIPHATE Barcelona Monte Cassino

Frankish Empire at accession of Charlemagne, 768
Conquests of Charlemagne to 814
Marches

△ Archbishopric

✚ Important monastery

✚ Notable Carolingian school (and monastery)

Copyright © 1996 Angus Hudson Ltd / Three's Company

M E D I T E R R A N E A N   S E A

0   250   500 km

0   100   200   300 miles

CHARLEMAGNE

Charlemagne (Charles the Great, c. 742-814) was crowned the first Holy Roman Emperor by Pope Leo III in 800. After his accession to the Frankish throne in 771, Charles extended his realm, mainly eastwards across Saxony and Bavaria, and southwards across Lombardy. He gave military support to the Pope and enlarged the Patrimony of St Peter by granting it conquered lands. The alliance thus forged between church and state added considerable power to the papal institution over the next seven hundred years. In their aim to control the West, the Carolingian kings (750-887), and in particular Charlemagne, dreamed of reviving the Roman Empire. A renaissance of Latin culture saw the building of new schools in which calligraphy was restyled, and renowned ancient works, both religious and

INVASIONS OF EUROPE, 7TH TO 10TH CENTURIES

ATLANTIC OCEAN

NORTH SEA

Lindisfarne

Dublin

York

V I K I N G S

BALTIC SEA

KIEVAN RUSSIA

Kiev

Bremen

Hamburg

Cologne

Elbe

S L A V S

Rouen

Paris

Rheims

Trier

Rhine

Orleans

FRANCE

Danube

M A G Y A R S

Bordeaux

Valence

BLACK SEA

Arles

Pisa

BYZANTINE EMPIRE

EMIRATE OF CORDOBA

CORSICA

Rome

Constantinople

Cordoba

SARDINIA

Bari

Taranto

Seville

BALEARIC ISLANDS

SICILY

MUSLIMS

Tunis

Kairouan

MEDITERRANEAN SEA

Western Christendom	Slav expansion, to 700 CE
Eastern Christendom	Viking invasions, 8th and 9th centuries
Pagan lands	Magyar invasions, 10th century
Islamic empire	Muslim invasions, 9th and 10th centuries

Copyright © 1996 Angus Hudson Ltd / Three's Company

---

profane, were copied. *The City of God* by St Augustine, for example, was painstakingly copied by monks. In this way, much of Latin literature was saved from the cultural extinction threatened by the Dark Ages.

INVASIONS OF EUROPE

As the Germanic barbarians migrated westwards, so a power vacuum in eastern Europe was filled by Slavic tribes in the seventh century. Their further migration southwards into the Balkans formed a barrier between Byzantium and the West by 700.

In western Europe during the ninth century, invasions came on all fronts and severely disrupted the political stability gained under Charlemagne. Vikings from Norway and Denmark plundered and colonized eastern parts of Britain and Ireland, and settled into what became the duchy of Normandy in

northern France. Magyar penetration through Germanic lands into the heart of France, and Saracen (Muslim) attacks from across the Mediterranean weakened the Frankish Empire.

Ironically the Vikings, who had attacked the northern frontiers, helped in the tenth century to rebuff the growing threat of Islam which had occupied most of Spain since 756.

IRISH/CELTIC AND BRITISH MISSIONS TO EUROPE, 6TH TO 8TH CENTURIES

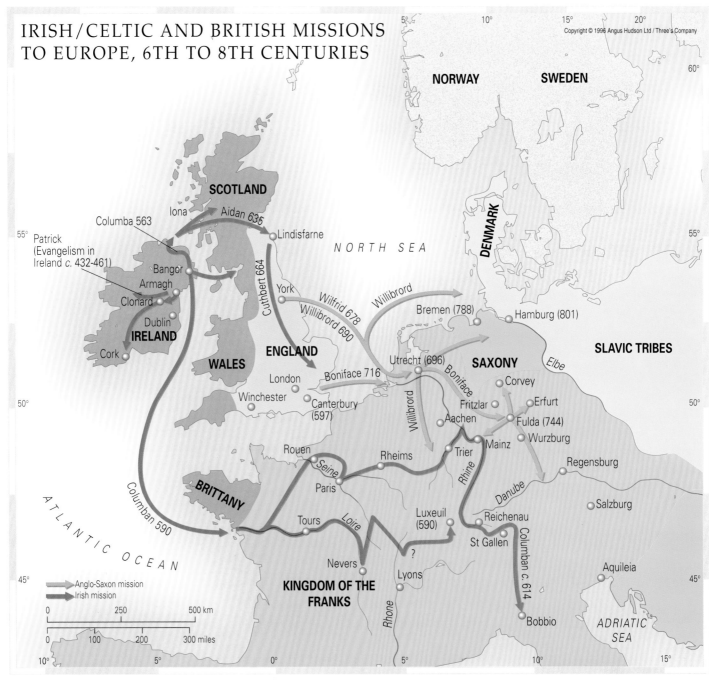

Copyright © 1996 Angus Hudson Ltd / Three's Company

NORWAY   SWEDEN

NORTH SEA

DENMARK

SCOTLAND
Iona   Aidan 635
Columba 563   Lindisfarne
Patrick (Evangelism in Ireland c. 432-461)
Bangor
Armagh
Clonard
Dublin
IRELAND
Cork

Cuthbert 664
York   Wilfrid 678   Willibrord
Willibrord 690
Bremen (788)   Hamburg (801)
WALES   ENGLAND
London   Boniface 716   Utrecht (696)   SAXONY   Elbe   SLAVIC TRIBES
Winchester   Canterbury (597)   Willibrord   Boniface   Corvey
Fritzlar   Erfurt
Aachen   Fulda (744)   Wurzburg
Rouen   Rheims   Trier   Mainz   Regensburg
Seine   Rhine   Danube
Paris   Reichenau   Salzburg
BRITTANY   Luxeuil (590)   St Gallen
Columban 590   Tours   Loire   ?   Columban c. 614
Nevers   Lyons   Aquileia
KINGDOM OF THE FRANKS   Rhone   Bobbio   ADRIATIC SEA

Anglo-Saxon mission
Irish mission
0   250   500 km
0   100   200   300 miles

ATLANTIC OCEAN

IRISH AND ANGLO-SAXON MISSIONS

The conversion to Christianity of the pagan peoples of northern Europe was the result of two major influences: Pope Gregory the Great's policy of evangelization through the Anglo-Saxons, and the '*peregrinatio*' (self-imposed exile in foreign lands) of Irish monks. From the centre founded by Columba on Iona, Aidan moved to Holy Island on Lindisfarne, and Columban took the gospel as far as Bobbio in Lombardy.

After Pope Gregory dispatched Augustine to England in 597 to become the first bishop of Canterbury, the two most successful missionaries to the continent were Willibrord, known as the Apostle to the Frisians, and Boniface, the outstanding Apostle to the Germans. They usually travelled in a group of monks, and established churches, holy days and the cult of saints to replace the shrines and superstitions of the pagan cults of the north, such as Thor, god of thunder.

There was also a political dimension involving the Frankish rulers and the papacy. The conversion and befriending of pagans on the eastern border of the Frankish Empire provided greater security and opened the way for expansion eastwards.

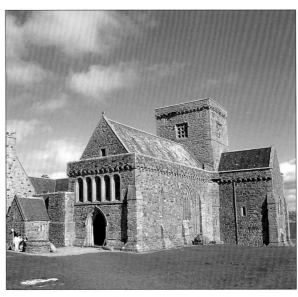

Iona became the focus for the spread of Celtic Christianity.

ROMAN MISSIONS IN WESTERN EUROPE

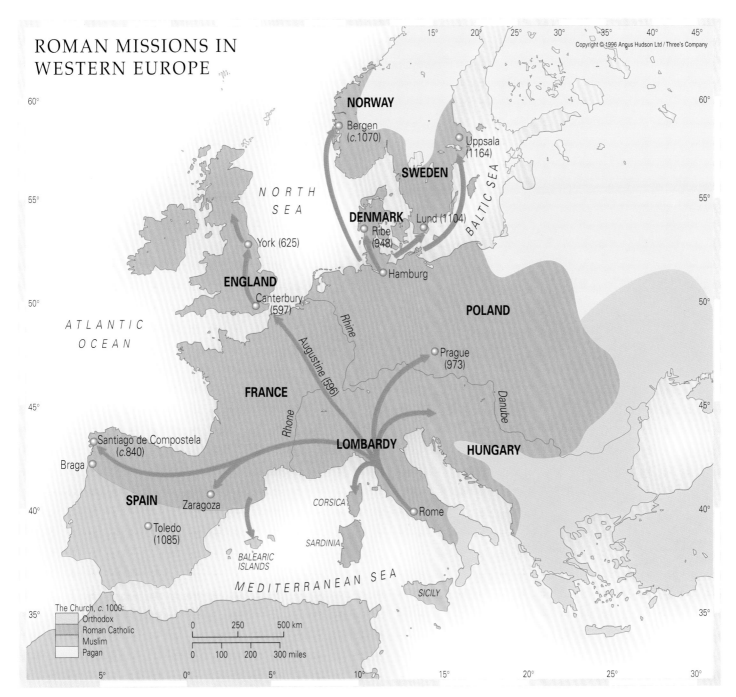

NORWAY

Bergen
(c.1070)

Uppsala
(1164)

SWEDEN

BALTIC SEA

NORTH
SEA

DENMARK Lund (1104)

York (625)

Ribe
(948)

Hamburg

ENGLAND

POLAND

ATLANTIC
OCEAN

Canterbury
(597)

Rhine

Prague
(973)

Augustine (596)

FRANCE

Danube

Rhone

Santiago de Compostela
(c.840)

LOMBARDY

HUNGARY

Braga

SPAIN Zaragoza

CORSICA

Rome

Toledo
(1085)

SARDINIA

BALEARIC
ISLANDS

MEDITERRANEAN SEA

SICILY

The Church, c. 1000:
Orthodox
Roman Catholic
Muslim
Pagan

0   250   500 km

0   100   200   300 miles

Boniface, the 'Apostle to the Germans'.

ROMAN MISSIONS IN WESTERN EUROPE

With the coronation of Charlemagne as the first Holy Roman Emperor in 800, western Europe experienced a period of evangelization. With crusader-like zeal and military might the frontier of Christendom was pushed steadily northwards and eastwards. The title of the emperor reflected the new ideal of a ruler that Charlemagne envisaged. Following the example of the Israelite King David, he conquered and converted, built churches and prayed to God. Missions from Rome fanned out in all directions in the wake of conquest in order to sustain a faith beyond nominal conversion.

To the south, the threat of Islam was upon every north Mediterranean shore. Rome itself was plundered in 846, Sicily was taken by 902 and Muslim strongholds were set up in southern Italy. Steady losses of Christians through conversion to Islam brought new missions to old lands. The important pilgrim centre of Santiago de Compostela was founded during this period.

ORTHODOX MISSIONS, 9TH TO 11TH CENTURIES

Copyright © 1996 Angus Hudson Ltd / Three's Company

Orthodox mission from Constantinople, with date
Area under patriarchate of Rome, c. 1050
Area under patriarchate of Constantinople, c. 1050
Islam, c. 1050
✤ Patriarchate

| 0 | 500 | 1000 km |
| 0 | 200 | 400 | 600 miles |

ORTHODOX MISSIONS

In eastern Europe the foundations of the modern Orthodox national churches were laid in the ninth century. Competition between Rome and Constantinople over territory thus far unclaimed continually brought into question the boundary of their Patriarchates. Missionaries from both East and West operated in the Balkans. The main missionary advance from Constantinople was led by Cyril and Methodius. Boris of Bulgaria adopted the eastern rite c. 870, whereupon Rastislav, prince of Moravia (now Slovakia), turned also to Byzantium. Byzantine Christianity became the official religion in Serbia by 891.

Unlike the Western church, which was unified by its dependence on a Latin liturgy, the Byzantines allowed each nation or people to foster its own independent church with a liturgy conducted in the local language.

Kariye Camii, built as a Byzantine church in Constantinople in the eleventh century, converted into a mosque, but today functioning as a church again in modern Istanbul.

CHRISTIANITY IN RUSSIA *c.*1050

Copyright © 1996 Angus Hudson Ltd / Three's Company

Extent of Kievan Russia, *c.*1050
Archbishopric
Bishopric

CHRISTIANITY COMES TO RUSSIA

The first recorded Russian convert was Olga, widow of Igor, who ruled from 945 to 964. There was no mass conversion, however, until the later ruler Vladimir, who established the Kievan state of Rus, saw the advantage of having a state religion. While on a trip to Constantinople he was impressed by the splendour of Byzantine worship, architecture and culture, and his advisors are quoted in the Russian Chronicle as saying 'If the Greek faith were evil, it would not have been adopted by your grandmother, Olga, who was wiser than anyone.'

Vladimir returned to Kiev, and a mass baptism of his people followed in 988. Russia imported many features of Byzantine culture, including a literary language, aesthetic styles of masonry and mosaics, music and the liturgy as well as an elaborate theological system. Byzantium, for its part, greatly enlarged the extent of the patriarchate of Constantinople.

An artist's impression of a typical medieval monastery.

MONASTIC REFORM

Since the eighth century nearly all monasteries in the West followed the Benedictine Rule. However, in time reforms became necessary. In the tenth and eleventh centuries a major monastic reform movement spread through Europe following the Order of Cluny, founded in 910. Some houses found that this reform did not go far enough and a more austere model was founded at Cîteaux, near Dijon, in 1098. This gave rise to the new Order of Cistercian monasteries. These reforms returned to a strict observance of the Benedictine Rule.

The Cistercian monasteries were built in remote places to avoid contact with town dwellers. They cultivated wasteland and ran sheep farms to satisfy the growing demand for wool. Their financial success and growing popularity resulted in the establishment of 694 Cistercian monasteries in Europe by the end of the thirteenth century. There were five 'daughter' houses which together supervised standards among the other houses. One of the first to join the Cistercians was St Bernard who became abbot of Clairvaux.

The reforming monks wished to present to ordinary people a radical alternative way of life to that led by the clergy – a clergy who, in the opinion of many, were dissolute and too affluent. The Cluniac monks joined as young boys and received all their training in the cloister. The Cistercian monks, on the other hand, had already lived part of their adult lives in society before they rejected its values and joined the monastery. The Cistercians came to be more damning of the mores of contemporary society than were the more moderate Cluniacs. The Cluniac movement in turn had a major influence on reform in the Western Church, especially under Pope Gregory VII.

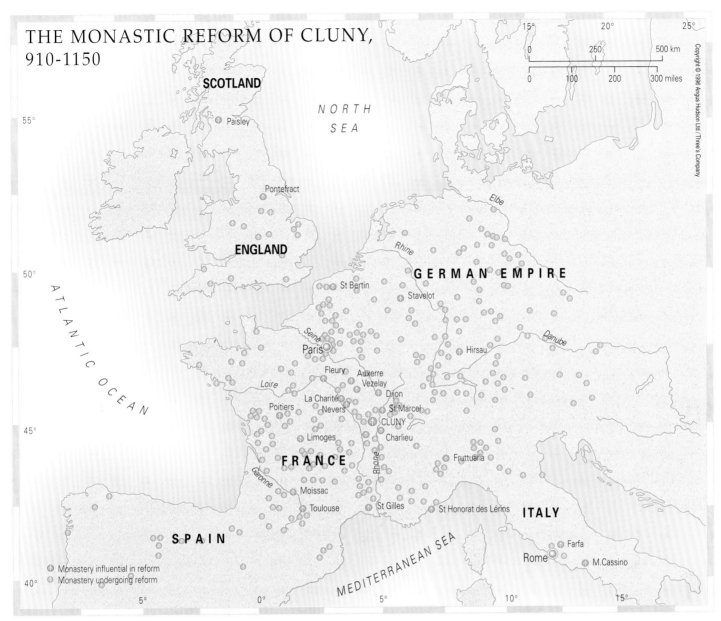

THE MONASTIC REFORM OF CLUNY, 910-1150

SCOTLAND

NORTH SEA

· Paisley

· Pontefract

ENGLAND

GERMAN EMPIRE

Elbe

Rhine

St Bertin

Stavelot

Danube

Seine

Paris

Hirsau

Fleury

Auxerre
Vezelay

Loire

Dijon

La Charité

St Marcel

Poitiers

Nevers

CLUNY

Limoges

Charlieu

FRANCE

Rhône

Fruttuaria

Garonne

Moissac

Toulouse

St Gilles

St Honorat des Lérins

ITALY

SPAIN

⊕ Monastery influential in reform
⊙ Monastery undergoing reform

Farfa

Rome

M.Cassino

ATLANTIC OCEAN

MEDITERRANEAN SEA

CISTERCIAN MONASTICISM, 12TH TO 13TH CENTURIES

SWEDEN

SCOTLAND

NORTH SEA

DENMARK

IRELAND

WALES

ENGLAND

GERMAN EMPIRE

ATLANTIC OCEAN

Clairvaux

Pontigny
Fontenay

Morimond

CÎTEAUX

La Ferté

FRANCE

⊕ One of five first
daughter monasteries
of Cîteaux

· Cistercian monastery

ITALY

SPAIN

MEDITERRANEAN SEA

The ruins of Tintern Abbey, a Cistercian house in England's Wye Valley.

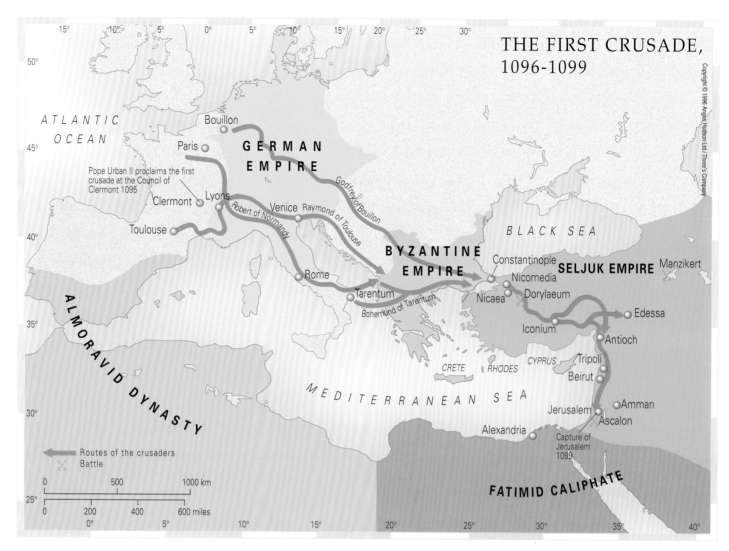

Copyright © 1996 Angus Hudson Ltd / Three's Company

Routes of the crusaders
Battle

0   500   1000 km
0   200   400   600 miles

THE CRUSADES

St Anne's Church, Jerusalem, was built by the victorious Crusaders.

The Crusades were a series of expeditions first intended to recover the Holy Land from Muslim occupation and to secure free access for pilgrims. The call to the First Crusade by Pope Urban II at the Council of Clermont in 1095 was prompted by an offensive deep into Asia Minor by the Seljuk Turks mounting pressure on Byzantium's eastern border. Those who joined the Crusades were granted indulgences and, in the event of death, were assured of martyrdom status.

In 1099 Jerusalem was captured. Over the next twenty years a series of Latin Crusader states was established in the Levant. Subsequent crusades were instigated to defend these kingdoms. Bernard of Clairvaux preached the Second Crusade (1147) to recapture Edessa. However, it was unsuccessful and the Muslim leader Saladin captured Jerusalem. As a result, the Third Crusade (1189-92) was raised, but it failed to recover the Holy City.

The Byzantines, meanwhile, were ambivalent to all this. On the one hand they had repeatedly requested help, and supported the Crusades because they relieved pressure on their eastern front; on the other hand, the establishment of Crusader states was more than they bargained for. Feuding broke out between East and West and led to the diversion of the Fourth Crusade, in 1202, to Constantinople; the capital was sacked and a Latin emperor enthroned. A Latin empire of Constantinople then held power from 1204 until 1261. A number of Byzantine centres of resistance were set up in exile, and the main one, at Nicaea, organized a campaign with help from Genoa and reduced the Latin presence to minor states in southern Greece.

THE SECOND CRUSADE, 1147-1149

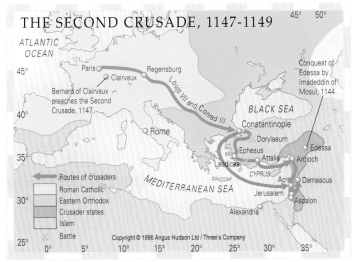

ATLANTIC
OCEAN

45°
50°

Paris
Clairvaux
Regensburg

Bernard of Clairvaux
preaches the Second
Crusade, 1147

Louis VII and Conrad III

BLACK SEA

Conquest of
Edessa by
Imadeddin of
Mosul, 1144

Rome

Constantinople

Dorylaeum

Ephesus
Attalia
Laodicea
Antioch

Edessa

CYPRUS

Acre
Damascus

Jerusalem
Ascalon

MEDITERRANEAN SEA

Alexandria

Routes of crusaders
Roman Catholic
Eastern Orthodox
Crusader states
Islam
Battle

Copyright © 1996 Angus Hudson Ltd / Three's Company

0° 5° 10° 15° 20° 25° 30° 35°

THE THIRD CRUSADE, 1189-1192

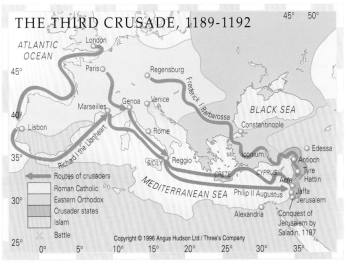

ATLANTIC
OCEAN

45°
50°

London

Paris
Regensburg

Frederick I Barbarossa

BLACK SEA

Marseilles
Genoa
Venice

Lisbon
Richard the Lionheart
Rome
Constantinople

Iconium
Edessa

SICILY
Reggio
CRETE
CYPRUS
Antioch
Tyre
Hattin
Acre

Philip II Augustus
Jaffa
Jerusalem

MEDITERRANEAN SEA

Routes of crusaders
Roman Catholic
Eastern Orthodox
Crusader states
Islam
Battle

Alexandria
Conquest of
Jerusalem by
Saladin, 1187

Copyright © 1996 Angus Hudson Ltd / Three's Company

0° 5° 10° 15° 20° 25° 30° 35°

THE CRUSADER STATES

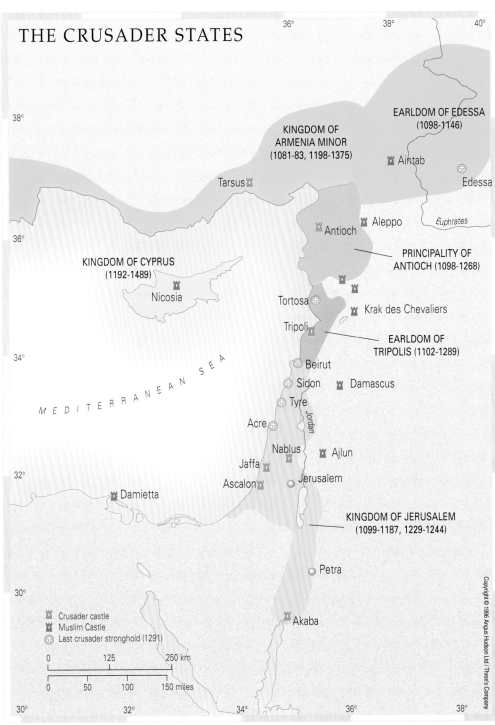

36°
38°
40°

EARLDOM OF EDESSA
(1098-1146)

KINGDOM OF
ARMENIA MINOR
(1081-83, 1198-1375)

Aintab

Tarsus

Edessa

Aleppo
Euphrates

Antioch

KINGDOM OF CYPRUS
(1192-1489)

PRINCIPALITY OF
ANTIOCH (1098-1268)

Nicosia

Tortosa
Krak des Chevaliers

Tripoli

EARLDOM OF
TRIPOLIS (1102-1289)

MEDITERRANEAN SEA

Beirut
Sidon
Damascus
Tyre
Jordan

Acre

Nablus
Ajlun
Jaffa
Ascalon
Jerusalem

Damietta

KINGDOM OF JERUSALEM
(1099-1187, 1229-1244)

Petra

30°

Crusader castle
Muslim Castle
Last crusader stronghold (1291)

0 125 250 km

0 50 100 150 miles

30° 32° 34° 36° 38°

**The vaulted gatehouse to the Crusader
stronghold at Caesarea.**

Copyright © 1996 Angus Hudson Ltd / Three's Company

Boundary of communion with Rome, c. 1050
Boundary of communion with Constantinople, c. 1050
Overlapping area of churches with allegiance to Rome or Constantinople
Norman invasions, 1057-85
Northern limit of Islamic rule, c. 1050

THE FINAL RIFT

The final break of Christendom into the Roman Catholic West and Orthodox East was the culmination of centuries of friction that stemmed from the western and eastern divisions of the Roman Empire. Culturally and linguistically diverse, and politically antagonistic, Rome and Constantinople had differences beyond religious questions. Even when under the mutual threat of

Norman invasions, a meeting for peace arranged in Constantinople in 1054 ended in bitter recrimination and a papal bull excommunicating the Eastern Church.

Relations over religious questions were rarely harmonious, for example during the iconoclast controversy (726 to 843), over the reverence to be paid to icons. Debate about the nature of the Trinity, whether the Holy Spirit proceeds from the Father *and the Son* (Western standpoint) or from the Father

through the Son (Eastern standpoint) became critical in the time of Photius (864). The final rift, though, was more political than theological, and concerned the supremacy of Rome. The pope claimed pre-eminence among the patriarchs, whereas Constantinople insisted on Rome as one among equals.

NORTH SEA

BALTIC SEA

ATLANTIC OCEAN

MEDITERRANEAN SEA

CORSICA

SARDINIA

SICILY

BALEARIC ISLANDS

Uppsala

Konigsberg

Aberdeen

St Andrews

Edinburgh

Jarrow

Wearmouth

Rievaulx

York

Dublin

Sempringham

Peterborough

Cambridge

Oxford

Canterbury

Groningen

Amsterdam

Leiden

Utrecht

Paderborn

Hildesheim

Corvey

Magdeburg

Wittenberg

Tournai

Marburg

Fulda

Prague

Rouen

Beauvais

Laon

Rheims

Metz

Mainz

Worms

Speyer

Strasbourg

Bamberg

Mont St Michel

Savigny

Paris

Chartres

Clairvaux

Regensburg

Danube

St Gall

Salzburg

Fontevrault

Tours

Poitiers

Cîteaux

Cluny

Grande Chartreuse

Geneva

Milan

Vercelli

Vicenza

Padua

Pavia

Piacenza

Parma

Reggio

Bologna

Ravenna

La Chaise Dieu

Rhone

Garonne

Toulouse

Montpellier

Aix

Pisa

Florence

Arezzo

Siena

Santiago de Compostela

Oviedo

Palencia

Valladolid

Salamanca

Avila

Alcalá

Tagus

Toledo

Lisbon

Lerida

Rome

Monte Cassino

Naples

Salerno

Seville

Granada

Palermo

Monreale

Messina

Rhine

Elbe

Seine

Loire

Legend:

Paris — Law school

✝ Centre of monastic reform

⭐ Important cathedral school

★ Important monastic school

University founded
- before 1300
- 1300–1500
- 1500–1700

0   250   500 km

0   100   200   300 miles

Copyright © 1996 Angus Hudson Ltd / Three's Company

THE CHURCH AND LEARNING

In Western Europe during the Middle Ages education was largely in the hands of the Church. Until about the tenth century, the exposition of doctrine was the responsibility of bishops or monks in monasteries. Over the next four centuries, however, they were gradually superseded by the masters who taught in new cathedral schools and universities.

Paris was the main centre of learning, and was adopted by Franciscans and Dominicans as their main training centre. Among the major scholars of this period who studied or taught at Paris were William of Ockham, Anselm of Bec, Peter Abelard, Peter Lombard, Albert the Great, Duns Scotus, Thomas Aquinas and Pope Innocent III. Their main legacy, in a systematic account known as scholasticism, was to harmonize the foundational theology of Augustine with the philosophy of classical Greek thinkers, especially Aristotle. Bringing together the Catholic articles of faith and the method of reasoning by logic was the crowning achievement of Thomas Aquinas in his *Summa Theologica*, which was to form the chief basis of future Catholic theology.

(Above) York Minster, England, at dusk; (right) Cologne Cathedral, Germany; (below) detail from the intricate stone carvings outside Chartres Cathedral, France.

MAJOR GOTHIC CATHEDRALS OF WESTERN EUROPE

- Origin of gothic architecture, 1130 – 1300
- Cathedral city with influential gothic style
- City with major gothic cathedral

GOTHIC CATHEDRALS

The Gothic style of cathedral building emerged in early twelfth-century France and became the dominant style of the Latin West. The new structural development was the use of external flying buttresses. By taking some of the weight of the main construction, they allowed masons to build to much greater heights and dispose of the massive, and less elegant, structural style typical of earlier cathedrals. At first only a select handful of masons and craftsmen knew this engineering secret, and so the earliest examples of Gothic architecture were confined to a region around Paris. The Gothic influence gradually spread to Germany, Italy, Spain, Sweden and elsewhere, where French architectural styles could be recognized.

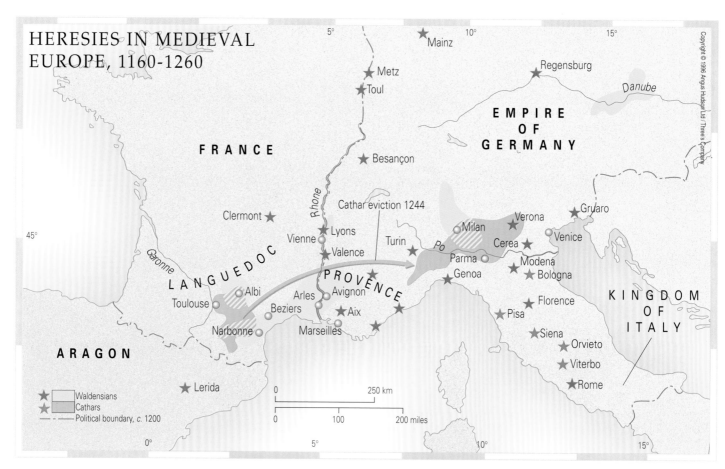

Mainz

Regensburg

Danube

Metz

Toul

EMPIRE
OF
GERMANY

FRANCE

Besançon

Rhone

Cathar eviction 1244

Verona

Gruaro

Clermont

Milan

Venice

Vienne

Lyons

Cerea

Valence

Turin

Po

Parma

LANGUEDOC

PROVENCE

Genoa

Modena

Bologna

Albi

Arles

Avignon

Toulouse

Beziers

Aix

Florence

KINGDOM
OF
ITALY

Narbonne

Marseilles

Pisa

ARAGON

Siena

Orvieto

Lerida

Viterbo

Rome

★ Waldensians
★ Cathars
Political boundary, c. 1200

0   250 km

0   100   200 miles

HERESY AND DISSENT

An increased emphasis on vows of
poverty among the reforming
monasteries inadvertently opened the
door for dissenters to challenge the
lifestyle of the more affluent clergy and
corrupt monasteries. One proponent of
the vow of poverty was a rich merchant
from Lyons, named Peter Valdes
(Waldo), who decided to sell everything
he owned. He translated the New
Testament into the local language and
preached to ordinary illiterate people,
who for the first time could understand
the gospel. The group became known as
the Waldensians. Their rejection of
ecclesiastical authority led to their
condemnation as heretics before 1200.
However, the movement grew and by
the end of the thirteenth century had
spread through much of Europe.

A much more menacing sect, called
the Cathars or Albigensians (from Albi),
whom in fact the Waldensians preached
against, appeared early in the eleventh
century. They spread rapidly and by the
1160s were established in two main
areas: Languedoc in southern France
(where they became known as the
Albigensians) and Lombardy. They

The fortress-like cathedral of Albi, France.

believed all creation and matter to be
evil, and the incarnation and crucifixion
both to be false. The path to salvation
was the release of the soul from the
cage of sinful flesh and its reunification
with God.

Innocent III launched a crusade in
1209 to combat the Albigensian and
Waldensian heretics by force. It turned
into a long struggle, taking on an
almost civil-war scale as many southern
Catholics supported the Albigensians in

defence of their property. A partial
peace was agreed in 1229. Pope Gregory
IX instigated a series of inquisitions in
1231 to root out heresy in France, Italy
and Germany. This marked the
beginning of a more repressive papal
regime.

LATIN KINGDOM OF CONSTANTINOPLE, 1205

BULGARIAN EMPIRE

BLACK SEA

Adrianople

Constantinople

Nicomedia

Nicaea

EPIRUS

THESSALONICA

AEGEAN SEA

LESBOS

CHIOS

NICAEAN EMPIRE

DUCHY OF ATHENS

ACHAEA

Athens

MEDITERRANEAN SEA

BYZANTIUM FALLS

After the recapture of Constantinople from Latin possession, various Western leaders pushed for further campaigns to regain it. Byzantine emperors had to appease the West, and particularly the pope of the day, to keep that ambition in check. Meanwhile the Byzantine rulers, who needed military help from the West to halt the Ottoman Turks, had to manoeuvre with great diplomatic skill. The Byzantine emperor John V (1354-91) appealed to the pope for help in 1355 when the Ottomans were poised to invade the Balkans. The popes were concerned for the Christian East, but wary of helping while the Byzantine Church remained in schism from Rome.

In 1371 the Ottomans defeated the Serbs near Adrianople. Serbia, Bulgaria and ultimately Byzantium, were forced to capitulate, becoming vassal states of the Ottoman Empire. Attempts to rebel against the Ottomans resulted in the eventual capture and sack of Constantinople in 1453.

THE DECLINE AND FALL OF BYZANTIUM

KINGDOM OF HUNGARY

GOLDEN HORDE

Belgrade

Cherson

BOSNIA

Danube

BLACK SEA

KINGDOM OF SERBIA

KINGDOM OF BULGARIA

Sophia

BALKANS

Philippopolis

Adrianople
1371

1453 Falls to the Ottomans

Constantinople (Istanbul)

Thessalonica

Nicomedia

Ankara

TURKS

Gallipoli

Nicaea

LEMNOS

Caesarea

AEGEAN SEA

Smyrna

ANATOLIA

Corinth

Athens

Edessa

Miletus

LESSER ARMENIA

RHODES

CYPRUS

Antioch

CRETE

Tripoli

MEDITERRANEAN SEA

Damascus

- - - - Boundary of Byzantine Empire in 1265
Byzantine Empire in 1355
Ottoman Empire in 1355
✕ Battle with date

0   250 km

0   100   200 miles

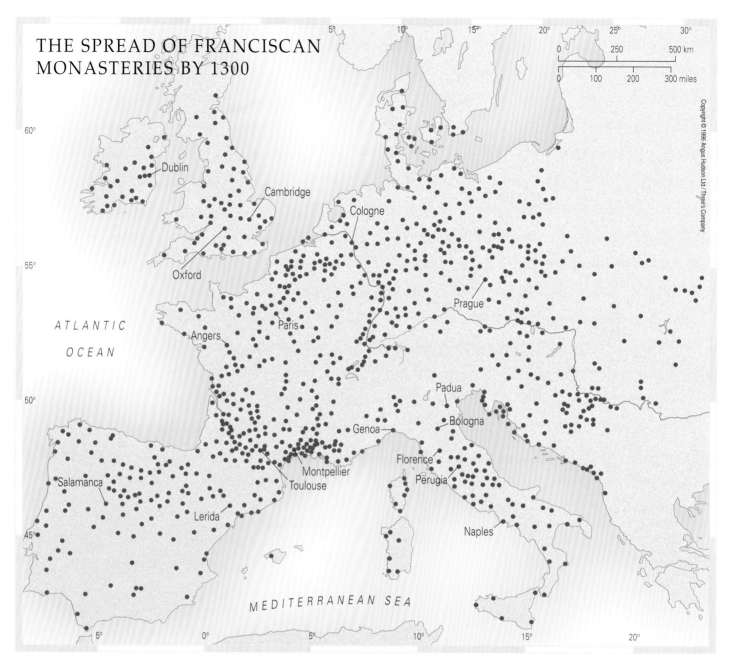

THE SPREAD OF FRANCISCAN MONASTERIES BY 1300

ATLANTIC
OCEAN

Dublin

Cambridge

Cologne

Oxford

Prague

Paris

Angers

Padua

Bologna

Genoa

Florence

Perugia

Montpellier
Toulouse

Salamanca

Lerida

Naples

MEDITERRANEAN SEA

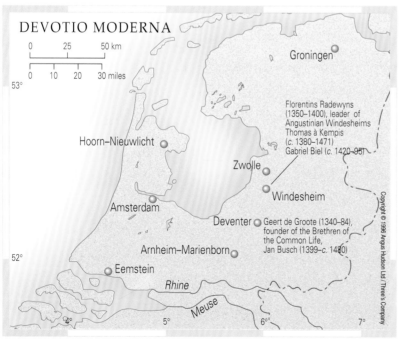

DEVOTIO MODERNA

Groningen

Florentins Radewyns
(1350–1400), leader of
Angustinian Windesheims
Thomas à Kempis
(c. 1380–1471)
Gabriel Biel (c. 1420–95)

Hoorn–Nieuwlicht

Zwolle

Windesheim

Amsterdam

Deventer Geert de Groote (1340–84),
founder of the Brethren of
the Common Life,
Jan Busch (1399–c. 1480)

Arnheim–Marienborn

Eemstein

Rhine

Meuse

THE FRANCISCANS

As towns and cities developed in medieval Europe, the cloistered monastery began to decline in importance. Some of the clergy felt the need for a way of working in the world while still living under a spiritual rule. Early in the thirteenth century new groups of ascetic preaching monks, known as friars, arose. One group, the Franciscans, sprang from the example and teaching of Francis of Assisi (1182-1226), who renounced his inheritance to live a life of prayer and poverty. Despite these ascetic beginnings, it was not long before the order began to own property and take on the trappings of an organisation.

THE SPREAD OF DOMINICAN MONASTERIES BY 1300

500 km
250
0
0   100   200   300 miles

65°
60°
55°
50°
45°

Trondheim

Skanninge

Visby

Lund

Edinburgh

Ribe
Roskilde
Stralsund

York
Cambridge
Norwich

Bremen
Lubeck

Magdeburg

Oxford
London

Krakow

Canterbury
Beauvais

Cologne
Mainz

Paris

Trier

Strasbourg

Vienna

Basel

A T L A N T I C

O C E A N

Limoges

Bern

Bologna

Rome

Naples

Toledo

M E D I T E R R A N E A N   S E A

5°   0°   5°   10°   15°   20°

The basilica of S. Francesco, Assisi.

THE DOMINICANS

Dominic de Guzman (1170-1221), a priest from Castile, recognized that clergymen needed better teaching in order to pass on the faith to the people. He founded the Dominican order, another order of friars, officially known as the Order of Preachers, to fulfil this need. The Dominicans went on to found colleges and seminaries to train the clergy, and produced such medieval thinkers as Albertus Magnus and Thomas Aquinas. The friars achieved a great deal in pastoral work, education and mission.

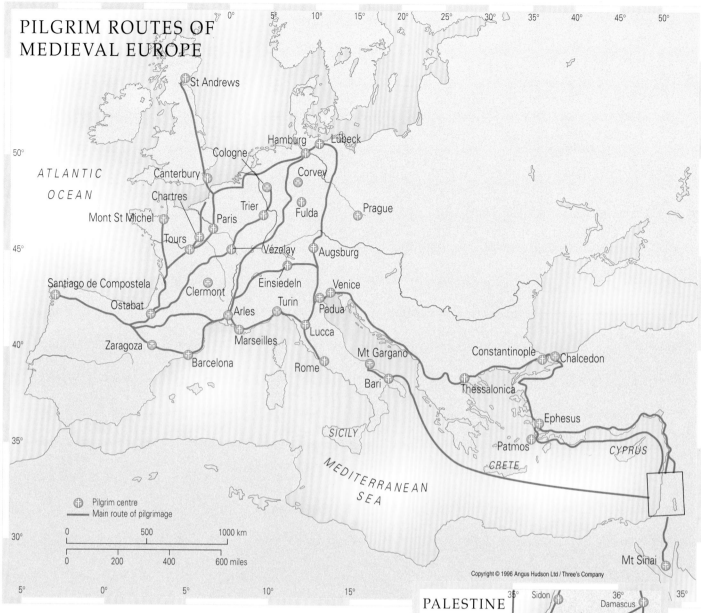

PILGRIM ROUTES OF MEDIEVAL EUROPE

St Andrews
Hamburg · Lübeck
Cologne
Canterbury · Corvey
Chartres · Trier
Mont St Michel · Paris · Fulda · Prague
Tours · Vézelay · Augsburg
Santiago de Compostela · Clermont · Einsiedeln · Venice
Ostabat · Arles · Turin · Padua
Zaragoza · Marseilles · Lucca
Barcelona · Rome · Mt Gargano · Constantinople · Chalcedon
Bari · Thessalonica
Ephesus
Patmos · CYPRUS
CRETE
Mt Sinai

ATLANTIC OCEAN

MEDITERRANEAN SEA

SICILY

⊕ Pilgrim centre
— Main route of pilgrimage

Copyright © 1996 Angus Hudson Ltd / Three's Company

PILGRIMAGES

Pilgrimages to holy sites had been made since the fourth century, but became more common in the medieval period, when they carried the specific aims of winning God's grace through penance, or even of gaining eternal life. Irish monks regarded the Christian life itself as a pilgrimage to heaven, ideally to be lived in exile. The self-denial of a long, arduous journey was symbolic of this personal quest. Pilgrimage could replace public penance as an act of absolving sin, and journeys to holy sites were organized on a large scale from the eleventh century.

Three main places were visited: Rome, with the traditional tombs of Saints Peter and Paul; Jerusalem, together with other sites in the Holy Land associated with Jesus; and Santiago de Compostela, where St James' tomb was believed to have been discovered around 830. The Holy Land became especially popular once the recapture of Jerusalem during the First Crusade (1099) and the instituting of the Orders of knights made travel there more secure. However, with the Muslim reconquest of Jerusalem in 1187, the number of pilgrimages to Rome and Santiago de Compostela greatly increased.

The routes through France via Tours and Vézelay were the most thronged, owing chiefly to Cluniac influence. The idea of the holiness of saints' relics and of their supernatural power developed, with the result that relics proliferated along these routes. A certain tourism was exploited. Local shrines, hospices and the owners of relics recovered from

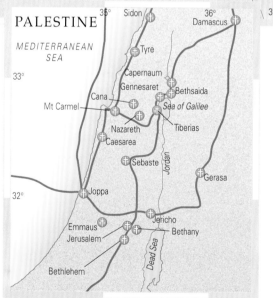

PALESTINE

MEDITERRANEAN SEA

Sidon
Damascus
Tyre
Capernaum · Bethsaida
Gennesaret · Sea of Galilee
Cana · Tiberias
Mt Carmel
Nazareth
Caesarea
Sebaste · Gerasa
Jordan
Joppa
Emmaus · Jericho
Jerusalem · Bethany
Bethlehem · Dead Sea

the Holy Land would grow affluent on the expenditure of people undertaking organized pilgrimage packages.

THE CHRISTIAN RECONQUEST OF SPAIN

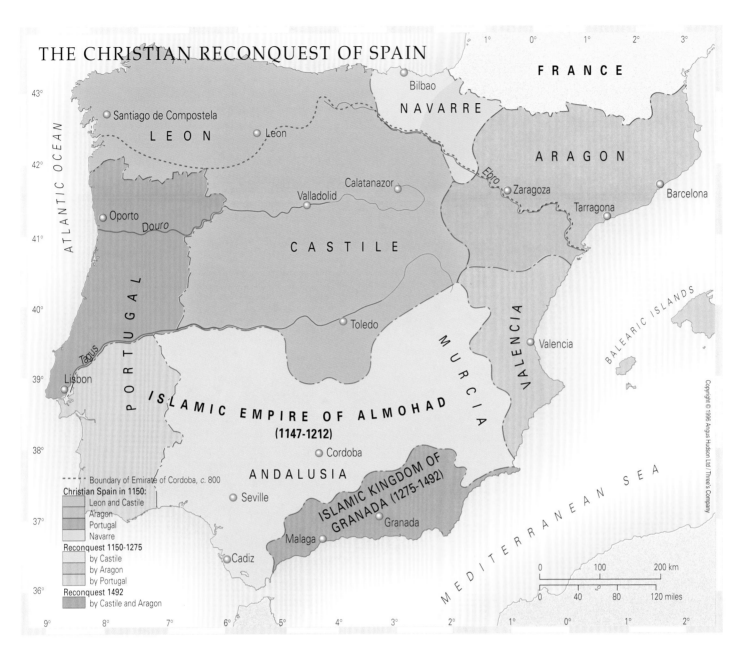

FRANCE

Bilbao

NAVARRE

ARAGON

ATLANTIC OCEAN

Santiago de Compostela

LEON

Leon

Calatanazor

Zaragoza

Barcelona

Valladolid

Tarragona

Oporto

Douro

CASTILE

Ebro

PORTUGAL

Toledo

MURCIA

VALENCIA

Valencia

BALEARIC ISLANDS

Tagus

Lisbon

ISLAMIC EMPIRE OF ALMOHAD
(1147-1212)

Cordoba

ANDALUSIA

ISLAMIC KINGDOM OF GRANADA (1275-1492)

Seville

Granada

- - - - Boundary of Emirate of Cordoba, *c.* 800
Christian Spain in 1150:
- Leon and Castile
- Aragon
- Portugal
- Navarre
Reconquest 1150-1275
- by Castile
- by Aragon
- by Portugal
Reconquest 1492
- by Castile and Aragon

Malaga

Cadiz

MEDITERRANEAN SEA

0   100   200 km
0   40   80   120 miles

Copyright © 1996 Angus Hudson Ltd / Three's Company

THE RECONQUEST OF SPAIN

The Alhambra Palace, Granada, a peak of Moorish cultural achievement.

The Christian reconquest of Spain began with victory at the Battle of Calatanazor in 1002, at a time when the ruling Umayyad Caliphate was embroiled in civil war. A long period of Christian assaults on successive Islamic dynasties resulted in the capitulation of Islamic power in 1236 at Cordoba. The Arabic state of Granada became a vassal to Castile for the next 250 years, during which the great Alhambra Palace in the city of Granada was built, the peak of Moorish cultural achievement. The reconquest of Spain was completed in 1492.

With the gradual recovery of Spain came monastic influence from France. Many religious houses of the Cistercian and Cluniac orders were established and cathedrals in the Gothic style were built, for example at Léon and Toledo.

Many Muslims continued to live in Spain after 1492, until their final expulsion by edict in 1614. It was the end of a civilization which had brought great thinkers, such as Averroës, who lived as a judge in Cordoba, and had reintroduced to the West the lost classical philosophy of Aristotle.

THE JEWS IN MEDIEVAL EUROPE

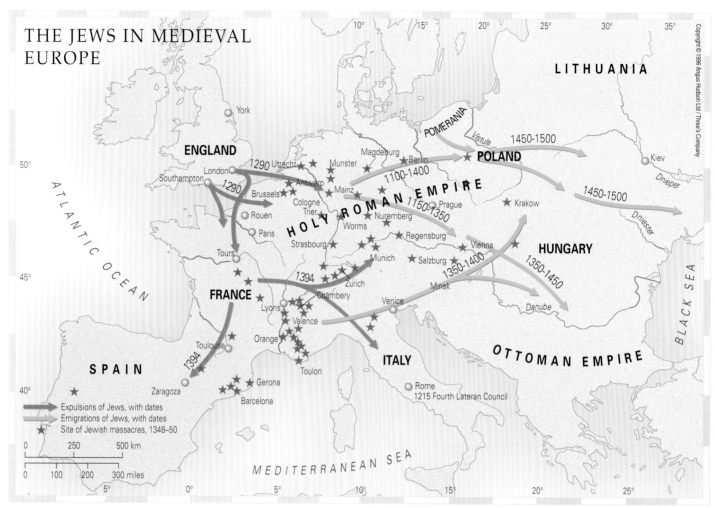

Expulsions of Jews, with dates
Emigrations of Jews, with dates
★ Site of Jewish massacres, 1348–50

THE JEWS IN MEDIEVAL EUROPE

During the Roman Empire Jews were already widespread throughout Mediterranean Europe. After the Jewish War of 66-73 in Palestine many fled the Holy Land to find new homes. The Frankish Emperor Charlemagne (724-814) actively encouraged Jewish immigration. Jewish merchants were treated favourably, because of their trade connections with the Mediterranean and the East, and they soon developed good business relations, especially as money lenders, with the kings and nobles of western Europe. The Jews were 'useful', since usury was forbidden to Christians. Jewish settlements spread out from north-eastern France along the valleys of the Rhine, the Elbe and the Danube, and across the English Channel to London.

The Jews of northern Europe were known as the Ashkenazim. There was also an equally large Jewish colonization in Spain and Portugal, known as the Sephardim. By 1100 the Ashkenazim and Sephardim together far outnumbered the ancient Jewish communities of the Middle East.

Resentment of their increasing numbers and their economic rise in society grew steadily among the townsfolk, and Jews were frequently scapegoated. The advent of the Crusades provided the excuse for intensified discrimination against Jews, and two centuries of persecutions and expulsions followed. Jews were attacked by mobs in the Rhineland during the First Crusade. They were expelled from England in 1290 and from France from the thirteenth century, culminating in a major expulsion in 1394. Pope Innocent III passed restrictive measures in the Fourth Lateran Council of 1215, requiring Jews to wear distinctive dress. They were also forced to live in separate districts, or ghettos.

The result was a steady migration of Jews eastwards across central Europe to Poland, Hungary, Lithuania and Russia.

The Rhine valley.

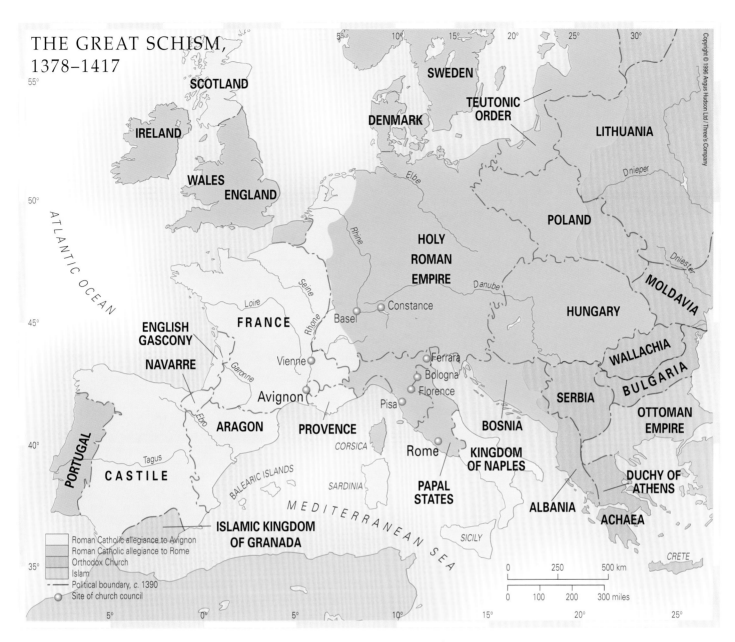

THE GREAT SCHISM, 1378–1417

SCOTLAND

IRELAND

WALES

ENGLAND

ATLANTIC OCEAN

ENGLISH GASCONY

FRANCE

NAVARRE

Vienne

Avignon

ARAGON

PROVENCE

PORTUGAL

CASTILE

Tagus

BALEARIC ISLANDS

SARDINIA

CORSICA

ISLAMIC KINGDOM OF GRANADA

MEDITERRANEAN SEA

SWEDEN

DENMARK

TEUTONIC ORDER

LITHUANIA

POLAND

HOLY ROMAN EMPIRE

Elbe

Rhine

Seine

Loire

Rhone

Garonne

Ebro

Basel

Constance

Danube

HUNGARY

MOLDAVIA

Dnieper

Dniester

WALLACHIA

BULGARIA

Ferrara

Bologna

Florence

Pisa

SERBIA

Rome

KINGDOM OF NAPLES

PAPAL STATES

BOSNIA

OTTOMAN EMPIRE

DUCHY OF ATHENS

ALBANIA

ACHAEA

SICILY

CRETE

Roman Catholic allegiance to Avignon
Roman Catholic allegiance to Rome
Orthodox Church
Islam
— · — Political boundary, c. 1390
◯ Site of church council

| 0 | 250 | 500 km |
| 0 | 100 | 200 | 300 miles |

THE GREAT SCHISM

The Great Schism was a division of Western Christendom into two camps, following the exile of the papacy at Avignon, known as the 'Babylonian Captivity'. In 1302 Pope Boniface VIII issued the bull 'Unam Sanctam', in which he declared the pope to have authority over any king. The next year he excommunicated Philip IV of France. Philip promptly ordered the arrest of Boniface, who died shortly afterwards.

Political instability in Italy and the Papal States, together with the need of protection from the French king, rendered the papal seat in Rome untenable. The papacy was moved to Avignon, where a succession of French Popes presided, under French control, in effect, from 1309 to 1377. These popes were resented in England and in the Holy Roman Empire, and pressure began to build from devout Christians who revered the See of St Peter as the true centre of the Roman church. Eventually, the Avignon Pope Gregory XI returned to Rome, where he died soon after. A fraught period of electing his successor was followed by the withdrawal of support from French cardinals, and soon rival popes divided the allegiance of Europe between them.

At one point there were three competing popes. A series of councils, led by conciliarists who sought to make council superior to pope, tried to heal the divide. It was not until the Council of Constance (1414-17) that the split was effectively healed. Martin V was acknowledged by nearly all as the sole and rightful pope, but antipopes did not die out until mid-century.

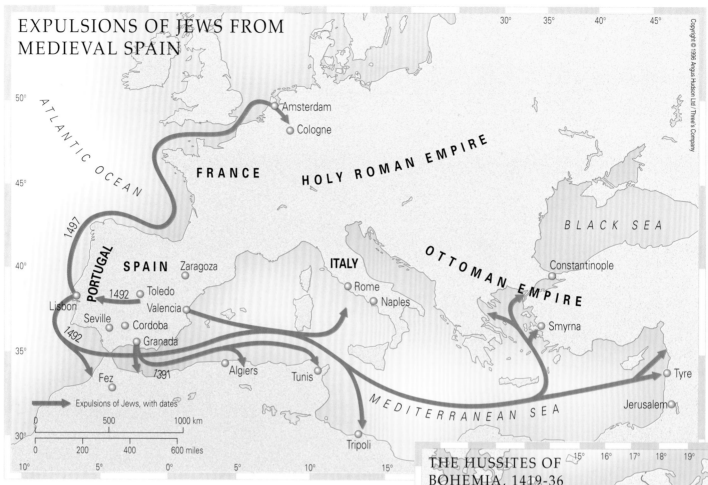

EXPULSIONS OF JEWS FROM MEDIEVAL SPAIN

Expulsions of Jews, with dates

THE EXPULSION OF THE JEWS FROM SPAIN

Until the second half of the fourteenth century the Jews of Spain, or the Sephardim, had been spared the persecutions which the Ashkenazi Jews of northern Europe had suffered. Most were unaffected by the Christian reconquest of Spain and lived in established communities. However, growing political instability, and the sermons of church leaders, turned the populace against them. In 1391 anti-Jewish violence in Seville spread through Castile and Aragon.

Instead of martyrdom, tens of thousands of Jews opted to convert to Christianity and became labelled by their enemies as *marranos* ('swine'). They reconstructed their communities, but by the middle of the fifteenth century had aroused hostility again. The genuineness of their new 'Christian' faith was tried by councils of the Spanish Inquisition, often with barbaric methods, and secret Jews were rooted out. With the capture of the Alhambra of Granada, the last bastion of Islam, in 1492, a decree was issued by

Ferdinand and Isabella banishing all Jews from Spain.

Between 100,000 and 150,000 Jews departed. Some went across the border to Portugal, but most set sail for North Africa and Ottoman Turkey.

THE HUSSITES

As well as ending the Great Schism, the Council of Constance was called to combat heresy. One of those condemned to death was Jan Hus (John Huss) (*c.* 1372-1415). Hus was a reformer from Bohemia whose preaching against the morals of the clergy angered the church authorities but won him wide support among the townsfolk.

He became a national hero on his death and the Czech people established the Hussite church. This church formed a national focus for rebellion against both the papacy and the Holy Roman Empire. It was also known as the Bohemian Brethren. It survived until the Hapsburgs restored the Roman

THE HUSSITES OF BOHEMIA, 1419-36

Main Hussite territory
Hussite campaign
Boundary of Holy Roman Empire

Catholic church in 1620. Remnants regrouped and became influential in Moravia.

THE BAKER
atlas
of
CHRISTIAN
HISTORY

THE MODERN CHURCH

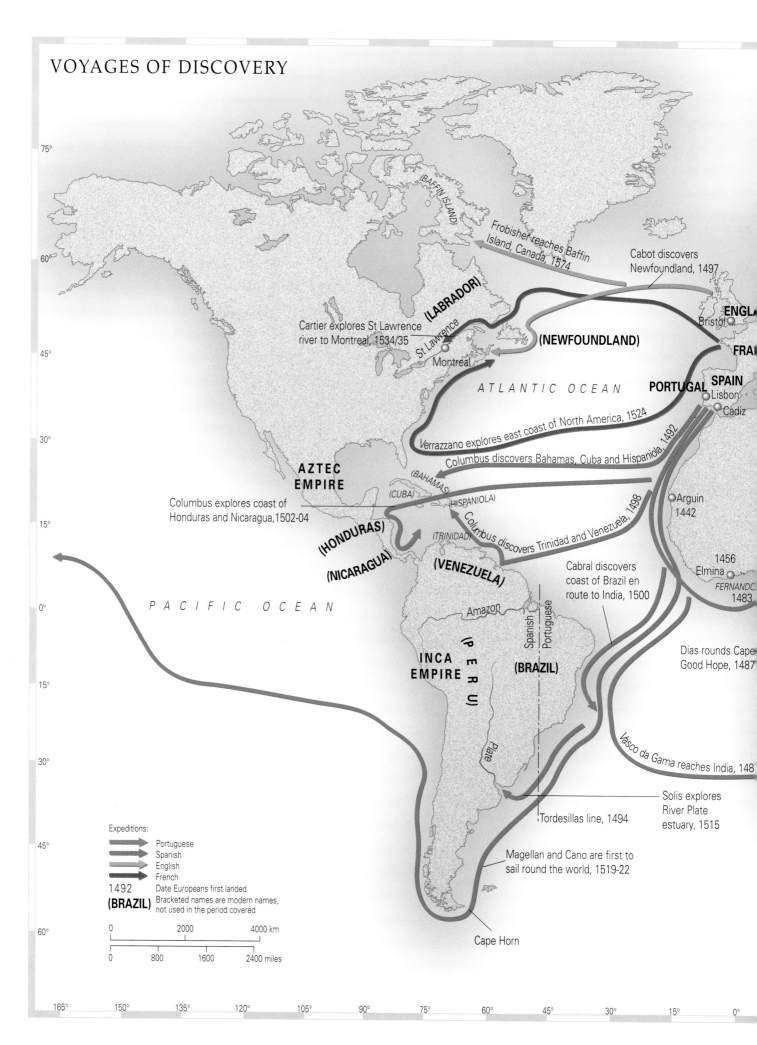

VOYAGES OF DISCOVERY

Frobisher reaches Baffin Island, Canada, 1574

Cabot discovers Newfoundland, 1497

(BAFFIN ISLAND)

(LABRADOR)

Cartier explores St Lawrence river to Montreal, 1534/35

St Lawrence

(NEWFOUNDLAND)

ENGLA

Bristol

Montreal

ATLANTIC OCEAN

FRA

PORTUGAL **SPAIN**

Lisbon

Cadiz

Verrazzano explores east coast of North America, 1524

Columbus discovers Bahamas, Cuba and Hispaniola, 1492

AZTEC EMPIRE

(BAHAMAS)

(CUBA)

Columbus explores coast of Honduras and Nicaragua,1502-04

(HISPANIOLA)

Arguin
1442

(HONDURAS)

(TRINIDAD)

Columbus discovers Trinidad and Venezuela,

1456

Elmina

FERNANDO

(NICARAGUA)

(VENEZUELA)

Cabral discovers coast of Brazil en route to India, 1500

1483

PACIFIC OCEAN

Amazon

Spanish Portuguese

Dias rounds Cape Good Hope, 1487

INCA EMPIRE

(P E R U)

(BRAZIL)

Plate

Vásco da Gama reaches India, 148

Solis explores River Plate estuary, 1515

Tordesillas line, 1494

Magellan and Cano are first to sail round the world, 1519-22

Expeditions:

Portuguese
Spanish
English
French

1492 Date Europeans first landed

(BRAZIL) Bracketed names are modern names, not used in the period covered

0		2000		4000 km
0	800	1600	2400 miles

Cape Horn

| 165° | 150° | 135° | 120° | 105° | 90° | 75° | 60° | 45° | 30° | 15° | 0° |

75°
60°
45°
30°
15°
0°
15°
30°
45°
60°

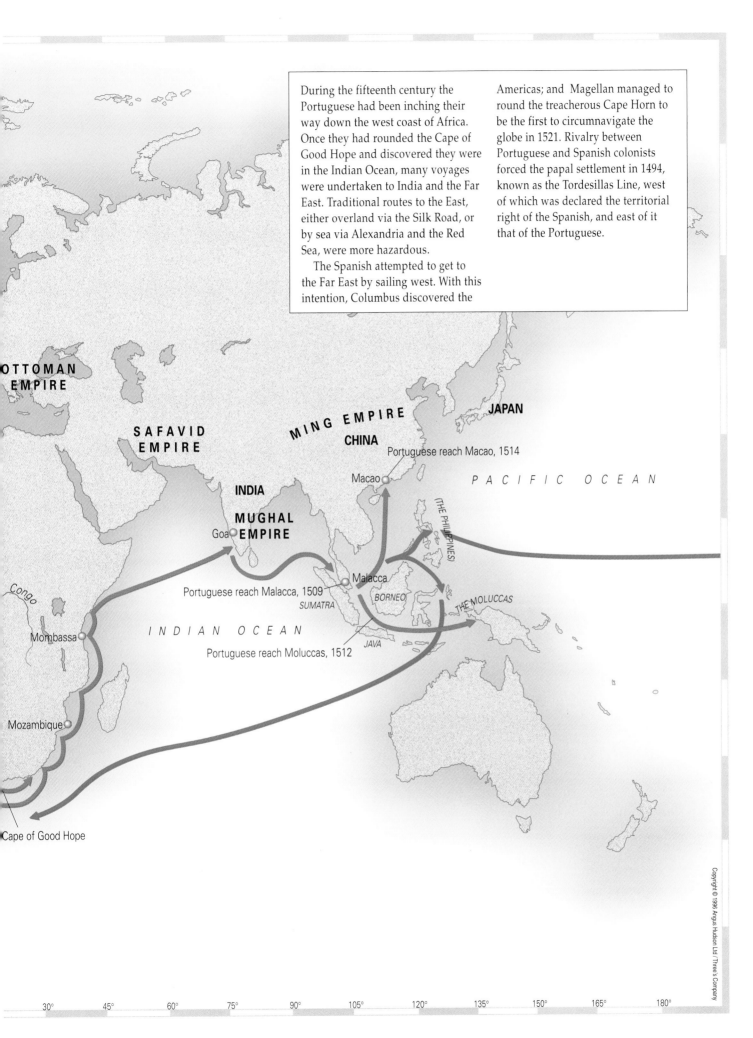

During the fifteenth century the Portuguese had been inching their way down the west coast of Africa. Once they had rounded the Cape of Good Hope and discovered they were in the Indian Ocean, many voyages were undertaken to India and the Far East. Traditional routes to the East, either overland via the Silk Road, or by sea via Alexandria and the Red Sea, were more hazardous.

The Spanish attempted to get to the Far East by sailing west. With this intention, Columbus discovered the Americas; and Magellan managed to round the treacherous Cape Horn to be the first to circumnavigate the globe in 1521. Rivalry between Portuguese and Spanish colonists forced the papal settlement in 1494, known as the Tordesillas Line, west of which was declared the territorial right of the Spanish, and east of it that of the Portuguese.

OTTOMAN EMPIRE

SAFAVID EMPIRE

MING EMPIRE
CHINA

JAPAN

Portuguese reach Macao, 1514

Macao

PACIFIC OCEAN

INDIA

MUGHAL EMPIRE

Goa

(THE PHILIPPINES)

Malacca

Portuguese reach Malacca, 1509

SUMATRA

BORNEO

THE MOLUCCAS

Congo

INDIAN OCEAN

Mombassa

Portuguese reach Moluccas, 1512

JAVA

Mozambique

Cape of Good Hope

30°   45°   60°   75°   90°   105°   120°   135°   150°   165°   180°

115

REFORMATION EUROPE

In 1517, Martin Luther posted his 95 Theses on the church door at Wittenberg. In 1520, Huldreich Zwingli of Zurich revolted against Rome, and John Calvin, in 1533, had a vision that he should lead a mission to restore the Church to its original purity, an objective he held in common with most of the Protestant reformers.

However, as much of the Reformation was motivated by politics as by religion. The opportunity was there for kings and leaders in Europe to take advantage of the Church's unpopularity and seize some of its wealth and power. Henry VIII declared himself absolute head of the Church of England in 1534. Many German princes supported Luther. After the condemnation of his teachings at the Diet of Worms by Emperor Charles V in 1521, the princes forced the Peace of Augsburg (1555), in which a prince was allowed to adopt either Catholicism or Lutheranism for his subjects. Luther was obliged to turn against the more radical dissenters in Germany, such as the Anabaptists, who precipitated the Peasants' Revolt in 1525. Calvinism took root in France, Poland, Hungary and Scotland; the Calvinist Church of Scotland being formed in 1560.

St Giles' Cathedral, Edinburgh, from which John Knox led the Scottish Reformation.

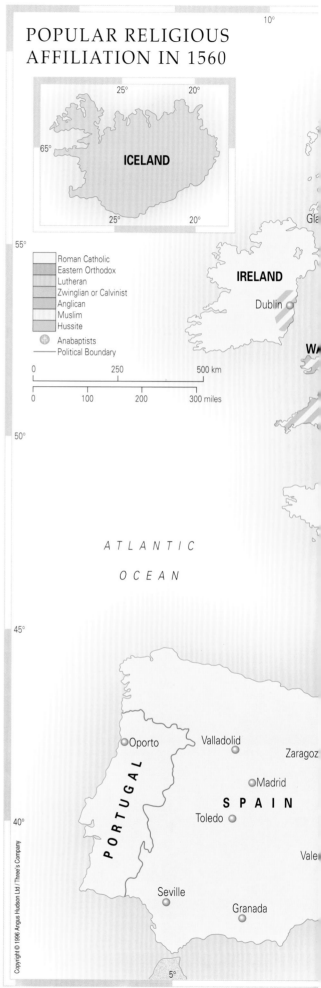

POPULAR RELIGIOUS AFFILIATION IN 1560

ICELAND

Roman Catholic
Eastern Orthodox
Lutheran
Zwinglian or Calvinist
Anglican
Muslim
Hussite
Anabaptists
Political Boundary

0   250   500 km
0   100   200   300 miles

IRELAND

Dublin

ATLANTIC

OCEAN

PORTUGAL

Oporto

Valladolid

Zaragoz

Madrid

SPAIN

Toledo

Vale

Seville

Granada

NORWAY

SWEDEN

FINLAND

ESTONIA

RUSSIA

LIVONIA

COURLAND

*BALTIC
SEA*

Stockholm

LITHUANIA

Konigsberg

PRUSSIA

Danzig

POLAND

Warsaw

*NORTH
SEA*

DENMARK

Copenhagen

Groningen

Bremen   Hamburg

Amsterdam

Magdeburg

Munster

Wittenberg

Antwerp

HOLY ROMAN

London

Canterbury

York

nburgh

TLAND

JGLAND

Zwickau

EMPIRE

Frankfurt

Edict of Worms, 1521,
condemns Lutheranism

Rouen

Rheims

Prague

BOHEMIA

MORAVIA

Brno

Regensburg

Paris

Worms

Augsburg

es

Tours

Munich

Vienna

Budapest

Zurich

Poitiers

Nevers

Salzburg

FRANCE

Peace of Augsburg, 1555,
recognizes existence of Lutheranism

HUNGARY

Lyons

Geneva

Milan

Venice

Avignon

Toulouse

Modena

Ferrara

Bucharest

rdeaux

*ADRIATIC
SEA*

Marseilles

Florence

OTTOMAN EMPIRE

CORSICA

**PAPAL
STATES**

Barcelona

Rome

**KINGDOM
OF NAPLES**

SARDINIA

Naples

BALEARIC ISLANDS

MEDITERRANEAN   SEA

SICILY

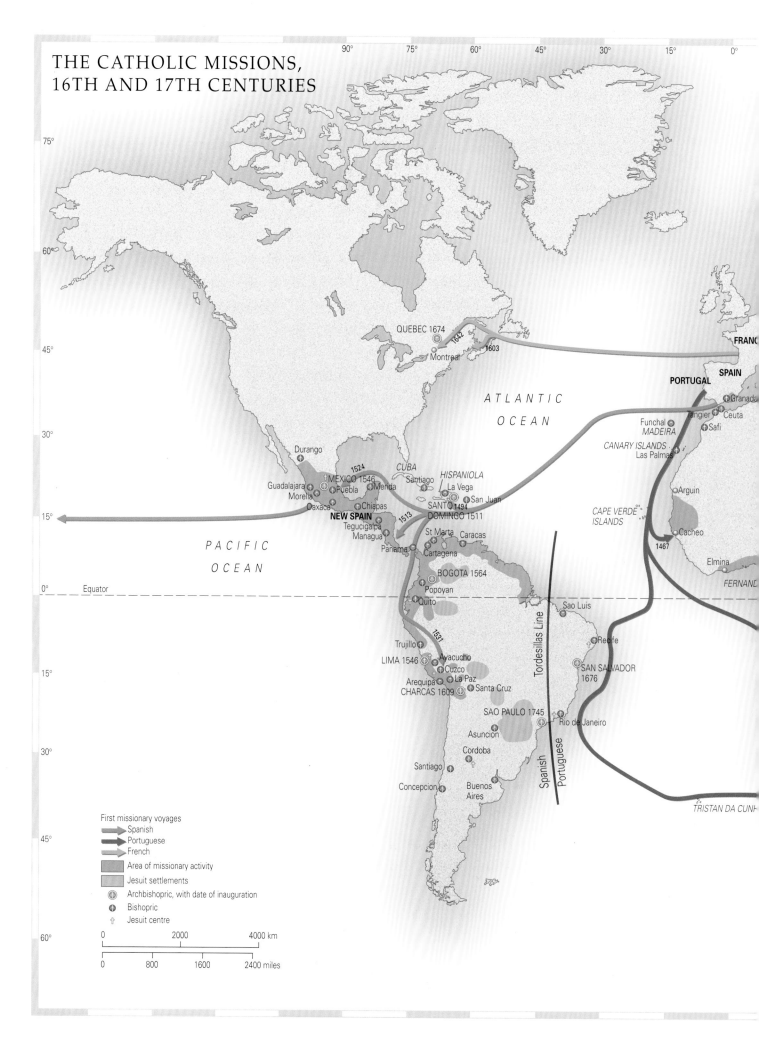

THE CATHOLIC MISSIONS,
16TH AND 17TH CENTURIES

QUEBEC 1674
Montreal
1642
1603

ATLANTIC
OCEAN

FRANC

SPAIN

PORTUGAL

Granada

Funchal
Tangier Ceuta
MADEIRA Safi

CANARY ISLANDS
Las Palmas

Durango

1524
CUBA
MEXICO 1546 Santiago HISPANIOLA
Guadalajara Puebla La Vega
Morelia Merida
Oaxaca Chiapas SANTO 1494 San Juan
NEW SPAIN DOMINGO 1511
Tegucigalpa 1513
Managua St Marta Caracas
Panama Cartagena

CAPE VERDE
ISLANDS

Arguin

Arguin

Cacheo

1467

Elmina

PACIFIC

OCEAN

BOGOTA 1564
Popoyan

Equator
Quito

FERNAND

Sao Luis

Trujillo
1531
Recife

LIMA 1546 Ayacucho
Cuzco
Arequipa La Paz
CHARCAS 1609 Santa Cruz

SAN SALVADOR
1676

Tordesillas Line

SAO PAULO 1745
Rio de Janeiro

Asuncion

Cordoba

Santiago

Spanish Portuguese

Concepcion Buenos
Aires

TRISTAN DA CUNH

First missionary voyages
Spanish
Portuguese
French
Area of missionary activity
Jesuit settlements
Archbishopric, with date of inauguration
Bishopric
Jesuit centre

0   2000   4000 km

0   800   1600   2400 miles

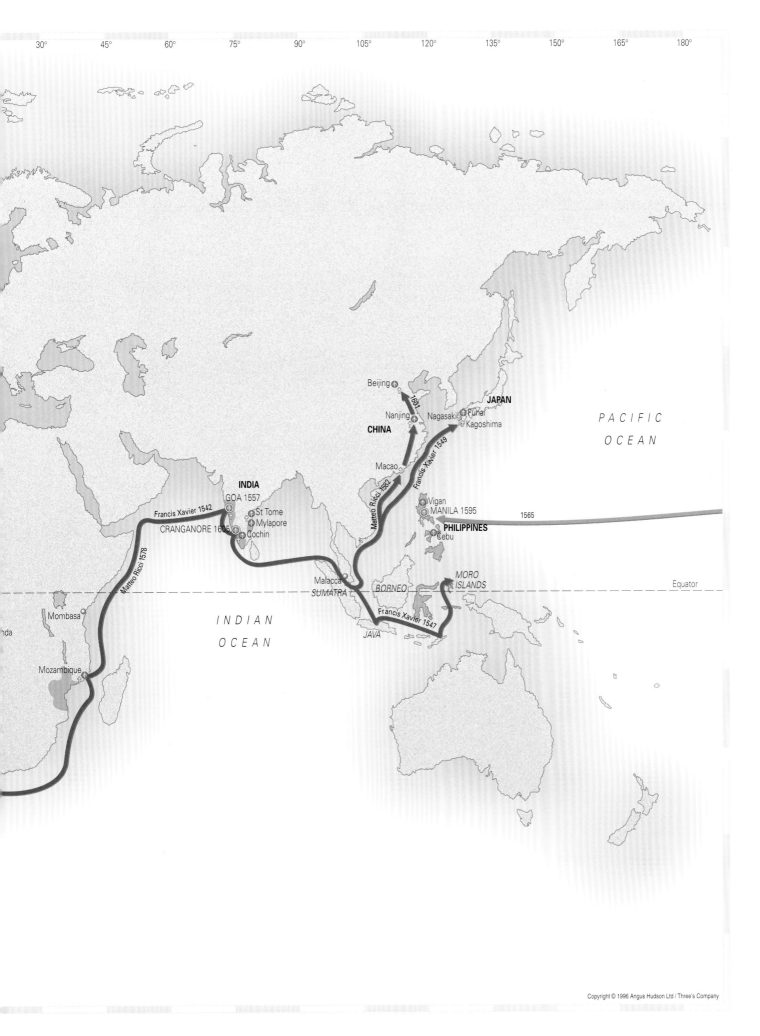

Beijing

1601

Nanjing

NANJING

CHINA

JAPAN

Nagasaki   Funai
Kagoshima

Macao

Matteo Ricci 1582

Francis Xavier 1549

PACIFIC
OCEAN

INDIA

GOA 1557

Francis Xavier 1542

St Tome

Mylapore

CRANGANORE 1605   Cochin

Vigan
MANILA 1595

1565

PHILIPPINES

Cebu

Matteo Ricci 1578

Malacca

SUMATRA

BORNEO

MORO
ISLANDS

Equator

Mombasa

INDIAN

OCEAN

JAVA

Francis Xavier 1547

Mozambique

Interior of the Gesù, Rome, mother church of the Jesuit order.

CATHOLIC MISSIONS

Part of the justification for the conquest of unknown lands by European powers was the opportunity it presented of extending the frontier of Christianity. The Pope instructed these powers to take missionaries with them, and to found bishoprics in a diocesan network.

One of the aims of the Jesuit Order was to evangelize the 'heathen'; and Jesuits, along with Dominicans, Franciscans, Augustinians and Capuchins, were the main missionary bodies in the Americas during the sixteenth and seventeenth centuries. One of the first Jesuit missionaries to the East was Francis Xavier, who reached Goa in India in 1542, and Japan in 1549. Matteo Ricci worked in China from 1582. However, in the Far East, some rulers became suspicious of the power of the Pope, and the Church was unable to lay any permanent foundations, especially in China, until future waves of missionaries arrived in the nineteenth century.

Likewise, in Africa, only a superficial impact was made in this earlier period, namely in the Congo and Mozambique.

Not till the time of the later explorer-missionaries of the nineteenth century was any lasting influence established. In South and Central America, wholesale conversions of indigenous communities were organized by missionary teams. The Jesuits invented a social order, known as a *'reduction'*, in which the indigenous population would live isolated from the outside world under the paternalist direction of European Jesuit priests.

The dome of St Peter's Rome.

THE CATHOLIC REFORMATION

The Catholic Reformation was the revival of the Roman Catholic Church in the face of growing support for Protestantism. Internal reform of the religious orders had begun in the 1520s. The Jesuit Society was founded in 1534 by Ignatius Loyola (1491-1556) to spearhead the revival, and was largely responsible for consolidating the Catholic faith in southern Europe. The Council of Trent (1545-63) was called to re-establish doctrines of the Catholicism which had been called into question as a result of Protestantism, and to renew disciplines of the spiritual life. The supremacy of the pope was confirmed. The Thirty Years War (1618-1648) was the final phase of the struggle between Catholics and Protestants. It was fought out in the Holy Roman Empire (Germany), with the Danes, English, Dutch and Swedes supporting German Protestant princes against the Catholic rulers. The main outcome was the recovery for Rome of southern Germany and Poland.

THE CATHOLIC RECOVERY,
c. 1650

RUSSIA

SCOTLAND

NORTH

SEA

SWEDEN

DENMARK–NORWAY

BALTIC
SEA

BALTIC
STATES

Vilnius

EAST
PRUSSIA

Copenhagen

Danzig
Konigsberg

IRELAND

Hamburg

Vistula

POLAND

WALES

ENGLAND

UNITED
PROVINCES

Elbe

Munster

Warsaw

London

Antwerp

HOLY
ROMAN
EMPIRE

Krakow

Mons

Prague

Douai

Liege

Rheims

Trier

Mainz

Wurzburg

Rouen

Paris

Verdun

Molsheim

Ingolstadt

Danube

HUNGARY

Budapest

Seine

Nancy

Dillingen

La Flèche

Pont-à-Mousson

Zurich

Vienna

OTTOMAN
EMPIRE

ATLANTIC

Loire

Tours

Bourges

Dôle

SWISS
CONFEDERATION

MILAN

REPUBLIC OF
VENICE

Graz

OCEAN

Geneva

SAVOY

Milan

FRANCE

Lyons

Genoa

Venice

Bordeaux

Rhône

Ravenna

Colonies
of Venice

Garonne

Avignon

PARMA

Florence

PAPAL
STATES

Santiago de Compostela

Toulouse

GENOA

MODENA

Ebro

CORSICA

TUSCANY

Rome

PORTUGAL

Valladolid

Salamanca

Naples

Madrid

Tagus

Toledo

Sassari

KINGDOM
OF TWO
SICILIES

Lisbon

SPAIN

Valencia

BALEARIC ISLANDS

SARDINIA

Cagliari

Seville

Palermo

Messina

M E D I T E R R A N E A N   S E A

Catholic
Protestant
Eastern Orthodox
Muslim
☐ Important Jesuit centre
— Political Boundary

0	250	500 km
0	100	200	300 miles

GERMAN PROTESTANTISM IN 1618

DENMARK

BALTIC SEA

NORTH SEA

MECKLENBURG

BREMEN

Elbe

Berlin

BRANDENBURG

POLAND

UNITED PROVINCES

Rhine

MUNSTER

Wittenberg

Cologne

SAXONY

SILESIA

SPANISH NETHERLANDS

HESSE

GERMAN (HOLY ROMAN) EMPIRE

Dresden

Frankfurt

BOHEMIA

Worms

PALATINATE

Nuremberg

MORAVIA

WURTTEMBERG

Strasbourg

BAVARIA

Danube

FRANCE

FRANCHE-COMTE

Augsburg

AUGSBURG

Munich

AUSTRIA

Vienna

HUNGARY

Basel

Lake Constance

Salzburg

STYRIA

SWISS CONFEDERATION

Zurich

SALZBURG

TYROL

CARINTHIA

OTTOMAN EMPIRE

Lake Geneva

Geneva

CARNIOLA

VENICE

Majority denomination:
- Catholic
- Lutheran
- Calvinist and Zwinglian
- Muslim area
- Political Boundary

0   125   250 km

0   50   100   150 miles

MEDITERRANEAN SEA

ADRIATIC SEA

PAPAL STATES

GERMAN PROTESTANTISM

Protestantism reached its greatest extent in Germany under Emperor Maximilian II (1564-76), who was confessionally neutral. Many of the north German bishoprics converted to Protestantism during this time.

After the compromising formula of the Concordat of 1577, most Lutherans adopted a less politically aggressive stance than had been held earlier in the century. In Saxony, the heartland of Lutheran orthodoxy, Lutheranism became a quietistic faith of the common people. Calvinists, on the other hand, hardened their position. They won support from the princes of the Electoral Palatinate, which became common ground for German, French, Dutch and Bohemian Protestantism.

Archduke Ferdinand II led a brutal Catholic reaction in Styria, Carinthia and Carniola, with first the expulsion of, and then the execution of, many Protestants after 1596. Bohemia suffered badly in the Thirty Years War (1618-1648) in which many Protestant nobles either had their property confiscated, or were executed. This laid the foundation for Czech hatred of German domination.

FRENCH PROTESTANTISM

The Huguenot Wars were fought between 1562 and 1598. Peace came when Henry IV of Bourbon converted to Catholicism. The Edict of Nantes (1598) granted the Huguenots freedom of worship and political equality and France accepted a Protestant minority. The Huguenots established themselves in the south and around Poitou in the west.

However, the rise of Absolutism in France, with its ruling maxim of 'one king, one faith, one law', led to a renewed persecution of the Huguenots. Their last stronghold (Rochelle) was taken in 1628. The Revocation of the Edict of Nantes in 1685 prompted about half a million Huguenots to flee the country. Most went to Brandenburg in Germany, Holland and England.

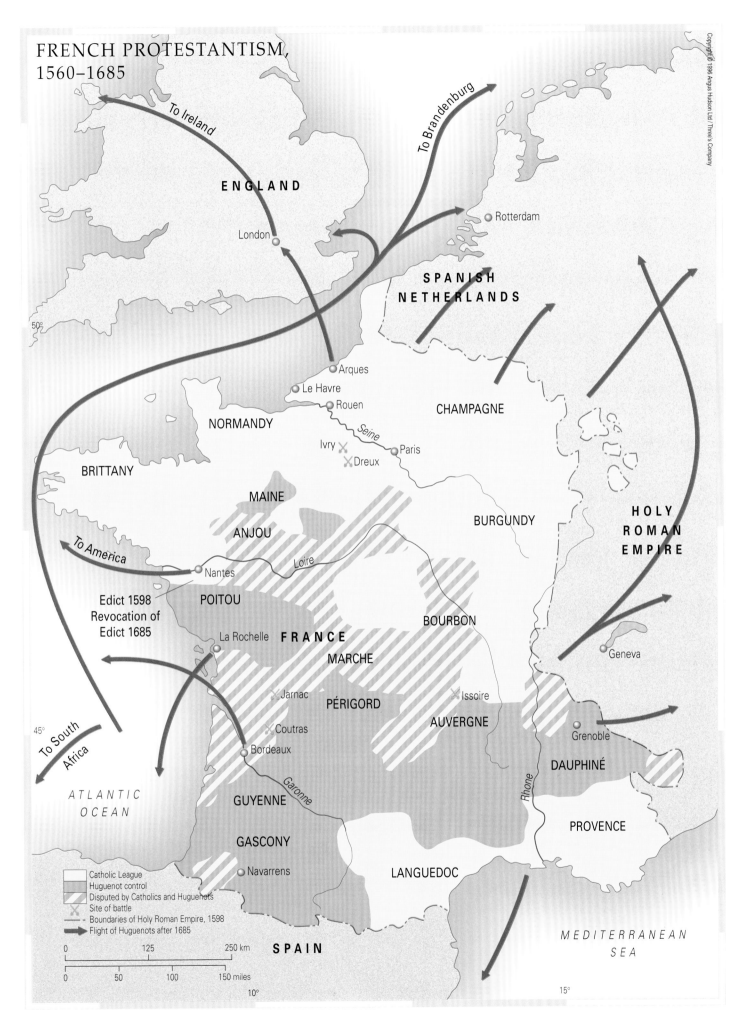

FRENCH PROTESTANTISM,
1560–1685

To Ireland

ENGLAND

London

To Brandenburg

Rotterdam

**SPANISH
NETHERLANDS**

Arques

Le Havre

Rouen

NORMANDY

Seine

CHAMPAGNE

Ivry

Dreux

Paris

BRITTANY

MAINE

ANJOU

BURGUNDY

To America

Loire

**H O L Y
R O M A N
E M P I R E**

Nantes

Edict 1598
Revocation of
Edict 1685

POITOU

FRANCE

BOURBON

La Rochelle

MARCHE

Geneva

Jarnac

PÉRIGORD

Issoire

To South
Africa

Coutras

Bordeaux

AUVERGNE

Grenoble

*ATLANTIC
OCEAN*

Garonne

GUYENNE

Rhone

DAUPHINÉ

GASCONY

PROVENCE

Navarrens

LANGUEDOC

Catholic League
Huguenot control
Disputed by Catholics and Huguenots
Site of battle
Boundaries of Holy Roman Empire, 1598
Flight of Huguenots after 1685

| | 0 | 125 | 250 km |

| | 0 | 50 | 100 | 150 miles |

S P A I N

10°

*MEDITERRANEAN
SEA*

15°

50°

45°

PROTESTANTISM IN THE NETHERLANDS, 1648

5° 6° 7° 8°

53°

NORTH SEA

GRONINGEN

FRIESLAND

DRENTHE

Zuider Zee

HOLLAND

OVERIJSSEL

Haarlem ○ ○ Amsterdam

UNITED PROVINCES
OF THE
NETHERLANDS

52°

○ Leiden UTRECHT

The Hague ○

○ Rotterdam

GELDERN

ZEELAND

HOLY
ROMAN
EMPIRE

○ Eindhoven

51°

○ Bruges ○ Antwerp

○ Ghent

LIEGE

SPANISH NETHERLANDS

○ Brussels ○ Maastricht

Rhine

○ Lille

○ Liege

Meuse

○ Mons

Arras ○

Majority denomination:

- Roman Catholic
- Calvinist

SPANISH
NETHERLANDS

50°

0 20 40 60 80 100 km

0 20 40 60 miles

2° 3° 4° 5° 6° 7° 8°

PROTESTANTISM IN THE NETHERLANDS

The Netherlands were divided into the Spanish south, which was Catholic, and the United Provinces of the north, which were Protestant. Early on the United Provinces followed Luther, but some Dutch Protestants became Anabaptists. The Melchiorites, named after Melchior Hoffmann, found supporters in Haarlem and Leiden. They turned from being a radical millenarian sect to a more quietistic group after the influence of the Frisian preacher Menno Simons (d. 1559). They became known as Mennonites, and spread from the Netherlands to Russia and North America.

From the 1560s, Calvinism became the focus for rebelling against Spanish rule, which had extended to the north. Strict Calvinism became the official creed in the United Provinces after the Council of Dort (1618-19).

PIETISM AND EVANGELICAL AWAKENING

Pietism was a movement within Lutheranism that modified Luther's doctrine of 'justification' by placing new emphasis on 'sanctification', believing that the in-dwelling Christ brings the believer to a life of holiness. Spener formed his 'assembly of piety' in 1669 and proposed prayer and Bible meetings. No distinct church formed, however, until Count Zinzendorf founded a colony, in 1722, on his estates in Saxony, whose inhabitants became known as the Moravian Brethren.

The Moravian Brethren were active missionaries in Europe and across the Atlantic. Through Moravian influence John Wesley, founder of the Methodists, had an evangelical experience of assurance of salvation in 1738 at Aldersgate Street in London; Wesley subsequently maintained links with the Brethren. One notable Pietist, August Francke (1663-1727), influenced devotion as far east as Moscow, and he educated Swedish students.

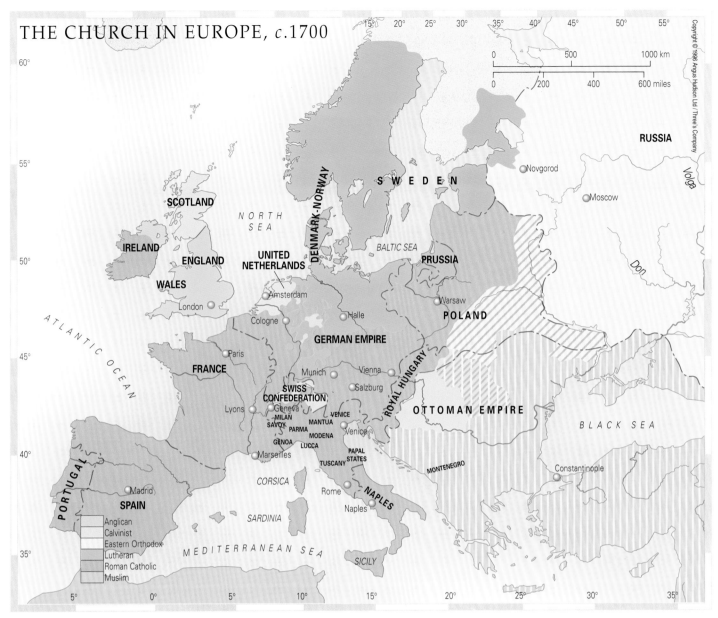

THE CHURCH IN EUROPE, c.1700

RUSSIA

Novgorod

Moscow

Volga

SCOTLAND

NORTH
SEA

IRELAND

ENGLAND

WALES

S W E D E N

DENMARK-NORWAY

BALTIC SEA

PRUSSIA

Amsterdam

Warsaw

UNITED
NETHERLANDS

POLAND

Cologne

Halle

GERMAN EMPIRE

ATLANTIC OCEAN

Paris

ROYAL HUNGARY

Don

FRANCE

Munich

Vienna

Salzburg

SWISS
CONFEDERATION

OTTOMAN EMPIRE

BLACK SEA

Lyons

Geneva

MILAN

VENICE

MANTUA

SAVOY

PARMA

Venice

MODENA

GENOA

LUCCA

Marseilles

PAPAL
STATES

TUSCANY

Constantinople

PORTUGAL

MONTENEGRO

CORSICA

Rome

NAPLES

Madrid

Naples

SPAIN

| Anglican |
| Calvinist |
| Eastern Orthodox |
| Lutheran |
| Roman Catholic |
| Muslim |

MEDITERRANEAN SEA

SARDINIA

SICILY

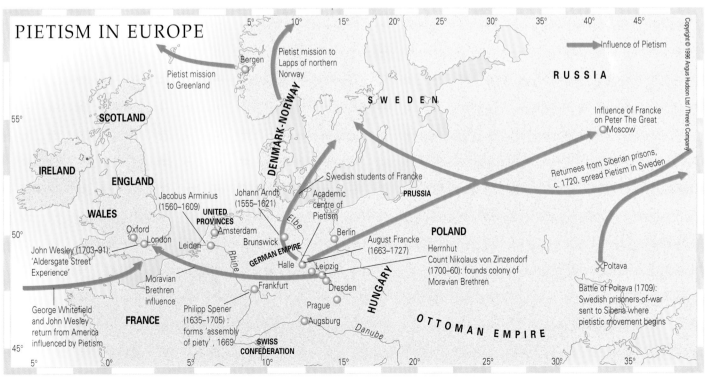

PIETISM IN EUROPE

Influence of Pietism

Pietist mission
to Greenland

Bergen

Pietist mission to
Lapps of northern
Norway

RUSSIA

DENMARK-NORWAY

S W E D E N

Influence of Francke
on Peter The Great
Moscow

SCOTLAND

IRELAND

ENGLAND

WALES

Jacobus Arminius
(1560–1609)

Johann Arndt
(1555–1621)

Swedish students of Francke

Academic
centre of
Pietism

PRUSSIA

Returnees from Siberian prisons,
c. 1720, spread Pietism in Sweden

UNITED
PROVINCES

Oxford

London

Amsterdam

Leiden

Berlin

POLAND

John Wesley (1703–91)
'Aldersgate Street
Experience'

Brunswick

August Francke
(1663–1727)

Herrnhut
Count Nikolaus von Zinzendorf
(1700–60): founds colony of
Moravian Brethren

Elbe

GERMAN EMPIRE

Rhine

Halle

Leipzig

Poltava

Moravian
Brethren
influence

Frankfurt

Dresden

HUNGARY

George Whitefield
and John Wesley
return from America
influenced by Pietism

FRANCE

Philipp Spener
(1635–1705):
forms 'assembly
of piety', 1669

Prague

Augsburg

Battle of Poltava (1709):
Swedish prisoners-of-war
sent to Siberia where
pietistic movement begins

OTTOMAN EMPIRE

SWISS
CONFEDERATION

Danube

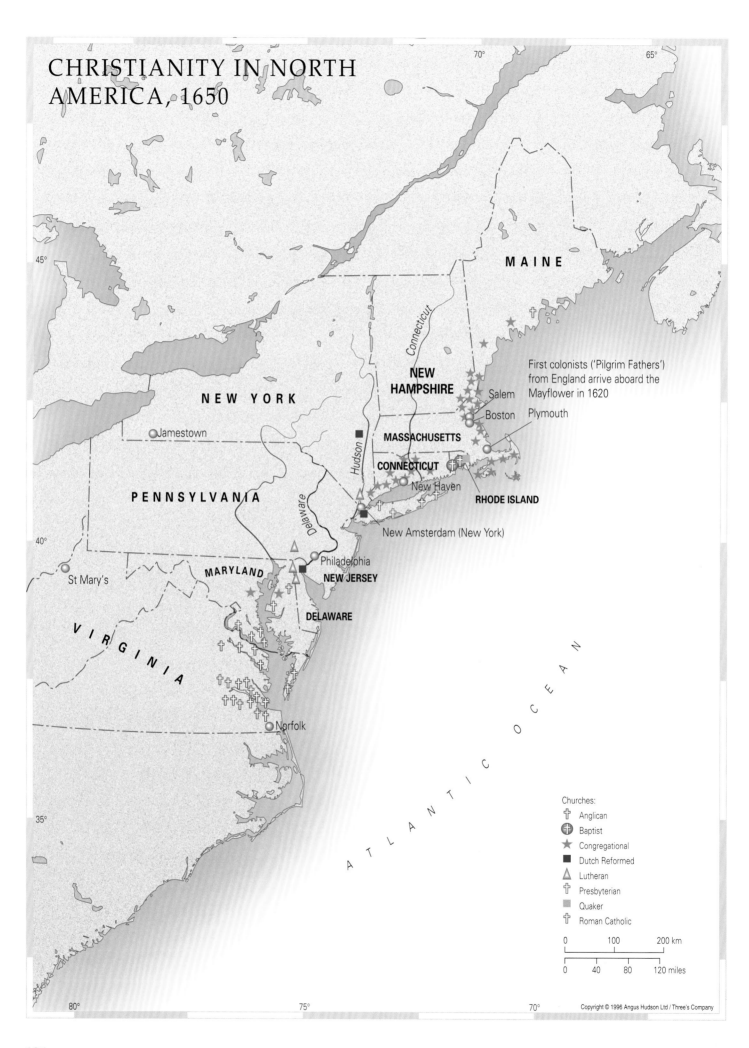

CHRISTIANITY IN NORTH AMERICA, 1650

MAINE

First colonists ('Pilgrim Fathers') from England arrive aboard the Mayflower in 1620

NEW HAMPSHIRE

Salem
Boston
Plymouth

NEW YORK

Jamestown

MASSACHUSETTS

CONNECTICUT

Connecticut

Hudson

New Haven

RHODE ISLAND

PENNSYLVANIA

Delaware

New Amsterdam (New York)

St Mary's

Philadelphia

MARYLAND

NEW JERSEY

DELAWARE

VIRGINIA

Norfolk

ATLANTIC OCEAN

Churches:

✝ Anglican
✠ Baptist
★ Congregational
■ Dutch Reformed
△ Lutheran
✝ Presbyterian
■ Quaker
✝ Roman Catholic

| 0 | 100 | 200 km |
| 0 | 40 | 80 | 120 miles |

Copyright © 1996 Angus Hudson Ltd / Three's Company

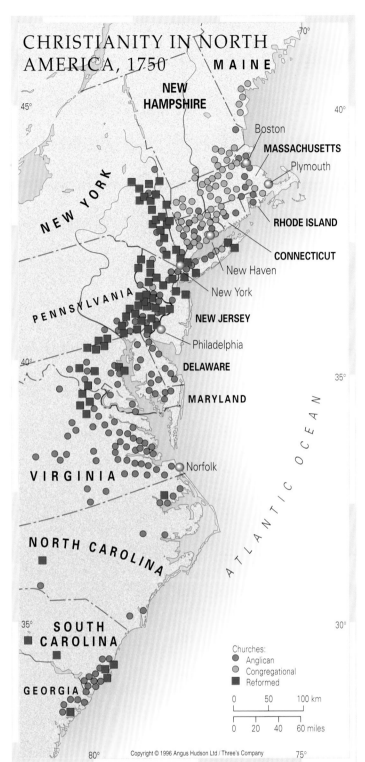

CHRISTIANITY IN NORTH
AMERICA, 1750

Churches:
- Anglican
- Congregational
- Reformed

0 50 100 km

0 20 40 60 miles

Copyright © 1996 Angus Hudson Ltd / Three's Company

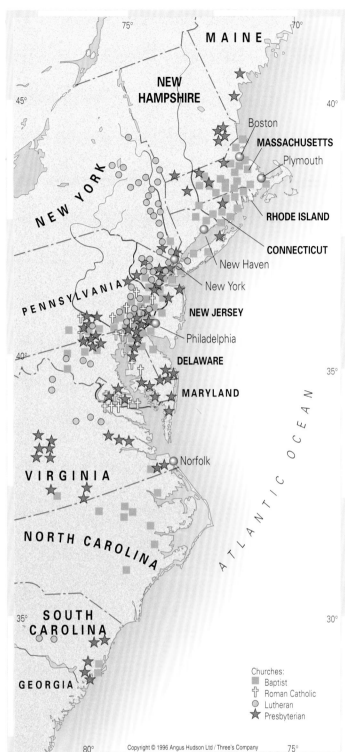

Churches:
- Baptist
- ✝ Roman Catholic
- Lutheran
- ★ Presbyterian

Copyright © 1996 Angus Hudson Ltd / Three's Company

CHRISTIANITY IN
NORTH AMERICA

Persecution of non-conformist churches in Europe resulted in flights to North America. The Pilgrim Fathers established a colony of Calvinists at Plymouth in 1620. After 1630 Puritans founded a colony at Massachusetts Bay. Rhode Island became a colony of religious toleration, and William Penn established Pennsylvania as a refuge for Quakers. Roman Catholics settled in Maryland from 1634.

A more pluralistic pattern emerged in the eighteenth century with the immigration of new groups, such as the Baptists, Methodists, Presbyterians, Lutherans and the Dutch Reformed. The First Great Awakening (*c.* 1726-70) was an evangelical revival that swept across the colonies, begun by the Dutch Reformed Church and taken up by the Presbyterians and Congregationalists. After the Independence of the USA in 1776, the state churches of the Church of England in the South, and Congregationalism in the North, were disestablished, and all the American churches became free and voluntary bodies.

Issues of social reform came to the fore after 1800, and denominations such as the Presbyterians, Methodists and Baptists became more politically active.

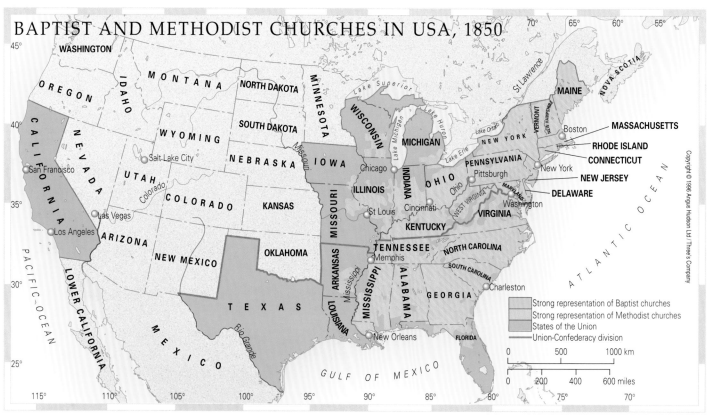

BAPTIST AND METHODIST CHURCHES IN USA, 1850

Strong representation of Baptist churches
Strong representation of Methodist churches
States of the Union
Union-Confederacy division

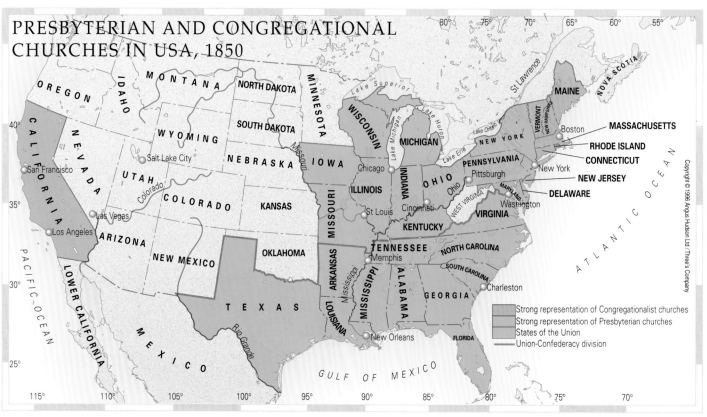

PRESBYTERIAN AND CONGREGATIONAL CHURCHES IN USA, 1850

Strong representation of Congregationalist churches
Strong representation of Presbyterian churches
States of the Union
Union-Confederacy division

MISSIONS TO CHINA

In 1865, James Hudson Taylor set up what became the largest mission in the world, the China Inland Mission. Thousands of volunteer missionaries offered their service, and by 1882 missionaries were resident in all but three of the provinces.

The Roman Catholics had continued to operate even in times of persecution. With official toleration concluded in the Convention of 1860 between China and France, Catholicism was able to expand faster than Protestantism. There were rapid advances after the setback of the Boxer rebellion in 1900, with the greatest growth in the Hubei and Guang-Dong provinces.

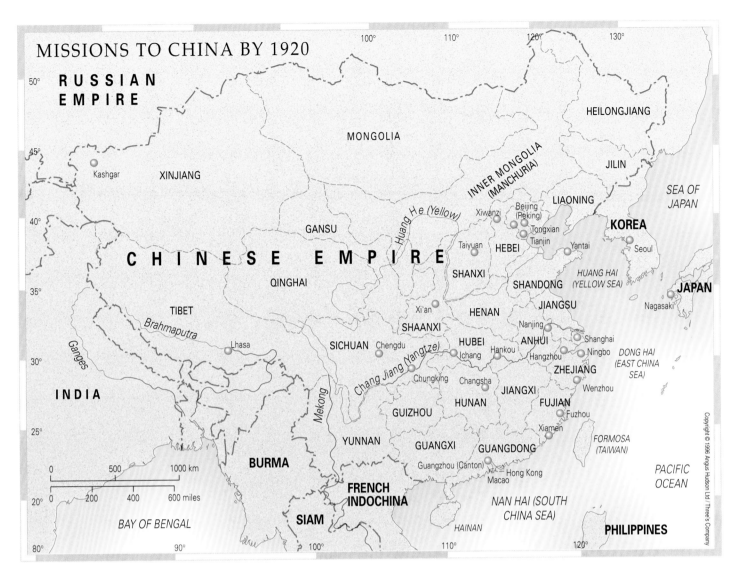

MISSIONS TO CHINA BY 1920

RUSSIAN EMPIRE

50°

Kashgar

XINJIANG

MONGOLIA

HEILONGJIANG

JILIN

45°

INNER MONGOLIA (MANCHURIA)

Xiwanzi

Beijing (Peking)

LIAONING

Huang He (Yellow)

Tongxian

Tianjin

40°

GANSU

Taiyuan

HEBEI

Yantai

Seoul

KOREA

SEA OF JAPAN

CHINESE EMPIRE

QINGHAI

SHANXI

SHANDONG

HUANG HAI (YELLOW SEA)

JAPAN

Nagasaki

35°

TIBET

Brahmaputra

Xi'an

HENAN

JIANGSU

Nanjing

Shanghai

Lhasa

SICHUAN

Chengdu

SHAANXI

HUBEI

Ichang

Hankou

Hangzhou

ANHUI

Ningbo

DONG HAI (EAST CHINA SEA)

30°

Ganges

Mekong

Chang Jiang (Yangtze)

Chungking

Changsha

ZHEJIANG

Wenzhou

INDIA

HUNAN

JIANGXI

FUJIAN

25°

GUIZHOU

Fuzhou

YUNNAN

GUANGXI

GUANGDONG

Xiamen

FORMOSA (TAIWAN)

PACIFIC OCEAN

BURMA

Guangzhou (Canton)

Hong Kong

Macao

FRENCH INDOCHINA

NAN HAI (SOUTH CHINA SEA)

20°

SIAM

BAY OF BENGAL

HAINAN

PHILIPPINES

0 500 1000 km

0 200 400 600 miles

Copyright © 1996 Angus Hudson Ltd / Three's Company

PROTESTANT MISSIONS

Shanghai	Hudson Taylor, founder of China Inland Mission, lands 1854
Yantai	Timothy Richard of Baptist Missionary Society (English) lands 1870
Mecao	Baptist missionaries (US) arrive 1835
Canton, Ningbo, Shanghai	Presbyterians (US)
Canton, Hong Kong, Xiamen, Shanghai	London Missionary Society by 1856
Canton, Fuzhou, Shanghai, Xiamen	American Board of Commissioners for Foreign Missions mission stations by 1857
Ningbo	Base of China Inland Mission 1865
Guangdong	Basel Mission, Rhenish Missionary Society expand from Hong Kong, 1895
Tianjin	Methodist New Missionary Society and evangelizes north
Yantai	Society for the Propagation of the Gospel in Foreign Parts from 1874
Ningbo, Wenzhou	English Methodist Free Church Mission 1864 (Ningbo), 1878 (Wenzhou)
Hangzhou	Mission of Presbyterian church (US), 1867
Yingkou, Mukden	Irish and Scottish Presbyterian missions, 1870s
Ichang	Church of Scotland mission, 1878
Taiwan	Canadian Presyterians, 1871
Sichuan	English Quakers, 1884
Nanjing	Ohio Yearly Meeting of Friends, 1887
Nanjing	Disciples of Christ, 1880s
Chengdu	Canadian Methodists, 1894
Fuzhou	Christian Endeavour movement (US), 1895
Guangzhou	United Brethren in Christ (US), 1889
Shandong, Jiangxi	Christian Brethren, 1895
Guangzhou	American Swedish Free Mission Society, 1888
Shanxi, Shaanxi, Henan	Swedish Mission in China, 1895
Valley of Han	Norwegian Lutheran China Mission Association
Wuchang, Ichang, Kashgar	Swedish Missionary Society, 1890s

ROMAN CATHOLIC MISSIONS

Chang Jiang lower reaches	Jesuits develop missions in 1850s
Hsien Hsien in Hebei	Northern centre of Jesuits from 1854
Xiwanzi	Lazarists found retreats in 1830s, Scheutveld Fathers (Belgian) establish HQ in 1866
Hong Kong	Seminary of Foreign Missions of Milan arrive in 1858
Southern Shandong	Society of the Divine Word 1882
Fujian, Taiwan	Dominicans dominant RC order
Chekiang, Kiangsi	Lazarists main missionary order in 1944
Guangdong, Guangxi, Guizhou, Yunnan, Sichuan, Manchuria, Tibet, Korea	Paris Societé des Missions Etrangéres main mission in 1914
Shandong, Shanxi, Shaanxi, Hubei, Henan	Franciscans dominant RC order
Most widespread women's mission	Franciscan Missionaries of Mary

TABLE OF ESTIMATED NUMBER OF CHRISTIANS IN CHINA (Western and Chinese)

[Statistics taken from Latourette]

Protestant:	1853 :	350
	1865 :	2,000
	1876 :	13,035
	1886 :	28,000
	1893 :	55,093
Roman Catholic:	1844 :	240,000
	1870 :	383,000
	1901 :	720,540
	1912 :	1,431,258

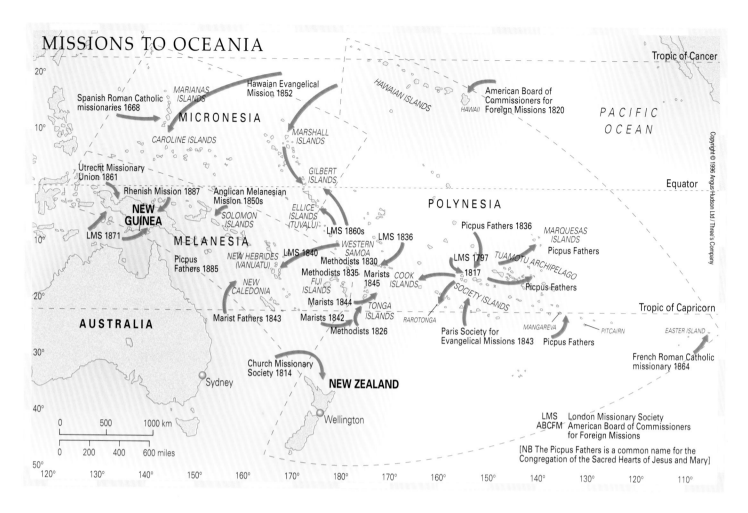

MISSIONS TO OCEANIA

The progression of missionary activity in the South Seas was generally from east to west. Favourable early reports of Tahiti meant that missionaries went there first, progressing eventually to the more hostile Melanesian Islands in the west. After the Society Islands, first encountered by the London Missionary Society (LMS), came the western islands of Polynesia – Tonga, Western Samoa and Fiji – first evangelized by the Methodists.

Spanish Roman Catholics had crossed from the Philippines to western Micronesia in the seventeenth century and converted the Marianas Islands, but no further Catholic evangelization occurred until late in the nineteenth century.

The main Catholic missionary bodies were French: in Melanesia, the Congregation of the Sacred Hearts of Jesus and Mary, known as the Picpus Fathers; and in Polynesia, the Marist Fathers. On many islands their arrival caused tension and sometimes conflict with the Protestant converts. In New Guinea, the island was divided by agreement into mission fields to avoid such confrontation.

French Catholics established themselves in New Caledonia and southern New Guinea, and also in the far eastern islands: Tahiti, the Marquesas Islands, Mangareva and Easter Island.

After the American Board converted the Hawaians, a huge enterprise crossing the Pacific was undertaken in 1852 to the Marshall Islands, and the Caroline and Gilbert Islands.

MISSIONS TO ASIA

William Carey of the Baptist Missionary Society led the way to evangelizing north India in 1793, when he landed at Calcutta. A major Christian centre was set up at nearby Serampore, from where missions spread along the Ganges Valley. By 1855, the Church Missionary Society had reached Peshawar. Large numbers of missions from Europe and North America landed in south India during the first half of the nineteenth century, where they encountered the Catholic Church founded by Francis Xavier and the Malabar Christian communities of Travancore, believed to date from about the sixth century.

The Cross tended to follow the flag. Where the European powers colonized, the missionary societies preached. The Netherlands Missionary Society was active in the Dutch East Indies. In China, the earliest missionary of this period was the Scot Robert Morrison, who arrived in Canton in 1807. However, China did not 'open' itself to the foreigner in any practical sense until the signing of the Treaty of Nanking in 1842, after the Opium Wars.

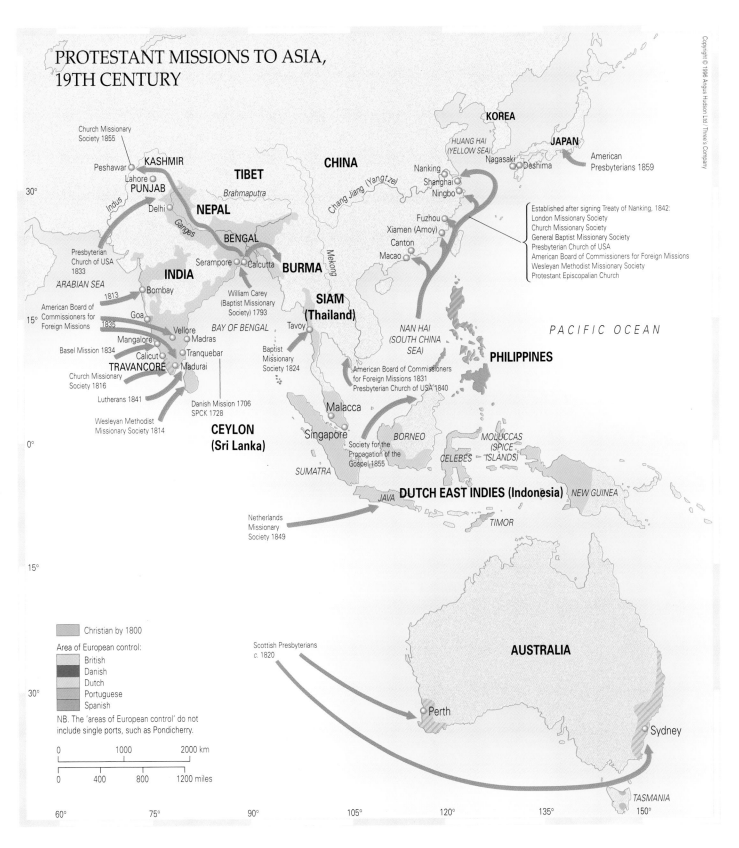

PROTESTANT MISSIONS TO ASIA, 19TH CENTURY

Church Missionary Society 1855

Peshawar

KASHMIR

CHINA

KOREA

HUANG HAI (YELLOW SEA)

JAPAN

Nagasaki
Deshima

American Presbyterians 1859

Lahore
PUNJAB

TIBET

30°

Delhi

Brahmaputra

NEPAL

Indus

Ganges

BENGAL

Nanking
Shanghai
Ningbo

Presbyterian Church of USA 1833

Serampore
Calcutta

BURMA

Fuzhou
Xiamen (Amoy)
Canton
Macao

Established after signing Treaty of Nanking, 1842:
London Missionary Society
Church Missionary Society
General Baptist Missionary Society
Presbyterian Church of USA
American Board of Commissioners for Foreign Missions
Wesleyan Methodist Missionary Society
Protestant Episcopalian Church

INDIA

ARABIAN SEA

Chang Jiang (Yangtze)

Mekong

1813

Bombay

American Board of Commissioners for Foreign Missions

15°

William Carey (Baptist Missionary Society) 1793

SIAM (Thailand)

NAN HAI (SOUTH CHINA SEA)

PACIFIC OCEAN

1835

Goa

BAY OF BENGAL

Tavoy

PHILIPPINES

Vellore
Madras

Mangalore

Basel Mission 1834

Calicut
Tranquebar

Baptist Missionary Society 1824

American Board of Commissioners for Foreign Missions 1831
Presbyterian Church of USA 1840

TRAVANCORE

Madurai

Church Missionary Society 1816

Danish Mission 1706
SPCK 1728

Lutherans 1841

0°

Wesleyan Methodist Missionary Society 1814

CEYLON (Sri Lanka)

Malacca

Singapore

BORNEO

MOLUCCAS (SPICE ISLANDS)

Society for the Propagation of the Gospel 1855

CELEBES

SUMATRA

DUTCH EAST INDIES (Indonesia) *NEW GUINEA*

JAVA

Netherlands Missionary Society 1849

TIMOR

15°

Christian by 1800

Area of European control:
British
Danish
Dutch
Portuguese
Spanish

NB. The 'areas of European control' do not include single ports, such as Pondicherry.

Scottish Presbyterians *c.* 1820

AUSTRALIA

0   1000   2000 km

0   400   800   1200 miles

30°

Perth

Sydney

60°   75°   90°   105°   120°   135°   150°

TASMANIA

Five 'treaty ports' – Canton, Xiamen (Amoy), Fuzhou, Ningbo and Shanghai – were designated cities for foreign settlement. British and American missions made inroads into China from there.

Japan remained hostile to the Westerner until the 1870s, and South Korea only received its first missionary in 1865. The Philippines had been colonized by the Spanish in the seventeenth century and most Filipinos had become Roman Catholic.

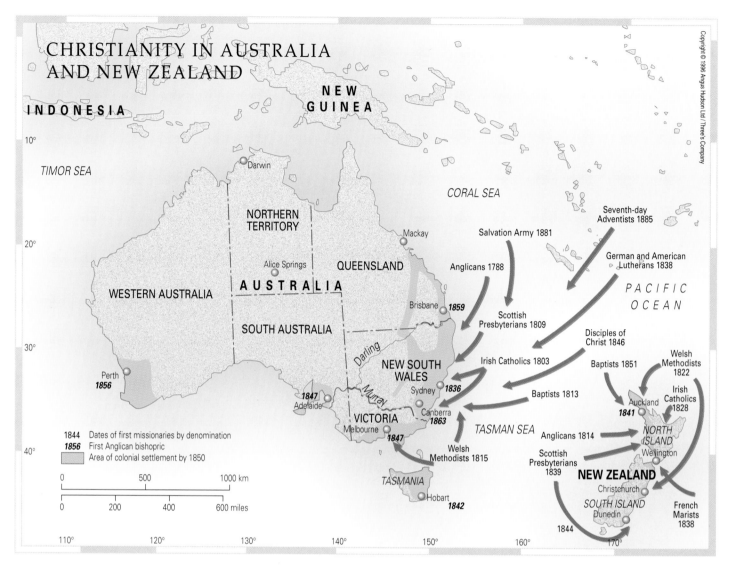

CHRISTIANITY IN AUSTRALIA AND NEW ZEALAND

INDONESIA

NEW GUINEA

TIMOR SEA

10°

Darwin

CORAL SEA

Seventh-day
Adventists 1885

20°

NORTHERN
TERRITORY

Mackay

Salvation Army 1881

German and American
Lutherans 1838

Anglicans 1788

Alice Springs

QUEENSLAND

AUSTRALIA

*PACIFIC
OCEAN*

WESTERN AUSTRALIA

Brisbane *1859*

Scottish
Presbyterians 1809

Disciples of
Christ 1846

30°

SOUTH AUSTRALIA

Darling

Perth
1856

Irish Catholics 1803

Baptists 1851

Welsh
Methodists
1822

NEW SOUTH
WALES

Irish
Catholics
1828

Murray

Sydney *1836*

Baptists 1813

Auckland
1841

1847
Adelaide

Canberra
1863

TASMAN SEA

NORTH
ISLAND

1844 Dates of first missionaries by denomination
1856 First Anglican bishopric
Area of colonial settlement by 1850

VICTORIA
Melbourne
1847

Welsh
Methodists 1815

Anglicans 1814

Scottish
Presbyterians
1839

Wellington

NEW ZEALAND

40°

0   500   1000 km

Christchurch

0   200   400   600 miles

TASMANIA

SOUTH ISLAND
Dunedin

French
Marists
1838

Hobart
1842

1844

110°   120°   130°   140°   150°   160°   170°

CHRISTIANITY IN AUSTRALIA AND NEW ZEALAND

James Cook charted the coasts of Australia and New Zealand in 1770. A Church of England chaplain sailed with the first convict ship for Australia in 1788. Wesleyan ministries began in 1815, and Presbyterians in 1823. The Church of England received special government grants of land to build churches and schools in New South Wales, though after 1836 grants were undenominational. By 1820, Roman Catholic priests were serving the predominantly Irish Catholic population.

The first European settlements in New Zealand were made in 1805, and the first missionaries arrived in 1814. Anglicans form the majority of the population, with large minorities of Scottish Presbyterians, Roman Catholics and Methodists.

MISSIONS TO AFRICA

Very little remained of the early Roman Catholic missions to Africa. The first wave of missionary activity to make deep inroads was in the 1830s and 1840s, especially in West Africa. Christianity was seen by many West African tribal rulers as a means to prosperity through trade with European countries. Missionaries set up stations and schools. Islam held sway over northern Africa. The ancient churches of the Copts in Egypt and the Ethiopian Church were exceptions.

The earliest missions to southern Africa in this period were naturally launched from the Cape of Good Hope, where there had long been European settlement. David Livingstone blazed trails from here which many other missions would follow. Roman Catholic missions were as active as Protestant ones in this period, especially the Holy Ghost Fathers (1848) and the White Fathers (1868).

Inter-denominational rivalry over mission fields intensified at the time of the European 'Scramble' for Africa, after 1880.

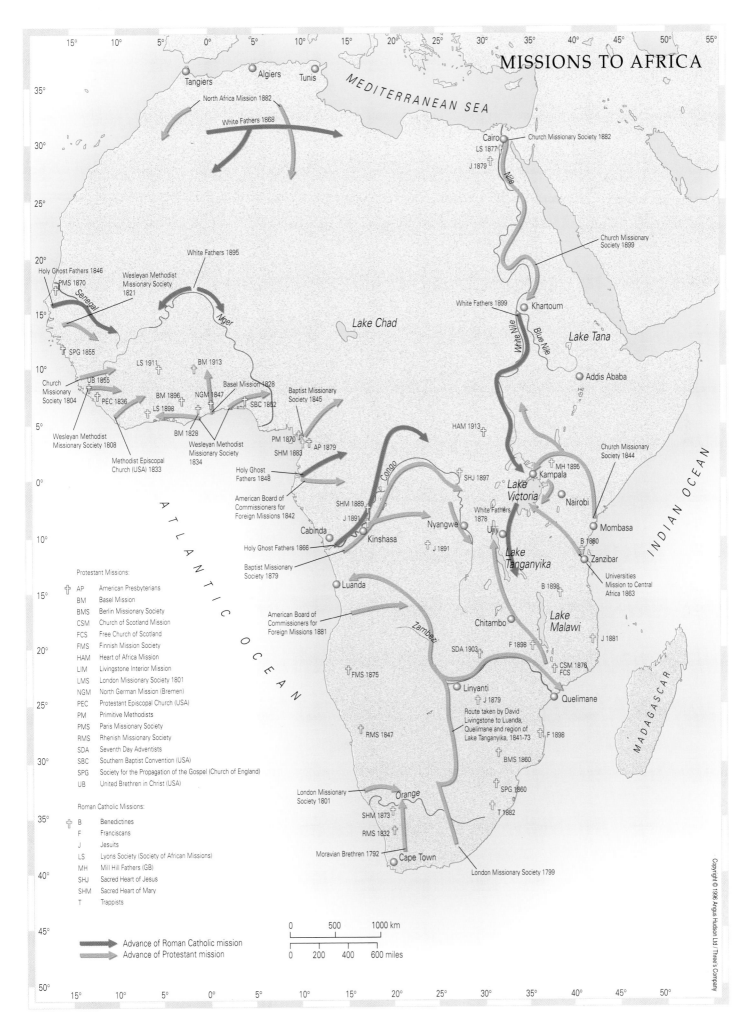

MISSIONS TO AFRICA

MEDITERRANEAN SEA

Tangiers
Algiers
Tunis

North Africa Mission 1882
White Fathers 1868

Cairo
Church Missionary Society 1882
LS 1877
J 1879

Church Missionary
Society 1899

White Fathers 1895

Holy Ghost Fathers 1846
PMS 1870
Wesleyan Methodist
Missionary Society
1821

White Fathers 1899
Khartoum

Senegal

Lake Chad
Lake Tana

SPG 1855
Niger

LS 1911
BM 1913
Addis Ababa

Church
Missionary
Society 1804
UB 1855
BM 1896
NGM 1847
Basel Mission 1828
Baptist Missionary
Society 1845

PEC 1836
LS 1898
SBC 1852
HAM 1913
Church Missionary
Society 1844

Wesleyan Methodist
Missionary Society 1808
BM 1828
Wesleyan Methodist
Missionary Society
1834
PM 1870
SHM 1883
AP 1879
SHJ 1897

White Fathers
1878
MH 1895
Kampala
Church Missionary
Society 1844

Methodist Episcopal
Church (USA) 1833
Holy Ghost
Fathers 1848
Lake
Victoria
Nairobi

American Board of
Commissioners for
Foreign Missions 1842
SHM 1889
Congo
Nyangwe
Ujiji
Mombasa

Cabinda
J 1891
Kinshasa
J 1891
B 1880
Zanzibar

Holy Ghost Fathers 1866
Lake
Tanganyika
Universities
Mission to Central
Africa 1863

Baptist Missionary
Society 1879
Luanda
B 1898
Lake
Malawi

American Board of
Commissioners for
Foreign Missions 1881
Zambezi
Chitambo
SDA 1903
F 1898
J 1881

FMS 1875
CSM 1876
FCS

Linyanti
J 1879
Quelimane

Route taken by David
Livingstone to Luanda,
Quelimane and region of
Lake Tanganyika, 1841-73
F 1898

RMS 1847
BMS 1860

Orange
SPG 1860

London Missionary
Society 1801
SHM 1873
T 1882

RMS 1832

Moravian Brethren 1792
Cape Town

London Missionary Society 1799

ATLANTIC OCEAN

INDIAN OCEAN

MADAGASCAR

Protestant Missions:

AP	American Presbyterians
BM	Basel Mission
BMS	Berlin Missionary Society
CSM	Church of Scotland Mission
FCS	Free Church of Scotland
FMS	Finnish Mission Society
HAM	Heart of Africa Mission
LIM	Livingstone Interior Mission
LMS	London Missionary Society 1801
NGM	North German Mission (Bremen)
PEC	Protestant Episcopal Church (USA)
PM	Primitive Methodists
PMS	Paris Missionary Society
RMS	Rhenish Missionary Society
SDA	Seventh Day Adventists
SBC	Southern Baptist Convention (USA)
SPG	Society for the Propagation of the Gospel (Church of England)
UB	United Brethren in Christ (USA)

Roman Catholic Missions:

B	Benedictines
F	Franciscans
J	Jesuits
LS	Lyons Society (Society of African Missions)
MH	Mill Hill Fathers (GB)
SHJ	Sacred Heart of Jesus
SHM	Sacred Heart of Mary
T	Trappists

0   500   1000 km
0 200 400 600 miles

→ Advance of Roman Catholic mission
→ Advance of Protestant mission

THE JEWISH DIASPORA FROM THE 6TH CENTURY BCE TO THE 20TH CENTURY

1	BELGIUM	300
2	NETHERLANDS	120
3	GERMANY	600
4	POLAND	800
5	CZECHOSLOVAKIA	900
6	SWITZERLAND	800
7	AUSTRIA	900
8	HUNGARY	100
9	ITALY	150
10	SLOVENIA	100
11	CROATIA	100
12	BOSNIA	100
13	YUGOSLAVIA	100
14	ROMANIA	165
15	BULGARIA	100
16	MACEDONIA	100
17	GREECE	100
18	GEORGIA	c. 1
19	AZERBAIJAN	c. 1
20	ARMENIA	c. 1

1898 Date of first known permanent settlement

Periods of settlement:
Exile – 500 CE
500 – 1000
1000 – 1500
1500 – 1900
After 1900

THE JEWISH DIASPORA

In the period of the biblical Exile (after the fall of Jerusalem in 587 BCE), Jews were to be found in many cities of the Ancient Near East. Up to the beginning of the Christian Era, Jewish Greek traders were moving around the Mediterranean and Black Sea areas, settling as merchants and farmers in what we know as Georgia, southern Ukraine and Russia. Jews of the Parthian Empire settled in Armenia and Azerbaijan. Jewish communities also flourished throughout the Carthaginian Empire in North Africa. By 1 CE Jews were beginning to spread to the Latin-speaking West of the Roman Empire. Alexandria was the centre of Greco-Jewish culture at this time.

Jewish settlement was widespread in Western Europe between 800 and 1200. Persecutions and expulsions forced migrations to Central and Eastern Europe after 1290. Sephardic Jews were finally expelled from Spain in 1492. They fled Europe for the newly discovered Americas. The Inquisition threatened the existence of many Jewish communities, and by 1640 the only safe refuges were those under Dutch rule. Under legal emancipation, Jewish culture was able to flourish in the Netherlands from the seventeenth century onwards.

The Chmielnicki massacres (1648-51) in Poland/Lithuania sent many Jews back westwards and southwards. However, a strong Jewish culture remained in central Europe until the Nazi holocaust.

Over-population and social tension in Europe led to the Great Migration to the Americas from 1881 to 1914. Over 2 million crossed the Atlantic, 85 per cent of them settling in the USA. Many more had emigrated from Europe by the outbreak of World War II.

Since the creation of the State of Israel in 1948, Jews from many parts of the world, and especially from Russia, have emigrated to Israel. Jews came from the Displaced Persons camps in Europe, detention camps in Cyprus, eastern Europe and northern Africa; and the entire Jewish populations of Yemen and Iraq migrated. The Jewish population of Israel increased from 650,000 in 1948 to 4,448,000 in 1995.

Tensions continued between Israel and the Arab nations, especially after

ISRAEL IN 1994

Israeli occupied in 1994; political status to be determined

JAPAN 1889

AUSTRALIA 1817

NEW ZEALAND 1840

LEBANON

Damascus

SYRIA

GOLAN HEIGHTS

Sea of Galilee

Haifa

Nazareth

MEDITERRANEAN SEA

Nablus

Jordan

Tel Aviv

WEST BANK

Jericho

Amman

Jerusalem

Palestinian autonomy created in May 1994

Gaza

Hebron

Dead Sea

GAZA STRIP

ISRAEL

JORDAN

Suez Canal

SINAI

GULF OF SUEZ

GULF OF AQABA

SAUDI ARABIA

EGYPT

Israeli conquests in 1967
Egyptian reoccupation in 1973
Israeli conquests in 1973
Israeli in 1994

| 0 | 50 | 100 km |

| 0 | 20 | 40 | 60 miles |

RED SEA

Copyright © 1996 Angus Hudson Ltd / Three's Company

the Sinai Campaign of 1956. The Six-Day War of 1967 between Israel and Egypt resulted in large territorial gains for Israel: the Sinai Peninsula, the Gaza Strip, eastern Palestine and the Golan Heights. Egypt and Syria attempted to recover lands in the Yom Kippur War of 1973, but without success.

The Camp David Accords of 1978 between Israel and Egypt, under the aegis of the USA, resulted in peace and the return to Egypt of the Sinai Peninsula. It was also agreed in principle that the Palestinians of the West Bank and Gaza Strip should be granted self-government. Only in May of 1994 did the Palestinians of the Gaza Strip, and the cities of Hebron and Jericho, achieve autonomy.

THE RISE OF PENTECOSTALISM

Country with significant Pentecostal minority,
with date of first Pentecostal church.

- pre-1900
- 1900-1919
- 1920-1939
- 1940-

0	2000	4000 km

0	800	1600	2400 miles

THE RISE OF PENTECOSTALISM

The modern Pentecostal movement is often reckoned to have begun in 1901 in Topeka, Kansas, USA, under the leadership of a former Methodist minister. Most early Pentecostals were active in the Methodist Church. They believed in the holiness of Christian life after conversion, maintaining that Christians should experience the same signs of spiritual power as did the Apostles on the Day of Pentecost.

The first Pentecostal denominations were in the southern USA: the Pentecostal Holiness Church, the Church of God and the predominantly black Church of God in Christ. In 1914 the Assemblies of God formed, and soon became the largest Pentecostal group in the USA.

The Pentecostal movement spread rapidly worldwide, being established in Europe and South America by 1920. It is the fastest growing Christian movement, both within its own specific Pentecostal churches and within the traditional denominations. In Roman Catholicism it is better known as 'Charismatic Renewal'. It is particularly popular in the Third World, notably in Latin America and among the African Independent churches.

SWEDEN

FINLAND

ROMANIA

ITALY

CENTRAL
AFRICAN
REPUBLIC

KENYA

WANDA

URUNDI

TANZANIA

MOZAMBIQUE

SOUTH
KOREA

PHILIPPINES

PACIFIC OCEAN

INDIAN
OCEAN

INDONESIA

PAPUA
NEW
GUINEA

30° 45° 60° 75° 90° 105° 120° 135° 150° 165° 180°

WORLDWIDE GROWTH RATE OF CHRISTIANITY *c.* 1995

GREENLAND

ICELAND

NORW

UNITED
KINGDOM

DENMARK

AUST

NETHERLANDS

IRELAND   BELGIUM

LUXEMBOURG

GERMANY   FRANC

SWITZERLAND

PORTUGAL   SPAIN   AND

ITA

MOROCCO   TUNISIA

ALGERIA

WESTERN
SAHARA

MAURITANIA

MALI

SENEGAL

GAMBIA   BURKINA
FASO

GUINEA-BISSAU   GUINEA

SIERRA LEONE   IVORY   GHANA
COAST   TOGO
BENIN
LIBERIA

CAMEROON

EQUATORIAL
GUINEA

GABON

ANGOLA

NAMIBIA

CANADA

U S A

MEXICO

CUBA   DOMINICAN
REPUBLIC

JAMAICA   PUERTO
RICO
BELIZE   HAITI
HONDURAS
GUATEMALA

EL SALVADOR   NICARAGUA

COSTA RICA   TRINIDAD &
TOBAGO

PANAMA   VENEZUELA   GUYANA   SURINAM
FRENCH GUIANA

COLOMBIA

ECUADOR

B R A Z I L

PERU

BOLIVIA

CHILE   PARAGUAY

A
R
G
E
N
T
I
N
A   URUGUAY

A T L A N T I C

O C E A N

P
A
C
I
F
I
C

O
C
E
A
N

Percentage annual Church growth, *c.* 1990

Very rapid (over 5%)
Rapid (3-5%)
Moderate (1-3%)
Little or nil (0-1%)
Decline (less than 0%)

0   2000   4000 km

0   800   1600   2400 miles

75°

60°

45°

30°

15°

0°

15°

30°

45°

60°

150°   135°   120°   105°   90°   75°   60°   45°   30°   15°   0°

SWEDEN

FINLAND

ESTONIA
LATVIA
LITHUANIA
RUSSIA

BELORUS
CZECH
REP.
»LAND
OVAKIA
UKRAINE
MOLDOVA
HUNGARY
ROMANIA
YUGOSLAVIA
BULGARIA
MACEDONIA
ALBANIA
GREECE
CROATIA
.OVENIA
CYPRUS
LEBANON
ISRAEL
JORDAN

GEORGIA
AZERBAIJAN
ARMENIA

TURKEY

SYRIA
IRAQ
KUWAIT
QATAR

R U S S I A

KAZAKHSTAN

UZBEKISTAN
TURKMENISTAN
TAJIKISTAN

KYRGYZSTAN

MONGOLIA

C H I N A

NORTH
KOREA

SOUTH
KOREA

JAPAN

I R A N

AFGHANISTAN

PAKISTAN

NEPAL

BHUTAN

BURMA
(MYANMAR)

TAIWAN
HONG KONG

.YA
EGYPT

SAUDI
ARABIA

ERITREA

UNITED
ARAB
EMIRATES

OMAN

YEMEN

I N D I A

BANGLADESH

LAOS

THAILAND VIETNAM

PHILIPPINES

CHAD

SUDAN

CENTRAL
AFRICAN
REPUBLIC

ETHIOPIA

SOMALIA

SRI
LANKA

CAMBODIA

MALAYSIA

BRUNEI

P A C I F I C   O C E A N

CONGO
UGANDA
KENYA
ZAIRE
RWANDA
BURUNDI
TANZANIA
MALAWI

I N D I A N

O C E A N

SINGAPORE

I N D O N E S I A

PAPUA
NEW
GUINEA

SOLOMON
ISLANDS

ZAMBIA

ZIMBABWE
BOTSWANA
SOUTH AFRICA
SWAZILAND
LESOTHO

MOZAMBIQUE

MADAGASCAR

VANUATU

FIJI

NEW CALEDONIA

AUSTRALIA

NEW
ZEALAND

30°   45°   60°   75°   90°   105°   120°   135°   150°   165°   180°

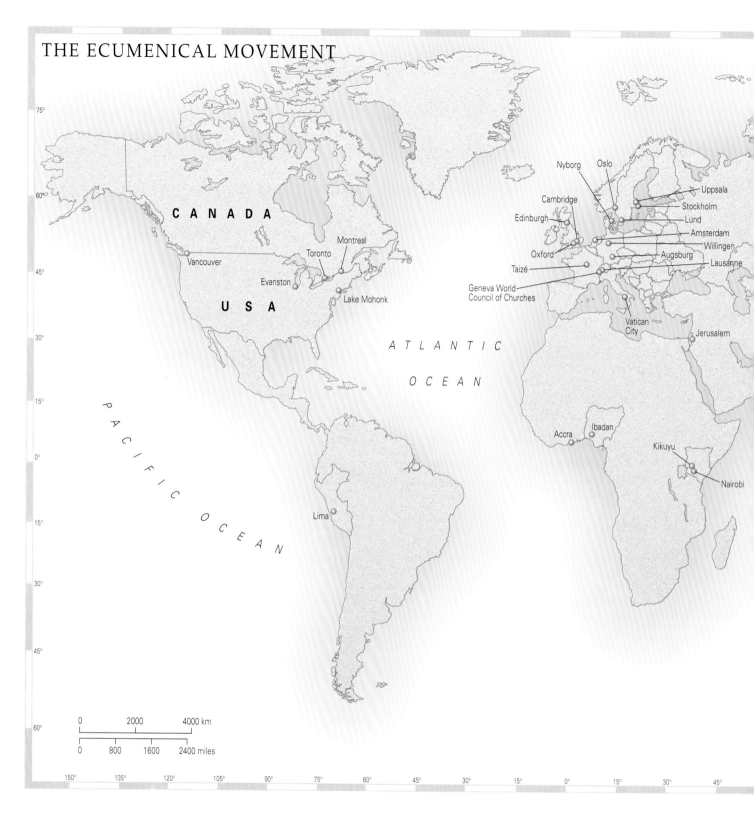

THE ECUMENICAL MOVEMENT

The ecumenical movement grew mainly out of Western Protestantism, for example among the Student Christian Movement and the YMCA, with the aim of promoting closer co-operation and understanding between the different branches of Protestantism. The World Missionary Conference of 1910 held at Edinburgh started the movement in earnest. By 1937 the Eastern Orthodox Church took an active part, as did churches of Africa and Asia. In 1948 the World Council of Churches was formed to lead the ecumenical movement, though without involvement from the Roman Catholics. At the Second Vatican Council (1962-65) the Roman Catholic standpoint shifted somewhat. Other communions became 'separated brethren' rather than being seen as outside the Church.

In some parts of the world successful unifications have been made. One notable example is South India in 1947, where Episcopal, Presbyterian and Congregational churches united. Sometimes denominational differences based on historical circumstances have ceased to be relevant today. In North

RUSSIA

New Delhi

PACIFIC OCEAN

INDIAN OCEAN

75° 90° 105° 120° 135° 150° 165° 180°

Cambridge 1893: Founding of Student Christian Movement (SCM) as the Inter-University Christian Union

Edinburgh 1910: World Conference of Protestant Missionaries

1913: Kikuyu conference, Kenya; federation of Anglican, Presbyterian and other Protestant churches proposed

Lake Mohonk 1921: Formation of International Missionary Council (NY, USA)

Oxford 1923: Second Conference of International Missionary Council

Oxford 1923: Second Meeting of International Missionary Council

Stockholm 1925: Universal Christian Conference on Life and Work, relating Christian faith to society, politics and economics

1925: Formation of United Church of Canada (union of Methodists, Presbyterians and Congregationalists)

Lausanne 1927: World Conference on Faith and Order, founding the Faith and Order Movement

Jerusalem 1928: Third Conference of International Missionary Council

Edinburgh 1937: Second World Conference on Faith and Order

Oxford 1937: Second World Christian Conference on Life and Work

Tambaram 1938: Fourth Conference of International Missionary Council

Amsterdam 1939: First World Conference of Christian Youth

1940: Foundation of Taizé (an ecumenical religious community) by Roger Schutz

1947: Foundation of the church of South India (union of Anglican, Methodist, Presbyterian, Congregationalist and Dutch Reformed churches)

Toronto 1947: Fifth meeting of International Missionary Council

Oslo 1947: Second World Conference of Christian Youth

Amsterdam 1948: Foundation of World Council of Churches, union of 'Life and Work' and Faith and Order movements

1948: Formation of National Council of Churches, (USA)

Travancore 1952: Third World Conference of Christian Youth, (India)

Willingen 1952: Sixth Meeting of International Missionary Council, (Germany)

Lund 1952: Third World Conference on Faith and Order, (Sweden)

Evanston 1954: Second Assembly of World Council of Churches, (USA)

Accra 1958: Final Assembly of International Missionary Council, (Ghana)

Ibadan 1958: First All African Christian Conference, (Nigeria)

Nyborg 1959: First Assembly of Conference of European Churches, (Denmark)

New Delhi 1961: Third Assembly of World Council of Churches; integration of International Missionary Council within WCC

1961: Russian Orthodox Church joins WCC

Montreal 1963: Fourth World Conference on Faith and Order

Vatican City 1965: Second Vatican Council Decree withdraws mutual excommunications of 1054 between Eastern and Western Churches

Geneva 1966: World conference on Church and Society

Uppsala 1968: Fourth Assembly of World Council of Churches

1970: Foundation of Church of North India (union of Anglicans, Congregationalists, Presbyterians, some Methodists, Baptists and Disciples of Christ)

1970: Foundation of Church of Pakistan (union of Anglicans, Methodists, Presbyterians and Lutherans)

Augsburg 1971: First Ecumenical Pentecost Meeting for Protestants and Catholics (Germany)

Lima 1971: Third Assembly of World Council of Christian Education

Nairobi 1975: Fifth Assembly of World Council of Churches

Vancouver 1983: Sixth Assembly of World Council of Churches

Canberra 1991: Seventh Assembly of World Council of Churches

America, non-denominational churches have been set up, and co-operative church ventures aimed at counselling in society, such as in prisons and hospitals, can break down denominational barriers.

The Student Christian Movement was founded in Cambridge.

BIBLE SOCIETIES WORLDWIDE

CANADA
1805, 1904

USA
1808, 1816

MEXICO
1878, 1963

CUBA *1820*

DOMINICAN *1807*, 1968
REPUBLIC

JAMAICA
1834, 1969

PUERTO *1807*
RICO

HAITI
1807

GUATEMALA
1988

HONDURAS *1807*

BARBADOS *1979*

NICARAGUA
1807, 1974

EL SALVADOR
1807

COSTA RICA
1967

1958, 1969
VENEZUELA

SURINAM *1907*

PANAMA
1807, 1974

COLOMBIA
1834, 1966

ECUADOR
1964

B R A Z I L
1862, 1948

PERU

1821, 1969

BOLIVIA
1905, 1966

1947, 1969

PARAGUAY

CHILE
1864, 1969

URUGUAY
1958

A R G E N T I N A

1825, 1963

A T L A N T I C

O C E A N

P A C I F I C   O C E A N

NORWAY
1816, 1816

ICELAND
1815, 1915

SCOTLAND
1805, 1861

DENMAR
1814, 18

NORTHERN
IRELAND
1807, 1808

ENGLAND
AND WALES
1804, 1804

1806, 1806 **IRELAND**
1836, 1946 **BELGIUM**

Crawley

NETHER
1814,

1710, 1948 **GERMANY**
1818, 1946
1804, 1955 **SWITZERLAND**
1850, 1970**AUSTRIA**

FRAN

PORTUGAL
1868, 1966

SPAIN
1806, 1975,

MOROCCO
1993

ALGE
1832, 1

CAMEROON
1870, 1965

1807, 1966 **SIERRA LEONE**

IVORY
COAST

GHANA

BENIN

1827, 1966 **LIBERIA**

1902, 1966

1807, 1975,

1807, 1966

Miami

Dates in *italic*: Beginning of organized work
Dates in plain type: Bible Society formed or office opened

✚ United Bible Societies Regional Service Centre

● World service centre

0	2000	4000 km
0	800	1600	2400 miles

75°

60°

45°

30°

15°

0°

15°

30°

45°

60°

150° 135° 120° 105° 90° 75° 60° 45° 30° 15° 0°

SWEDEN
1804, 1815

FINLAND
1812, 1812

ESTONIA *1813*, 1991
LATVIA 1989
LITHUANIA 1992
RUSSIA 1814

LAND
6, 1946
OVAK
REP.
1949-53
CZECH *1810*, 1948-1953
REP. UKRAINE
1991
MOLDOVA 1990
HUNGARY *1811*, 1948
ROMANIA
1992
YUGOSLAVIA *1818*
BULGARIA 1993 GEORGIA
MACEDONIA *1994*
GREECE ARMENIA AZERBAIJAN
1819, 1966 *1993* *1990*
TURKEY
1812, 1966
CYPRUS *1810*, 1968
BANIA
LEBANON
1827, 1966
1816, 1966 ISRAEL

R U S S I A
1 8 1 4

KAZAKHSTAN
1993, 1994

MONGOLIA
1991

UZBEKISTAN KYRGYZSTAN
1993 *1994*
TURKMENISTAN
TAJIKISTAN
1994

NORTH
KOREA
1883, 1940
SOUTH
KOREA

JAPAN
1875, 1938

EGYPT
1818, 1966

SUDAN
1866, 1967
ERITREA
1993, 1993

CENTRAL
AFRICAN
REPUBLIC

5, 1966

CONGO

ZAIRE
378, 1954

IRAN
1814, 1967

JORDAN
1972

AFGHANISTAN

PAKISTAN
1809, 1944

NEPAL
1950, 1976

INDIA
1811, 1944

BANGLADESH
1911, 1953

C H I N A

BURMA
(MYANMAR)
1889, 1966

THAILAND
1890, 1966

VIETNAM
1892, 1966

TAIWAN
1949, 1966

HONG KONG
1869, 1949

PHILIPPINES
1899, 1963

P A C I F I C   O C E A N

ETHIOPIA
1812, 1966

1896, 1966
UGANDA
KENYA
Nairobi
1869, 1970
RWANDA
1877, 1975
BURUNDI
1967, 1975
TANZANIA
1845, 1970

SRI
LANKA
1812, 1966

CAMBODIA
1892, 1968

MALAYSIA
1815, 1985

Singapore
1815, 1966

I N D I A N

O C E A N

MALAWI *1880*, 1966

A ZAMBIA
67 *1880, 1966*
ZIMBABWE
1880, 1984
BOTSWANA
1967
SWAZILAND

MOZAMBIQUE
1880, 1966

MADAGASCAR
1872, 1965

SOUTH AFRICA

LESOTHO
1967

1820, 1965

I N D O N E S I A
1814, 1951

PAPUA
NEW
GUINEA
1881, 1975

SOLOMON
ISLANDS

1816, 1975

VANUATU
FIJI

NEW CALEDONIA

AUSTRALIA
1817, 1925

NEW
ZEALAND
1846, 1946

The British and Foreign Bible Society was founded on
7 March 1804. By its centenary in 1904 it had
distributed 181 million copies of the Scriptures
worldwide.

In 1946 the United Bible Societies was formed to
coordinate the many Bible Societies throughout the
world. By the end of 1993, at least one book of the
Bible had been translated into 2,062 languages.

30°   45°   60°   75°   90°   105°   120°   135°   150°   165°   180°

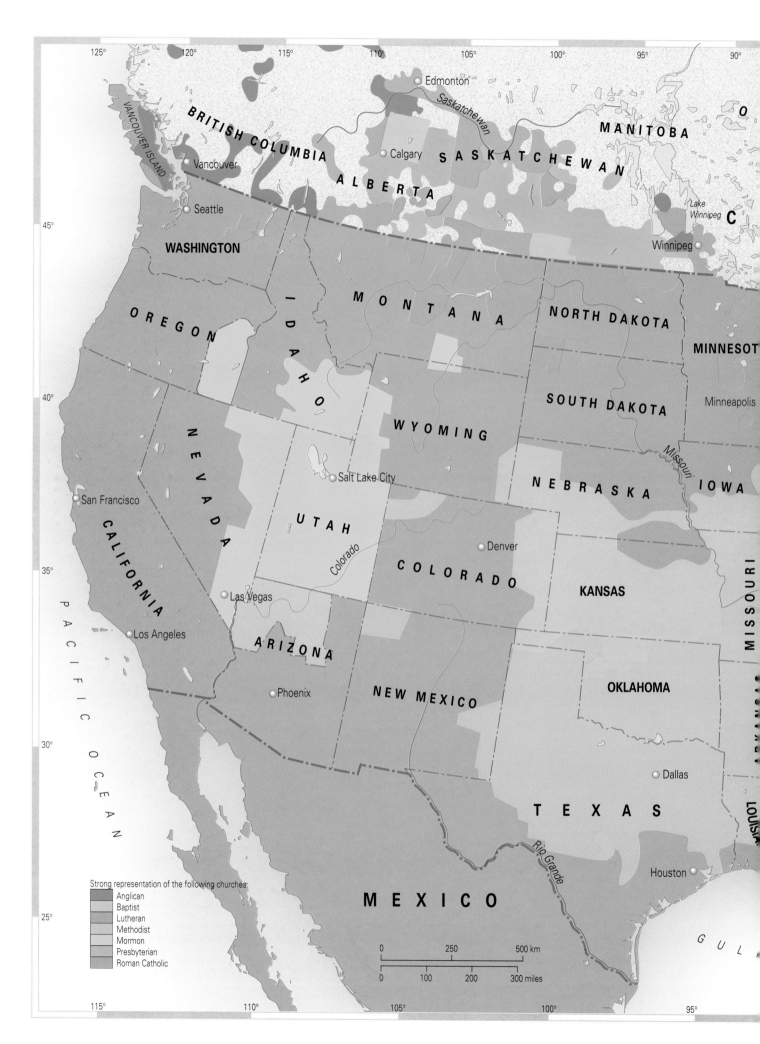

Strong representation of the following churches:

- Anglican
- Baptist
- Lutheran
- Methodist
- Mormon
- Presbyterian
- Roman Catholic

PACIFIC OCEAN

VANCOUVER ISLAND

BRITISH COLUMBIA

ALBERTA

SASKATCHEWAN

MANITOBA

Edmonton

Saskatchewan

Calgary

Lake Winnipeg

C

Winnipeg

Vancouver

Seattle

WASHINGTON

OREGON

IDAHO

MONTANA

NORTH DAKOTA

MINNESOT

SOUTH DAKOTA

Minneapolis

NEVADA

WYOMING

Salt Lake City

San Francisco

UTAH

NEBRASKA

IOWA

Missouri

Denver

Colorado

COLORADO

KANSAS

MISSOURI

Las Vegas

Los Angeles

ARIZONA

CALIFORNIA

Phoenix

NEW MEXICO

OKLAHOMA

Dallas

TEXAS

LOUISI

Rio Grande

Houston

MEXICO

GUL

0   250   500 km

0   100   200   300 miles

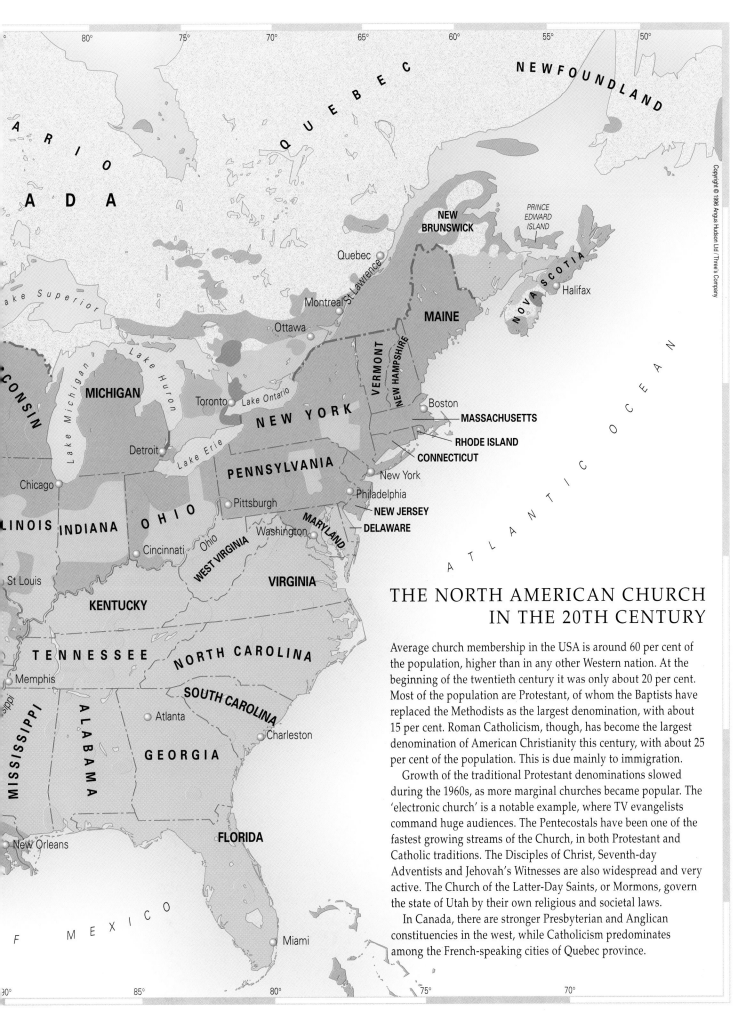

THE NORTH AMERICAN CHURCH IN THE 20TH CENTURY

Average church membership in the USA is around 60 per cent of the population, higher than in any other Western nation. At the beginning of the twentieth century it was only about 20 per cent. Most of the population are Protestant, of whom the Baptists have replaced the Methodists as the largest denomination, with about 15 per cent. Roman Catholicism, though, has become the largest denomination of American Christianity this century, with about 25 per cent of the population. This is due mainly to immigration.

Growth of the traditional Protestant denominations slowed during the 1960s, as more marginal churches became popular. The 'electronic church' is a notable example, where TV evangelists command huge audiences. The Pentecostals have been one of the fastest growing streams of the Church, in both Protestant and Catholic traditions. The Disciples of Christ, Seventh-day Adventists and Jehovah's Witnesses are also widespread and very active. The Church of the Latter-Day Saints, or Mormons, govern the state of Utah by their own religious and societal laws.

In Canada, there are stronger Presbyterian and Anglican constituencies in the west, while Catholicism predominates among the French-speaking cities of Quebec province.

AFRICAN INDEPENDENT CHURCHES

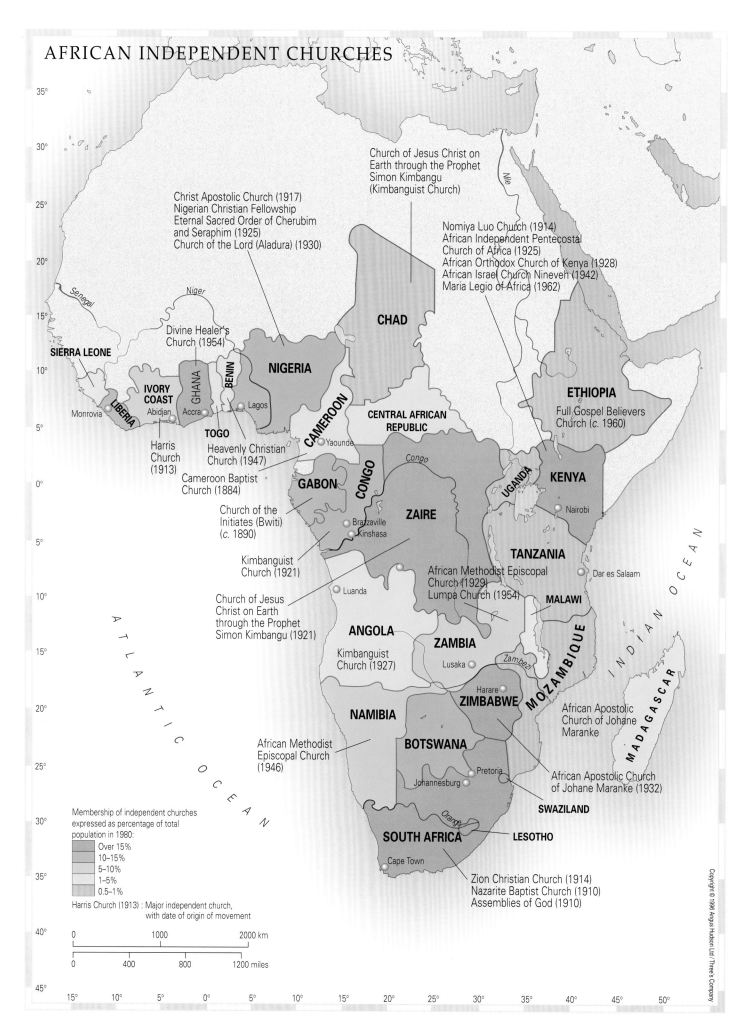

Church of Jesus Christ on Earth through the Prophet Simon Kimbangu (Kimbanguist Church)

Christ Apostolic Church (1917)
Nigerian Christian Fellowship
Eternal Sacred Order of Cherubim and Seraphim (1925)
Church of the Lord (Aladura) (1930)

Nomiya Luo Church (1914)
African Independent Pentecostal Church of Africa (1925)
African Orthodox Church of Kenya (1928)
African Israel Church Nineveh (1942)
Maria Legio of Africa (1962)

Divine Healer's Church (1954)

CHAD

SIERRA LEONE

NIGERIA

IVORY COAST

GHANA

BENIN

LIBERIA

Monrovia

Abidjan

Accra

Lagos

ETHIOPIA

Full Gospel Believers Church (c. 1960)

CAMEROON

TOGO

CENTRAL AFRICAN REPUBLIC

Harris Church (1913)

Heavenly Christian Church (1947)

Yaounde

Cameroon Baptist Church (1884)

GABON

CONGO

Congo

UGANDA

KENYA

Nairobi

Church of the Initiates (Bwiti) (c. 1890)

ZAIRE

Kimbanguist Church (1921)

Brazzaville

Kinshasa

Church of Jesus Christ on Earth through the Prophet Simon Kimbangu (1921)

Luanda

African Methodist Episcopal Church (1929)
Lumpa Church (1954)

TANZANIA

Dar es Salaam

MALAWI

ANGOLA

ZAMBIA

Kimbanguist Church (1927)

Lusaka

Zambezi

MOZAMBIQUE

Harare

ZIMBABWE

African Apostolic Church of Johane Maranke

NAMIBIA

African Methodist Episcopal Church (1946)

BOTSWANA

MADAGASCAR

African Apostolic Church of Johane Maranke (1932)

Pretoria

Johannesburg

SWAZILAND

Orange

SOUTH AFRICA

LESOTHO

Cape Town

Zion Christian Church (1914)
Nazarite Baptist Church (1910)
Assemblies of God (1910)

Senegal

Niger

ATLANTIC OCEAN

INDIAN OCEAN

Nile

Membership of independent churches expressed as percentage of total population in 1980:

Over 15%
10–15%
5–10%
1–5%
0.5–1%

Harris Church (1913) : Major independent church, with date of origin of movement

0   1000   2000 km

0   400   800   1200 miles

CHRISTIANITY IN AFRICA

Some 44 per cent of the African Christian population is Roman Catholic. Protestants represent the mainstream colonial churches: Anglican, Baptist, Congregational, Lutheran, Methodist and Reformed. Many churches are growing rapidly, including some of the African Independent churches (see below and opposite).

Roman Catholicism is strongest in the Central African republics that were ruled by Catholic colonial regimes, such as Congo under the French, Zaire under the Belgians, and Angola under the Portuguese. Likewise, the country with the largest Protestant population is Namibia, a former German and South African colony. Denominational strength also reflects colonial legacy: for example, the Lutheran church in Namibia; the Dutch Reformed in South Africa; the Anglican church in East Africa.

The complexity, though, of African Christianity defies neat pigeon-holing. Whilst origins may be useful starting points, African religion is so multifarious and changeable that the depiction of any pattern is of limited value. Christians are still a minority in Africa, and animism is a major religious force. In some churches formal organization can be virtually absent, and Christian doctrine may be wedded to traditional beliefs.

AFRICAN INDEPENDENT CHURCHES

Many of the indigenous African churches have their origins in the mainstream mission churches. Their independence has allowed them to integrate Christian teaching with traditional African ideas and values. They are usually Pentecostal, and emphasize the power of healing and exorcism. Many have a charismatic prophet as leader, such as the Kimbanguist Church in Zaire, founded by Simon Kimbangu, and the Harris Church in the Ivory Coast, named after William Harris. Some of the largest and best-known in Nigeria are the Aladura (or 'praying people') churches.

South Africa has perhaps the most successful independent tradition. Here, as elsewhere in Africa, many developed as a protest against white control of the historic churches.

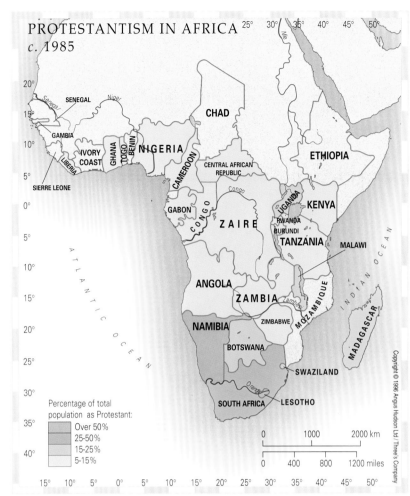

PROTESTANTISM IN AFRICA *c.* 1985

Percentage of total population as Protestant:
Over 50%
25-50%
15-25%
5-15%

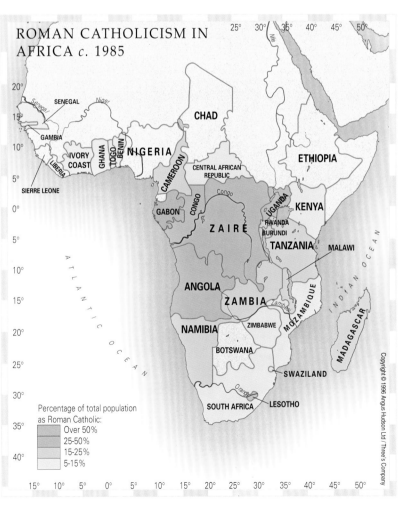

ROMAN CATHOLICISM IN AFRICA *c.* 1985

Percentage of total population as Roman Catholic:
Over 50%
25-50%
15-25%
5-15%

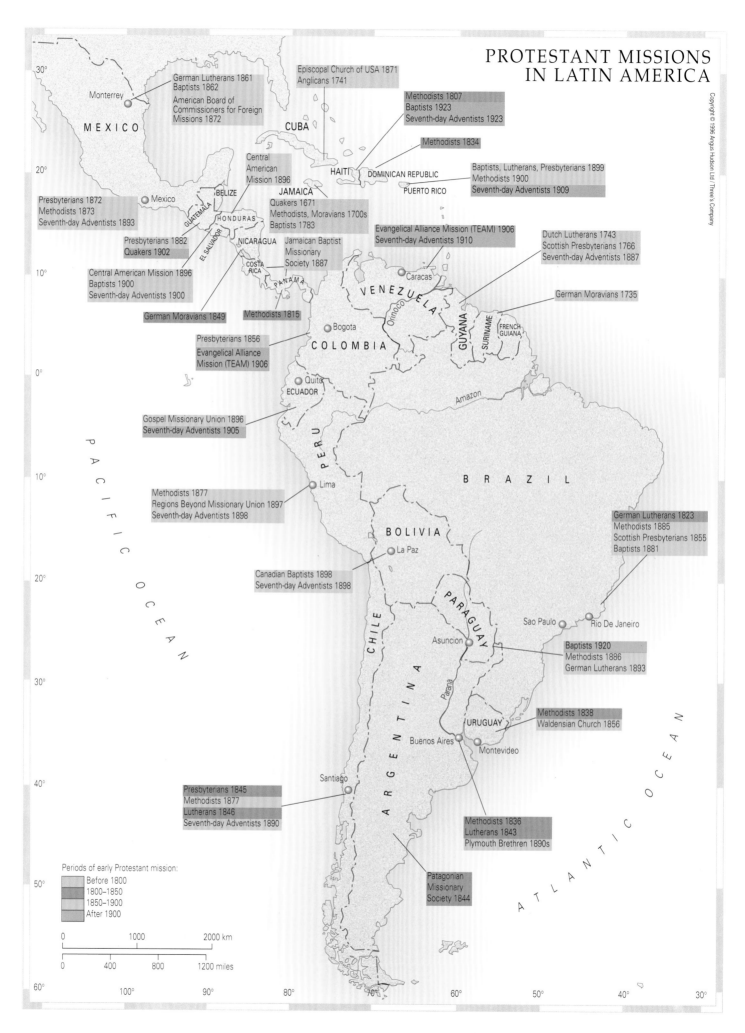

PROTESTANT MISSIONS IN LATIN AMERICA

German Lutherans 1861
Baptists 1862

American Board of
Commissioners for Foreign
Missions 1872

Episcopal Church of USA 1871
Anglicans 1741

Methodists 1807
Baptists 1923
Seventh-day Adventists 1923

Methodists 1834

Baptists, Lutherans, Presbyterians 1899
Methodists 1900
Seventh-day Adventists 1909

Monterrey

MEXICO

CUBA

HAITI

DOMINICAN REPUBLIC

PUERTO RICO

Central
American
Mission 1896

JAMAICA

Presbyterians 1872
Methodists 1873
Seventh-day Adventists 1893

Mexico

BELIZE

GUATEMALA

HONDURAS

Quakers 1671
Methodists, Moravians 1700s
Baptists 1783

Presbyterians 1882
Quakers 1902

NICARAGUA

EL SALVADOR

Jamaican Baptist
Missionary
Society 1887

Evangelical Alliance Mission (TEAM) 1906
Seventh-day Adventists 1910

Dutch Lutherans 1743
Scottish Presbyterians 1766
Seventh-day Adventists 1887

Central American Mission 1896
Baptists 1900
Seventh-day Adventists 1900

COSTA
RICA

PANAMA

VENEZUELA

Caracas

GUYANA

SURINAME

FRENCH
GUIANA

German Moravians 1735

German Moravians 1849

Methodists 1815

Orinoco

Presbyterians 1856

Evangelical Alliance
Mission (TEAM) 1906

Bogota

COLOMBIA

Quito

ECUADOR

Amazon

Gospel Missionary Union 1896
Seventh-day Adventists 1905

PERU

BRAZIL

Methodists 1877
Regions Beyond Missionary Union 1897
Seventh-day Adventists 1898

Lima

BOLIVIA

German Lutherans 1823
Methodists 1885
Scottish Presbyterians 1855
Baptists 1881

La Paz

Canadian Baptists 1898
Seventh-day Adventists 1898

PARAGUAY

Sao Paulo

Rio De Janeiro

CHILE

Asuncion

Baptists 1920
Methodists 1886
German Lutherans 1893

Parana

ARGENTINA

URUGUAY

Methodists 1838
Waldensian Church 1856

Buenos Aires

Montevideo

Santiago

Presbyterians 1845
Methodists 1877
Lutherans 1846
Seventh-day Adventists 1890

Methodists 1836
Lutherans 1843
Plymouth Brethren 1890s

PACIFIC OCEAN

ATLANTIC OCEAN

Periods of early Protestant mission:

Before 1800
1800–1850
1850–1900
After 1900

Patagonian
Missionary
Society 1844

0   1000   2000 km

0   400   800   1200 miles

30°

20°

10°

0°

10°

20°

30°

40°

50°

60°

100°   90°   80°   70°   60°   50°   40°   30°

CHRISTIANITY
IN LATIN AMERICA

MEXICO

CUBA

Baptists
Seventh-day Adventists

Assemblies of God

Anglicans

JAMAICA

HAITI

DOMINICAN REPUBLIC

PUERTO RICO

Pentecostal Church of God
Methodists
Seventh-day Adventists

Presbyterians

GUATEMALA

BELIZE

Assemblies
of God

HONDURAS

Anglicans
Baptists
Seventh-day Adventists

Assemblies of God
Central American Church
Presbyterians

EL SALVADOR

NICARAGUA

Moravians
Assemblies of God

Assemblies of God

Anglicans

Moravians

COSTA
RICA

PANAMA

Assemblies
of God

International Church of the
Foursquare Gospel

International Church of
the Foursquare Gospel

VENEZUELA

Orinoco

GUYANA

SURINAME

FRENCH
GUIANA

Assemblies of God
Baptists

United Pentecostal Church

COLOMBIA

Evangelical Missionary
Union Church
International Church of
the Foursquare Gospel

ECUADOR

Amazon

PERU

Assemblies of God
Seventh-day Adventists

B R A Z I L

PACIFIC OCEAN

BOLIVIA

Seventh-day Adventists
Evangelical Christian Union

PARAGUAY

Mennonites

CHILE

Paraná

Pentecostal Methodist Church
Seventh-day Adventists

A R G E N T I N A

URUGUAY

Assemblies of God
Waldensian Church

ATLANTIC OCEAN

Christian Assemblies
Plymouth Brethren

Over 90% of population Roman Catholic
50%-90% of population Roman Catholic
More Protestants than Roman Catholic
Fast-growing Protestant minority, with percentage of
population that is Protestant
Pentecostal minority church } the largest named first
Protestant minority church

30°
20°
10°
0°
10°
20°
30°
40°
50°
60°

120°   90°   80°   70°   60°   50°   40°   30°

PROTESTANT MISSIONS IN LATIN AMERICA

CHRISTIANITY IN LATIN AMERICA

Protestant missionaries came to Latin America from the USA to revive Christianity in the nineteenth century at a time when North American Protestant values were attractive to the middle-class liberals who had steered the Latin American republics to independence. Since the ejection of earlier Roman Catholic missions, a shortage of priests had brought decline in the Christian faith. The Methodists and Baptists came to the Caribbean on the tide of the anti-slavery movement. The Assemblies of God and Seventh-day Adventists were two of the more aggressively evangelistic missions at the beginning of the twentieth century. By the outbreak of World War I, all the Latin American republics had established Protestant missions. However, with only half a million converts in the entire region, they represented only a tiny fraction compared with the residual Catholic population.

In 1970, about half of the Roman Catholic clergy were foreigners. Many supported indigenous political movements that strove for justice against repressive governments. With less dependence on their bishops, and often stipends paid by their missionary societies, foreign clergy were in an easier position to challenge the authorities. Increasingly, the indigenous clergy, and some bishops, notably Archbishop Romero of Salvador, openly denounced their governments from the pulpit. Reactionary persecutions of the Church followed. Between 1964 and 1978, 260 foreign missionaries were expelled from Latin American states, and over 450 priests arrested.

Similar authoritarian attitudes prevailed at first against Protestant missions. However, through the 1960s, relations improved and Protestant growth escalated, especially in poor urban districts. Latin America was, in truth, a mission region, with a great majority of the population only nominally Catholic. The most spectacular Protestant growth has been among the Pentecostal groups, especially in Brazil, Chile, Mexico and Guatemala. Indeed, Latin America has been the most successful mission field in the world for the Pentecostal churches.

The most widespread Pentecostalist church is the Assemblies of God, whilst the Seventh-day Adventists are the most consistently successful of the evangelical groups.

Christian students in Campinas, Brazil, lead a service in a *favela* in the city.

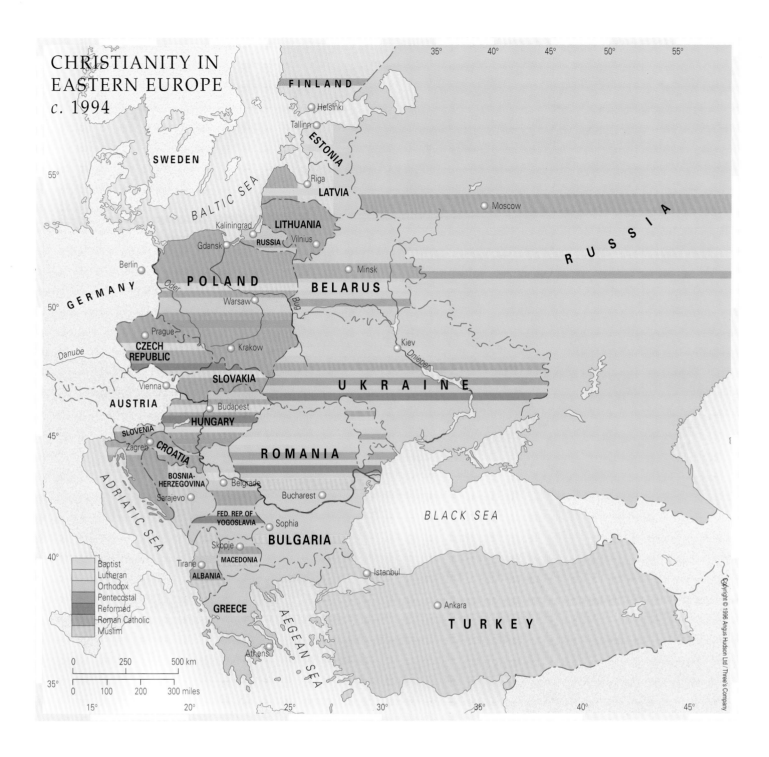

CHRISTIANITY IN EASTERN EUROPE
c. 1994

Baptist
Lutheran
Orthodox
Pentecostal
Reformed
Roman Catholic
Muslim

CHRISTIANITY IN EASTERN EUROPE

The main division in eastern Europe, between Roman Catholic and Eastern Orthodox, has persisted since the eleventh century.

By the 1920s most of the national Orthodox churches in the Balkans had come into being. Each church is independent but acknowledges the primacy of the Patriarchate of Constantinople. The traditional Protestant denominations have in several republics been overtaken by Pentecostals this century, though Lutheranism still holds sway in the far north. Roman Catholicism is still strong in central Europe, especially in Poland, where it is professed by over 90 per cent of the population.

In Estonia, Latvia and Bosnia, there is no majority confession. The main denominational allegiances are shown in equal parts.

PREDOMINANT RELIGIOUS AFFILIATION OF WORLD POPULATION *c.* 1990

NORTH AMERICA

SOUTH AMERICA

PACIFIC OCEAN

ATLANTIC OCEAN

Majority of population:
- Christian
- Muslim
- Buddhist
- Hindu
- Buddhist, Confucian and Taoist
- Buddhist and Shintoist
- Jewish
- Sikh
- Animist

0	2000	4000 km

0	800	1600	2400 miles

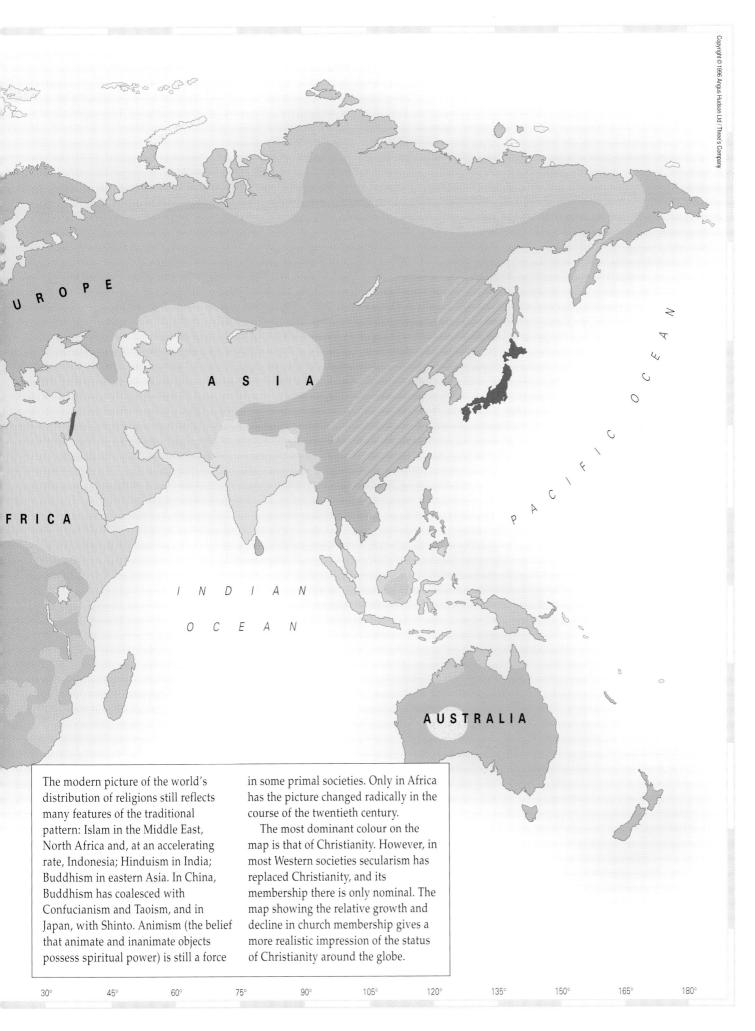

EUROPE

ASIA

PACIFIC OCEAN

AFRICA

INDIAN

OCEAN

AUSTRALIA

The modern picture of the world's distribution of religions still reflects many features of the traditional pattern: Islam in the Middle East, North Africa and, at an accelerating rate, Indonesia; Hinduism in India; Buddhism in eastern Asia. In China, Buddhism has coalesced with Confucianism and Taoism, and in Japan, with Shinto. Animism (the belief that animate and inanimate objects possess spiritual power) is still a force in some primal societies. Only in Africa has the picture changed radically in the course of the twentieth century.

The most dominant colour on the map is that of Christianity. However, in most Western societies secularism has replaced Christianity, and its membership there is only nominal. The map showing the relative growth and decline in church membership gives a more realistic impression of the status of Christianity around the globe.

| 30° | 45° | 60° | 75° | 90° | 105° | 120° | 135° | 150° | 165° | 180° |

BRANCHES OF CHRISTIANITY IN ASIA

Majority denomination:

Syria	Greek Orthodox
Jordan	Greek Orthodox
Iran	Armenian Apostolic
Georgia	Georgian Orthodox
Armenia	Armenian Apostolic
Azerbaijan	Russian Orthodox
Kazakhstan	Russian Orthodox
Uzbekistan	Russian Orthodox
Kyrgyzstan	Russian Orthodox
Qatar	Orthodox churches
Bahrain	Anglican
India	Estimated 16 million (1.91%) Protestants and 14.5 million (1.76%) Roman Catholics (1990) Other minority churches, each with over 1 million members: Church of South India Council of Baptist Churches of North East India Malankara Orthodox Syrian Church of the East United Evangelical Lutheran Churches in India Church of North India
Nagaland	85% Christian
Manipur	34% Christian
Mizoram	85% Christian
Burma	Burma Baptist Convention
China	Estimated over 10 million Protestants, and 6 million Roman Catholics (1990)
South Korea	Presbyterian churches Other minority churches, each with over ½ million members: Roman Catholic Church, Korean Methodist Church
Philippines	Minority church of over 3 million members: Philippine Independent Church
Indonesia	Protestant Church in Indonesia Minority of over 2 million members: Roman Catholic Church
Papua New Guinea	Evangelical Lutheran Church of Papua New Guinea Minority of over 1/2 million members: Roman Catholic Church

Main branches of Christianity in those countries with significant Christian population:

- Eastern Orthodox
- Protestant
- Roman Catholic

Size of Christian population:
- Less than 1 million
- 1–10 million
- More than 10 million

Copyright © 1996 Angus Hudson Ltd / Three's Company

CHRISTIANITY IN ASIA

After the 1966 Cultural Revolution in China Christianity was driven 'underground'. This gave rise to the secret house church movement, which spread rapidly.

With the relaxing of government control over religious worship churches have re-opened. However, estimates of present numbers of practising Christians are difficult to obtain and vary enormously. Some researchers have put the figure as high as 75 million Protestants and Catholics in 1992. In central Asia, Christianity tends to be confined to the Slavic immigrants, who are normally Eastern Orthodox; the most populous state being Kazakhstan. Islam thrives in many of the republics.

In southern Asia, India has sizeable Christian communities. Perhaps the most notable are those enclaves bordering Burma: Nagaland and Mizoram, where some 85 per cent of the population are Christian. Many of the boat people escaping the regime in Vietnam were Roman Catholic, though there remains a significant Christian community. Although in Indonesia the Church is stronger and officially tolerated, there have been Muslim reactions to Protestant evangelism, resulting in persecutions. In South Korea, on the other hand, the government has been completely favourable to the growth of the Church. Most there are Evangelicals. The Philippines still has one of the densest Roman Catholic populations in Asia.

154

INDEX

Page numbers in *italics* denote illustrations

157

158

NORTH AMERICA

SOUTH AMERICA

ATLANTIC OCEAN

PACIFIC OCEAN

Majority of population:
- Christian
- Muslim
- Buddhist
- Hindu
- Buddhist, Confucian and Taoist
- Buddhist and Shintoist
- Jewish
- Sikh
- Animist

0	2000	4000 km

0	800	1600	2400 miles

WORLDWIDE RELIGIOUS AFFILIATION